Max-Planck-Institut für ausländisches öffentliches Recht und Völkerrecht

Beiträge zum ausländischen öffentlichen Recht und Völkerrecht

Begründet von Viktor Bruns

Herausgegeben von
Jochen Abr. Frowein · Helmut Steinberger
Rüdiger Wolfrum

Band 117

Rudolf Bernhardt (Ed.)

Interim Measures Indicated by International Courts

Springer-Verlag
Berlin Heidelberg New York London Paris
Tokyo Hong Kong Barcelona Budapest

ISBN 978-3-642-08199-6

Die Deutsche Bibliothek – CIP-Einheitsaufnahme

Interim measures indicated by international courts / Rudolf Bernhardt (ed.). [Max-Planck-Institut für Ausländisches Öffentliches Recht und Völkerrecht]. – Berlin ; Heidelberg ; New York ; London ; Paris ; Tokyo ; Hong Kong ; Barcelona ; Budapest : Springer, 1994
(Beiträge zum ausländischen öffentlichen Recht und Völkerrecht ; Bd. 117)

NE: Bernhardt, Rudolf [Hrsg.]; GT

Satz (Datenkonvertierung): Konrad Triltsch, Graphischer Betrieb, 97070 Würzburg

Preface

Professor Hermann Mosler, former Director of the Max Planck Institute for Comparative Public Law and International Law, former Judge and Vice-President of the European Court of Human Rights, Judge of the International Court of Justice from 1976 to 1985, celebrated his 80th birthday at the end of the year 1992.

On 22nd January 1993, the Max Planck Institute organized a colloquium in honour of Hermann Mosler, on a topic which is of theoretical as well as practical interest: Interim Measures Indicated by International Courts. The participants of the colloquium were outstanding scholars and experts in the area of international dispute settlement.

The present publication is based on the colloquium of January 1993. It contains four reports, namely on the International Court of Justice (Thirlway), the Court of Justice of the European Communities (Jacobs), the Inter-American Court of Human Rights (Buergenthal) and the European Court of Human Rights (Bernhardt). Three of the reports were orally presented and discussed, and they have been revised and expanded for this publication; the report by Thomas Buergenthal could only be submitted in writing.

In preparing the colloquium the authors were requested to concentrate their contributions on the following questions:

1. Legal bases for the indication of interim measures (convention, statute, rules of court).
2. Conditions for the indication of interim measures (jurisdiction, competence, admissibility, urgency, necessity – irreparable damage – ; request of the parties and/or indication by the court *proprio motu*).
3. Permissible content of interim measures (connection between interim measures and potential result of the dispute?).
4. Binding force and enforceability of interim measures.
5. Legal consequences of measures later found unjustified.

Besides the reports mentioned above, the present publication also contains the oral addresses and the contributions to the discussion during the colloquium.

This publication on an important subject of public international law and international adjudication honours an outstanding international jurist.

Heidelberg, December 1993 RUDOLF BERNHARDT

Contents

Preface V
List of Abbreviations XI

Part One: Reports 1

The Indication of Provisional Measures by the International Court of Justice 1

H. W. A. Thirlway

I. The legal basis for the indication of provisional measures – Powers of the President of the Court 2
II. The purpose of provisional measures 5
A. Preservation of rights 7
B. Prevention of irreparable prejudice 8
C. Non-anticipation of Court's decision 11
D. Non-aggravation or extension of dispute 12
E. Preservation of evidence 16
III. The conditions for the indication of provisional measures . . . 16
A. Existence of jurisdiction 17
B. Existence of a *prima facie* case 23
C. Urgency 25
IV. The content of provisional measures: the "interim judgment" . 27
V. Binding or non-binding effect of provisional measures 28
VI. The consequences of measures 33
Addendum 34

Interim Measures in the Law and Practice of the Court of Justice of the European Communities 37

Francis G. Jacobs

Introduction 37
I. Legal bases for the grant of interim measures 38

A. The founding Treaties 38
1. Article 185 of the EEC Treaty 39
2. Article 186 of the EEC Treaty 40
3. Articles 187 and 192 of the EEC Treaty 41
B. The Statutes of the Court of Justice 41
C. The Rules of Procedure of the Court of Justice 42
II. Conditions for the grant of interim measures 44
A. Conditions of admissibility of an application for interim measures 44
B. Conditions of substance concerning the grant of interim measures 47
1. The admissibility of the main action 47
2. The pleas of fact and law establishing a *prima facie* case for the interim measures applied for 48
3. Urgency: the risk of serious and irreparable harm . . . 51
(a) The concept of urgency 51
(b) The burden of proof 52
(c) The imminent nature of the harm 52
(d) The characteristics of the harm 53
(i) The requirement of harm to the applicant in person 53
(ii) Non-material harm 54
(iii) Potential harm 55
(iv) Financial harm 55
4. The balance of interests 56
III. Permissible content of interim measures 59
IV. Binding force and enforceability of interim measures 60
V. Legal consequences of measures later found unjustified 62
VI. Interim measures in respect of Community provisions in the national courts 63
A. Interim measures in national courts to protect Community rights 64
B. Interim measures in national courts to suspend national measures implementing Community regulations 65
C. Interim measures in national courts and the duty to adopt coercive measures required by Community law . . 66
Concluding remarks 68

Interim Measures in the Inter-American Court of Human Rights 69

THOMAS BUERGENTHAL

Introduction 69
I. Jurisdictional Issues 71
II. The Scope of Article 63(2) 77
III. The Nature of Provisional Measures 81
IV. Inherent Powers 83
V. Legal Effect of Provisional Measures 84
VI. Procedural Issues 89
Conclusion 93

Interim Measures of Protection under the European Convention on Human Rights 95

RUDOLF BERNHARDT

Introduction 95
I. Texts and Practices under the European Convention 97
II. The Case of Cruz Varas and the Obligation of States to Adopt Interim Measures of Protection 100
III. General Problems of Interim Measures in Human Rights Matters 101

Annex: Extracts from the Statements in the Case *Cruz Varas* . 104
1. Opinion of the Commission of 7 June 1990 104
2. Judgment of the Court of 20 March 1991 109

Part Two: Colloquium 115

Opening Address 115

JOCHEN ABR. FROWEIN

Discussion 119

Steinberger, Chairman (119, 120), Tomuschat (120), Rodríguez Iglesias (121), Pescatore (121), von Mangoldt (122), Golsong (124), Hailbronner (125), Herdegen (126), Mosler (127), Delbrück (129), Mosler (129), Zemanek

(129), Klein (130), Stein (131), Partsch (132), Sir Ian Sinclair (133), Macdonald (134), Seidl-Hohenveldern (134), Bos (135), Thirlway (135), Jacobs (137), Thirlway (139), Bernhardt (140), Doehring (140), Frowein (141), Schiedermair (142), Tomuschat (143), Rodríguez Iglesias (143), Puente Egido (144), Oellers-Frahm (146), Pescatore (147), Hailbronner (147), von Mangoldt (148), Bernhardt (149), Thirlway (150), Jacobs (151), Steinberger (152)

List of Participants 153

List of Abbreviations

A. J. I. L.	American Journal of International Law
All ER	All England Law Reports
CMLR	Common Market Law Reports
CMLRev	Common Market Law Review
CSFR	Czech and Slovak Federal Republic
ECHR	European Convention on Human Rights
ECR	European Court Reports
ECSC	European Coal and Steel Community
EEC	European Economic Community
ELRev	European Law Review
Emory J. Int'l Disp. Res.	Emory Journal of International Dispute Resolution
EuGRZ	Europäische Grundrechte Zeitschrift
Eur. Court H. R.	European Court of Human Rights
Fordham Int'l L. J.	Fordham International Law Journal
Germ. YB. Int'l L.	German Yearbook of International Law
Hastings Int'l & Comp. L. Rev.	Hastings International and Comparative Law Review
ICJ	International Court of Justice
ILO	International Labour Organization
NJW	Neue Juristische Wochenschrift
PCIJ	Permanent Court of International Justice
RCADI	Recueil des Cours de l'Académie de Droit International
UN	United Nations
UNCITRAL	United Nations Commission on International Trade Law
UNESCO	United Nations Education, Scientific and Cultural Organization
WHO	World Health Organization

Part One: Reports

The Indication of Provisional Measures by the International Court of Justice*

H. W. A. THIRLWAY

Mr. Chairman, Ladies and Gentlemen: before starting on the scientific part of what I have to say, I should like just to refer to the fact which the Chairman has already mentioned, that unfortunately the workload of the International Court of Justice at the present time is such that it is and has been quite impossible for any of its Members to get away for this colloquium. May I convey to you on behalf of the Members of the Court their great regret that this has not been possible, regret not only because of the extreme interest of the subject chosen for today's study, but also because of the fact that it is being held to mark the 80th birthday of Judge Hermann Mosler. Judge Mosler is remembered with great respect and affection by all the Members of the Court whose term of office coincided or overlapped with his, and, if I may also add, by all the members of the Registry who had the pleasure of working with him.

When Professor Bernhardt did me the honour of inviting me to present a paper today on the subject of provisional measures in international courts, as it concerns the International Court of Justice at The Hague, he very kindly supplied a schema of the sort of points that might be covered in the various papers offered in connection with the various courts. I think the most useful

* Note: The following text is an edited transcript of the communication as delivered orally at the Colloquium in honour of Judge Hermann Mosler. Footnotes have been added, and some additional material, which could not be included for reasons of time, has been reproduced in a different style of type, in order to indicate what material was, and what was not, offered as the basis for the discussion that follows. Also included is an Addendum commenting on the Court's Order in the case concerning *Application of the Convention on the Prevention and Punishment of the Crime of Genocide (Bosnia and Herzegovina v. Yugoslavia (Serbia and Montenegro)*, delivered after the Colloquium but before the present volume went to press.

thing I can do is to follow that schema, in other words to present a sort of *tour d'horizon* of all the various questions arising on provisional measures in the International Court, even though in doing so I shall of course probably be telling most of those present what they already know! I hope however that this will provide a framework for the discussion which will follow. What I shall however try to do on that basis is to put a little emphasis on the recent jurisprudence of the International Court in this field; and by "recent" in that context I mean since 1984. One practical reason for this is that 1984 saw the first Order indicating provisional measures (in the Nicaragua *v.* United States case) subsequent to the publication in 1983 of the excellent work on the subject by Professor Sztucki[1], which covers the earlier ground in an entirely admirable way. What I have to say might thus be regarded to some extent as a pendant to, or an updating of, that book.
The schema of the present paper is therefore as follows:

I. The legal basis for the indication of provisional measures – Powers of the President of the Court
II. The purpose of provisional measures
   A. Preservation of rights
   B. Prevention of irreparable prejudice
   C. Non-anticipation of Court's decision
   D. Non-aggravation or extension of dispute
   E. Preservation of evidence
III. The conditions for the indication of provisional measures
   A. Existence of jurisdiction
   B. Existence of a *prima facie* case
   C. Urgency
IV. The content of provisional measures: the "interim judgment"
V. Binding or non-binding effect of provisional measures
VI. The consequences of measures.

I. The legal basis for the indication of provisional measures

Turning then to the first head, as it were, that is, the legal basis on which measures are indicated by the International Court of Justice, that is of course, as we all know, Article 41 of the Statute of the Court. The Statute also provides that the Court may make rules of procedure[2], and it has done so: as you will know, there are a number of rules on the subject of provisional measures[3]. Now straight away we have to note a question of terminology:

---

[1] Jerzy Sztucki, *Interim Measures in the Hague Court* (Kluwer, 1983).

[2] Statute, Article 30, paragraph 1: "The Court shall frame rules for carrying out its functions. In particular, it shall lay down rules of procedure".

[3] Rules, Articles 73–78.

I am using the expression "provisional measures" which is that of the Statute: "The Court shall have the power to indicate, if it considers that circumstances so require, any provisional measures which ought to be taken to preserve the respective rights of either party". So far as the rules are concerned, there has been a change of usage: the 1946 Rules, like those of the Permanent Court of International Justice, referred to "interim measures of protection". The wording of the rules was brought into line with the Statute when they were revised in 1978.

This was brought home to me when, in preparation for today, I asked our documentary department to give me a complete set of the Orders made by the Court in this field, so that I could have them with me in a convenient form. They sent me only a handful of Orders, so I asked what had happened to the rest. A junior member of the documentary department said: "You asked for Orders on provisional measures, and there you have them; but we do have Orders on something called 'interim measures of protection'"!

In 1978 the Court decided to unify the terminology and the Rules now refer, like the Statute, to provisional measures. This is perhaps not in fact the most happy rendering of "mesures conservatoires", because it does not have the idea of preservation which as we all know is probably the most essential element of the concept.

The fact that there is a provision for provisional measures in the Statute renders it unnecessary to go into the otherwise very interesting question of whether an international tribunal has an inherent power to indicate measures of this kind, in the absence of express authorization in its constituent instrument[4]. This is a controversial point, but as far as the International Court is concerned it is virtually an academic one, except to the extent that the kind of measures which the Court has on occasion claimed the power to indicate might be thought to go in some respects beyond the exact wording of the Statute. An interesting question is thus whether there is here an inherent power, or more probably an implied power, lying behind the words of the Statute, a matter we shall come to in a moment.

The only source of the power to indicate measures is in Article 41 of the Statute; the Rules spell out in more detail, for example, that the Court may indicate measures *proprio motu*[5], and that it may consider the indication of measures which are not those asked for by the parties[6], but I think it is clear that these powers still remain subject to Article 41. The exercise of the power under the Rules to indicate measures *proprio motu* cannot justify the Court in indicating measures which it would not have had power to do under Article 41. I mention the point because there has been a suggestion in a recent

[4] See for instance, Dumbauld, *Interim Measures of Protection in International Controversies*, pp. 180 et seq. (1932).

[5] Rules, Article 75, paragraph 1.

[6] Rules, Article 75, paragraph 2.

opinion appended by a judge to an Order on provisional measures which seems to point in the direction of a wider *proprio motu* power[7]; and I have doubts whether this can be justified.

Powers of the President

The President has certain powers given by the Rules; I shall pass over these, we can deal with them in discussion perhaps later, but I would like to try and keep this opening statement within reasonable bounds.

For a time the Rules of the Permanent Court of International Justice conferred on the President the power to indicate measures while the Court was not sitting[8]; but when the Rules were revised in 1931 it was generally accepted that the power to indicate measures could not be delegated[9]. In 1936, a provision was included for the President, "pending the meeting of the Court and a decision by it" to "take such measures as may appear to him to be necessary in order to enable the Court to give an effective decision"[10]. This provision was taken over in 1946 by the post-war Court; in 1978, the revised Rules replaced it with the following (Article 74, paragraph 4):

> "Pending the meeting of the Court, the President may call upon the parties to act in such a way as will enable any order the Court may make on the request for provisional measures to have its appropriate effects".

The omission of the words "and a decision by it" is noteworthy; this suggests an intention to limit the President's powers to the period before the Court meets, presumably on the basis that, once assembled, the Court itself can take all appropriate action. Since, however, the Rules do not confer or recognize a power of the Court to do anything other than indicate measures; and since measures can only be indicated after a hearing, a date for which has to be fixed "which will afford the parties an opportunity of being represented at it" (Article 74, paragraph 3), there is in most cases an interregnum between the date the Court assembles and the date on which its decision on the request is given. No President has, since 1978, however purported to exercise his powers under Article 74, paragraph 4, after the Court has assembled.

From 1972 on, successive Presidents have shown themselves very ready to address a communication to the parties, when provisional measures have been requested, calling in very general terms for restraint *pendente lite*; this has frequently been promp-

[7] *Questions of Interpretation and Application of the 1971 Montreal Convention arising from the Aerial Incident at Lockerbie*, dissenting opinion of Judge Ajibola: "The Parties have based much of their argument on the issue of *legal rights*. Without doubt, I think that the issue of legal rights is relevant and important to the Application of Libya and that the Applicant must clearly establish these rights to succeed on the merits. That is why Article 41 talks of the preservation of the respective *rights* of either party. However, Article 75 of the Rules of Court does not refer to the issue of *rights* but merely grants the Court the power to indicate provisional measures *proprio motu* against *any* or *all* parties if after due examination the circumstances of the case so require. In my view the Court should exercise the power conferred by Article 75 in this case." (*I. C. J. Reports* 1992, 92.)

[8] 1922 Rules of Court, Article 57.

[9] *P. C. I. J., Series D, No. 2, 2nd addendum*, 181 et seq.

[10] 1936 Rules, Article 61, paragraph 3.

ted by a request by a party, though usually the President's communication is less far-reaching than that requested. It is clear that the President can act *proprio motu*, but now that it has become common practice to ask him to act, it would be exceptional for him to see more urgency than the party concerned[11].

Such a communication was in recent years beginning to look like a normal, automatic, part of the procedure, and there was therefore a risk that it would be regarded as no more than a formality to which no particular attention need be paid. In two more recent cases, however, there was no request that the President exercise his powers in this respect; in each of them, while urgency was claimed to justify the indication of measures, that urgency was not so pressing that action was needed even before the Court could meet and take a decision. In the case of the *Arbitral Award of 31 July 1989*[12], Guinea-Bissau sought to restrain Senegal from asserting maritime jurisdiction in disputed sea areas; if the Court had not rejected the request as insufficiently connected with the claims of the Application, it would probably have found no immediate risk of irremediable damage. In the case of *Passage through the Great Belt*, similarly, the urgency was not immediate: indeed the main reason for the Court's rejection of the request was lack of urgency[13].

In the two Lockerbie cases, however, requests were made for the exercise of the presidential powers under Article 74, paragraph 4, of the Rules; but Vice-President Oda, Acting President in the two cases[14], declined to do so. His decision was announced at the opening of the hearings, and recorded in the opening paragraphs of the Court's Orders; no reasons were given, it being merely stated that

> "after the most careful consideration of all the circumstances then known to him [the Vice-President] had come to the conclusion that it would not be appropriate for him to exercise the discretionary power conferred on the President"[15].

It is respectfully suggested that the Vice-President was right to give no reasons; to do so would hardly be compatible with what is, as he stated, a discretionary power, and would have set an undesirable precedent.

In the absence of reasons, the question of the soundness of this decision does not lend itself to discussion; but it is a satisfying development in establishing that an indication by the President under Article 74, paragraph 4, is not a mere formality, and that any communication which a President does make under this provision, "after the most careful consideration of all the circumstances known to him", deserves to receive equally careful consideration from the State to which it is addressed.

II. The purpose of provisional measures

For the next main head to be considered, the purpose of measures, again the Statute gives us the starting point. To quote Article 41 once more: "The Court shall have the power to indicate, if it considers that circumstances so

---

[11] As Sztucki points out (*op. cit.*, note 1 above, 163–164), there has in these cases been no opportunity for a President to consider for himself whether such a communication should be sent.

[12] *I. C. J. Reports 1990*, 64.

[13] *I. C. J. Reports 1991*, 12: see in particular 18, para. 27.

[14] The President, being of British nationality, was debarred by Article 32, paragraph 1, of the Rules of Court from presiding in the case brought against the United Kingdom, and therefore found it appropriate to cede the presidency to the Vice-President in the closely-linked case brought against the United States.

[15] *I. C. J. Reports 1992*, 8–9, para. 17; 120, para. 18.

require, any provisional measures *which ought to be taken to preserve the respective rights of either party*". There is here a very clear statement of the essential purpose.

There have been various jurisprudential glosses, not to mention scholarly glosses, on that text, and a useful one to take as a starting point is afforded by the *Fisheries Jurisdiction* cases, which marked the beginning of the sort of wave of provisional measures requests with which the Court has been confronted over the last twenty years. In the Orders made in those cases on 17 August 1972, the Court included a very important paragraph, spelling out in more detail what is, as it were, implied in the Statute:

> "Whereas the right of the Court to indicate provisional measures as provided for in Article 41 of the Statute has as its object to preserve the respective rights of the Parties pending the decision of the Court, and presupposes that irreparable prejudice should not be caused to rights which are the subject of dispute in judicial proceedings, and that the Court's judgment should not be anticipated by reason of any initiative regarding the measures which are in issue"[16].

That definition, if we can call it that, contains three elements: (i) the indication is intended to preserve the respective rights of the parties; (ii) irreparable prejudice should not be caused to disputed rights; and (iii) the Court's judgment should not be anticipated by reason of any initiative regarding the measures – or perhaps better, regarding the rights which it sought to protect. Those three ideas reappear in various conjunctions in the Orders which the Court has made in this field since 1972, but the expression of their relationship to each other has not always been very consistent.

However, if I might open a small parenthesis at this point, the judgments of the Court are, as you know, the judgments of a Court of 15, or possibly 16 or 17 Members, and you know how difficult it is to get a consistent and coherent text out of that. Provisional measures Orders are prepared under pressure of time and in order to deal with the immediate situation. If I may unveil the secrecy of the deliberations sufficiently to say – and I feel sure that Judge Mosler will bear me out – the result is that the texts of such Orders should not be put under the magnifying glass on the assumption that every word has been weighed with the scholarly care which you might employ if you were writing a paper. As Professor Sztucki has in fact pointed out in his book[17], the extent of the interpretations of terms or phrases in these Orders which scholars have sometimes built upon them has perhaps gone rather beyond what is likely to have been intended. That little note of caution should be sounded before I go on to discuss the way in which the texts of provisional measures vary.

---

[16] *I. C. J. Reports 1972*, 16, para. 21; 34, para. 22.

[17] Sztucki, *op. cit.*, note 1 above, 278, commenting on the Orders in the *Fisheries Jurisdiction* cases.

A. Preservation of rights

The Statute itself contains the essential element of preservation of rights. A point of history to be noted in passing is that, as you will recall, the texts which existed in 1922 whereby other bodies enjoyed powers analogous to that of indicating provisional measures, and which may have given inspiration to the draftsmen of the Statute, were the 1907 Washington Convention which produced the Central American Court and the United States treaties called the Bryan Treaties. It is rather striking that the 1907 Convention, which referred to "a Court", did not mention preservation of rights, but referred to "non-aggravation of the dispute" – a concept which has come up very much in more recent work of the International Court – and that of the preservation of the *status quo*. The idea of preservation of rights is found in connection, not with a Court, but with a commission, the Arbitration Commission contemplated by the Bryan Treaties. I would suggest there was or may well have been a deliberate choice in 1922 of "preservation of rights" as the dominant idea, rather than "non-aggravation of the dispute".

What then is "preservation" of rights? The Permanent Court in the *South-Eastern Greenland* case was faced as early as 1932 with the fact that "preservation of rights" is to some extent an unfortunate way of expressing what is intended, because it is not easy to destroy a right; you can infringe a right, and you can act in violation of a right, but the right continues to exist, however much it is breached[18]. If proceedings are brought claiming that State A has a right and State B is breaching it or is threatening to breach it, that does not mean that the *right* needs to be preserved from destruction. On the other hand, if all that is needed for the indication of measures is to show that a right is being, or is going to be, infringed, is that not going to throw the door much too wide open for the indication of provisional measures in virtually every case? The decision in the *South-Eastern Greenland* case in fact adopted a fairly narrow line on that; the Court refused measures basically on the ground, or as one of the grounds, that the rights were not going to be damaged.

However, obviously something more was meant by the terms of the Statute, because otherwise there would be very few cases in which you could indicate provisional measures. It would have to be shown that the right was going to disappear, or conceivably that the subject-matter of the right was

[18] "Whereas, having regard to the character of the alleged rights in question, considered in relation to the natural characteristics of the territory in issue, even 'measures calculated to change the legal status of the territory' could not, according to the information now at the Court's disposal, affect the value of such alleged rights, once the Court in its judgment on the merits had recognized them as appertaining to one or other of the Parties ..." *Legal Status of the South-Eastern Territory of Greenland, P. C. I. J., Series A/B, No. 48*, 288; cf. also *ibid.*, 285.

[19] *Pleadings*, 11.

going to vanish totally, so that the right could thereafter only have a sort of theoretical, *in posse*, existence.

B. Prevention of irreparable prejudice

Hence the idea of irreparable prejudice comes into the picture, which was of course the second element in the *Fisheries Jurisdiction* dictum which I have quoted. The problem however still remains: what do you mean by irreparable? But that is a point I would like to reserve for the moment.

In its request in the *United States Diplomatic and Consular Staff in Tehran* case, the United States described as follows the "international legal rights of the United States" for the protection of which the measures were requested:

> "the rights of its nationals to life, liberty, protection and security; the rights of inviolability, immunity and protection for its diplomatic and consular officials; and the right of inviolability and protection for its diplomatic and consular premises"[19].

The measures of protection requested were, in short[20], the release of hostages, the vacation by Iranian intruders of the Embassy premises, and protection and free movement of diplomatic and consular personnel, none of whom should be put on trial.

In what way would the rights asserted be "preserved" by the measures requested? Setting aside for the moment the rights of individuals concerned, the other rights had already been grossly and flagrantly infringed; it was certainly right that the infringement should cease, but whether this took place following an order of interim measures or following judgment on the merits would not be a question of *preservation* of the rights, but rather a damage-limitation exercise. In neither event would the injury suffered be an irreparable one[21].

Turning to the rights of individual life and liberty, nothing could be more irreparable than the taking of life[22]. Prima facie, the right of each individual diplomat to life was an individual right; but there must be equally a right of the national State, protected by international law, not to have its citizens murdered. This may be tested by supposing that some of the persons seized in the Embassy, and threatened with execution, were nationals of some other State; the United States could then not have asked for provisional measures to protect those persons, though their own national State could[23]. The killing of a United States citizen, and perhaps *a fortiori* a United States diplomat, is thus an injury to the rights conferred by international law on the

---

[20] Set out in full in *Pleadings*, 12.

[21] It is not impossible to imagine an irreparable injury in this context; if the Iranian intruders had not already gained access to the secret files in the Embassy vaults, to prevent them doing so would be to forestall an injury which would be irreparable; once the cat is out of the bag, no monetary compensation will make up for the impossibility of putting it back in again.

[22] Referred to by the counsel for the United States as "the ultimate in irreparable injury" (*Pleadings*, 30).

[23] On the facts of the case as they stood, there was a difficulty in extending the Court's protection to two United States citizens who had been seized who were not diplomatic or consular officials, and therefore not covered by the 1973 and 1975 Vienna Conventions: see *I. C. J. Reports 1980*, 26–27, para. 50.

United States; there must, in effect, be as many distinct rights as there are nationals, since otherwise the killing of one national would not affect the continued existence of the general right, so that no special measures would be needed to "preserve" it from extinction.

How did the Court handle the matter in its Order indicating provisional measures? Much of that Order is taken up with resounding statements of the need for diplomatic and consular intercourse, and the pertinent obligations in that respect, which are not here to the purpose. It then devoted a single paragraph to the aspect now under study:

> "Whereas continuance of the situation the subject of the present request exposes the human beings concerned to privation, hardship, anguish and even danger to life and health and thus to a serious possibility of irreparable harm[24]".

The Court thus moved imperceptibly from the international legal rights of the United States to the injury to the persons, health and life of the individuals concerned; the Order provides no link between these two considerations.

The Order made by the Court in 1984 indicating provisional measures in the proceedings brought by Nicaragua against the United States[25] is rather disappointing in its treatment of the linked questions of "preservation of rights" and "irreparable prejudice". The statement in the Order of the purpose of measures is in the shortest possible form:

> "Whereas the power of the Court to indicate provisional measures under Article 41 of the Statute has as its object to preserve the respective rights of either party pending the decision of the Court"[26],

thus omitting both the reference to "irreparable prejudice" and to non-anticipation of the Court's judgment, to be found in previous Orders.

The Order then continues:

> "and whereas the legal rights for the protection of which Nicaragua claims that provisional measures are required are stated by it to be as follows:
> - the rights of Nicaraguan citizens to life, liberty and security;
> - the right of Nicaragua to be free at all times from the use or threat of force against it by a foreign state;
> - the right of sovereignty of Nicaragua;
> - the right of Nicaragua to conduct its affairs and to determine matters within its domestic jurisdiction without interference or intervention of any foreign state;
> - the right of self-determination of the Nicaraguan people';

and whereas furthermore the Republic of Nicaragua claims that the urgent need for the requested measures is shown by the fact that 'the lives and property of Nicaragua, the sovereignty of the State and the health and progress of the economy are all immediately at stake', that the United States has given no indication that it is willing to 'desist from its unlawful actions', but is seeking the resources to continue and intensify its activities;[27]"

The Court then turns to the question of the possible relevance of the regional diplomatic effort known as the Contadora Process, and the United States objections based upon it; having disposed of those objections, the Court simply states as its conclusion that:

---

24 *I. C. J. Reports 1979*, 20, para. 42.

25 *Military and Paramilitary Activities in and against Nicaragua (Nicaragua* v. *United States of America) I. C. J. Reports 1984*, 169.

26 *I. C. J. Reports 1984*, 182, para. 32.

27 *I. C. J. Reports 1984*, 182, para. 32.

"Whereas in the light of the several considerations set out above, the Court finds that the circumstances require it to indicate provisional measures, as provided by Article 41 of the Statute of the Court, in order to preserve the rights claimed . . .[28]".

There is thus no indication of how the Court regarded the measures indicated as necessary to preserve the rights claimed; the impression given is that it was content to accept Nicaragua's assertion on this point. It is material to note that the United States had based its opposition to the granting of measures essentially on its assertion of lack of jurisdiction, and its objectives associated with the Contadora Process; and on the facts it had in effect confined itself to a blanket statement of non-admission[29]. On the other hand, the Court did not take over the Nicaragua case to the extent of indicating the precise provisional measures requested[30].

A better example of the preservation of a party's rights is afforded by the two recent Lockerbie cases, between Libya and the United Kingdom, and Libya and the United States. In effect, the argument of Libya in requesting provisional measures was that the Montreal Convention, by imposing an obligation either to extradite or to prosecute persons accused of crimes to which the Convention applied, had simultaneously conferred a right to a free choice by the State concerned between these two means of bringing an offender to book. Accordingly, to force a State in this position to surrender an alleged offender would not merely infringe this right to choose, but nullify it, since once the offender had been handed over, the option of prosecuting him by the State's own authorities would in effect disappear completely. The Court's decision was in effect that, as a result of the adoption of Security Council resolution 748 (1992), the alleged right to choose appeared, prima facie, to have been taken away, so that it was no longer there to be preserved. The situation which existed prior to the adoption of resolution 748 (1992) raised more difficult questions, and four members of the majority voting in favour of the Court's Order made a joint declaration which seems to imply that they might, had it not been for the resolution, have been in favour of provisional measures[31].

Even in this hypothetical situation, however, the idea of preservation of rights from threatened annulation presents difficulties. Libya would only irrevocably lose its right of choice if it in fact surrendered the two accused to another State for trial, i.e., by an act of its own. That act would, in Libya's contention, be effected under duress resulting from pressure by the other States, which might take forms which were in themselves unlawful, or might remain within the limits of legality. To simplify the problem, let us suppose that such pressure used only lawful means; provisional measures would then be requested to require a State to refrain from acts which not merely *might*, in the eventual judgment of the Court, be found to be lawful, but would be recognized by the Court, even at the time of indicating measures, to be lawful. Such acts would, furthermore, be banned not because they in themselves caused the disappearance of, or injury to, the rights claimed, but because they could induce the State claiming them to abandon them.

---

[28] *I. C. J. Reports 1984*, 186, para. 39. The paragraph continues with reference to the operative clauses of the Orders made in the *Fisheries Jurisdiction* cases; the significance of this is obscure.

[29] *I. C. J. Reports 1984*, 181–182, para. 30.

[30] Cf. the statement of these at 171–172 of the Order with the measures indicated at 186–187.

[31] Joint declaration of Judges Evensen, Tarassov, Guillaume and Aguilar Mawdsley, *I. C. J. Reports 1992*, 24–25.

C. Non-anticipation of Court's decision

"Preservation of rights" means that it must be shown that there is a right, and that something is going to happen in connection with that right (I would like at this stage to be vague as to just what is envisaged), which has got to be prevented, and that it is not going to be sufficient to wait and recompense the holder of the right afterwards. Reverting to the *Fisheries Jurisdiction* formula, which is a wider definition of purpose, the formula comprises reference to irreparable prejudice, but also contains the idea that the Court's judgment should not be anticipated. What is the significance of "anticipation" of a court's judgment? Apparently it means solely that something is going to be done by the Respondent which he claims to be entitled to do, but which the Applicant considers he is not entitled to do, and that the Respondent wishes to act on his own idea of what is the situation, without waiting for the Court to rule on the matter. Now since there is a rule, to be examined in a moment, that the rights sought to be protected must be, to put it at its lowest, closely linked with the rights which are the subject of dispute in the main proceedings, to some extent an "anticipation" is only to be expected in every case. The *degree* of anticipation necessary to justify measures has therefore to be found.

Furthermore, the inevitable result of compliance with a measure inspired by such a criterion of "non-anticipation" will be that both parties must act on the assumption that the view of the legal position taken by the State requesting measures is the correct one. In itself, therefore, this is insufficient to justify measures; there must be a material difference between the results of the temporary application of the one view or the other, making it more just or more appropriate to impose the one view over the other. In this respect, the word "initiative" is significant: it is one thing to restrain one party from taking some step to change the status quo, and quite another to require a form of restraint which itself involves a departure from the status quo. This emerges from the *Passage through the Great Belt* case, to be examined in a moment.

This element of the definition of the object of the Court's power to indicate provisional measures was applied to the facts in the *Fisheries Jurisdiction* cases by the immediately following paragraph of the Order, as follows:

> "Whereas the immediate implementation by Iceland of its [Fishery] Regulations would, by anticipating the Court's judgment, prejudice the rights claimed by the United Kingdom and affect the possibility of their full restoration in the event of a judgment in its favour"[32].

The brevity of this finding, perhaps justified in an interlocutory Order, is however perhaps to be regretted as liable to cause misunderstanding. It was not the mere fact that Iceland's threatened action would "anticipate the Court's judgment" that would affect the possibility of full restoration of the United Kingdom's rights. In its request, the United Kingdom had explained very clearly the economic consequences of exclusion of British vessels from the Icelandic fishing grounds, and why those consequences would be irreversible[33]. It was, it is suggested, this that justified the Court's

[32] *I. C. J. Reports 1972*, 16, para. 21; 34, para. 22.

[33] See *Pleadings*, Vol. I, 75–76.

finding that provisional measures should be indicated. Even if the economic consequences had been purely transitory, and therefore capable of redress by monetary reparation, the Icelandic action would have been just as much an anticipation of the Court's judgment.

Non-anticipation is thus another way of putting the idea of preserving the *status quo*; but what is the *status quo* and is it necessarily the *status quo* that has to be preserved in order to protect the relevant rights?

A good example of this protection is furnished by the *Passage through the Great Belt* case, recently before the Court. To recall briefly the facts in that case, Denmark wished to construct a bridge over the Great Belt, which was its own internal waters, between two parts of its land territory. Finland claimed that the construction of the bridge as planned would prevent Finland from exercising a right which it claimed of passage through the Great Belt, for – in particular – oil drilling rigs, which were much higher than the bridge was going to be. Finland therefore asked not only for a judgment that Denmark was not entitled to interfere with the right of passage, but also for provisional measures to stop the bridge construction works.

Now the actual interference with the rights was only going to occur once the bridge was in place, or possibly at some late stage during the construction. So what was the *status quo*, and when was the *status quo* going to change? It could be said that the *status quo* was the fact of the Great Belt remaining open; but Finland argued in effect that the mere continuation of the works was creating a situation in which it would be, as it were, too late for Denmark to turn back, and that therefore the *status quo* was a *status quo* in which Denmark was not planning a bridge, or was at least not proceeding with construction works of a bridge. On that basis Finland sought to stop the works long before they were going to reach the stage when the Great Belt would be blocked. As you know the Court rejected that request for interim measures; it found that the actual interference was not going to take place until after the Court would foreseeably have given judgment on the merits[34]. So in the view of the Court the *status quo* was, as it were, in fact the *status quo* of the Great Belt, and not the *status quo* of Denmark's plans.

D. Non-aggravation or extension of dispute

I turn now to a further aspect of the jurisprudence on the question of the purpose of measures. The definition which I read out from the *Fisheries Jurisdiction* cases does not mention any question of aggravation or extension of the dispute, which was, as just mentioned above, to be found in the 1907 Washington Convention. This is however an element which has figured quite largely in the Orders made by the Court ever since the *Electricity*

[34] *Passage through the Great Belt, I. C. J. Reports 1991*, 18, para. 27.

Company of Sofia and Bulgaria case before the Permanent Court just before the war; and this must raise some questions as to exactly how that indication relates to the basic purpose of measures, namely the protection of rights.

The request for measures in the *Electricity Company* case was hurried on with great speed, and the Order was issued the very day after the matter was heard. That Order indicated measures which were that the rights of the parties should not be prejudiced, but also that there should be no extension or aggravation of the dispute. The measures indicated by the Court in the *Electricity Company* case were, first that

> "the State of Bulgaria should ensure that no step of any kind is taken capable of prejudicing the rights claimed by the Belgian Government or of aggravating or extending the dispute submitted to the Court"[35].

That provision was justified in a recital of the Order which quoted Article 41 of the PCIJ Statute, which was of course for practical purposes identical with the current Statute. The recitals of the Order continued as follows:

> "Whereas the above quoted provision of the Statute applies the principle universally accepted by international tribunals and likewise laid down in many conventions to which Bulgaria has been a party – to the effect that the parties to a case must abstain from any measure capable of exercising a prejudicial effect in regard to the execution of the decision to be given and, *in general, not allow any step of any kind to be taken which might aggravate or extend the dispute*"[36].

The last provision is thus presented by the Permanent Court as an aspect of a universal principle of which the Statute is an application, so it may be regarded either as a restatement of something which in the Permanent Court's view was inherent in judicial procedures, or as something which was implied in Article 41 of the Statute. I think in this opening statement I should do no more than throw out that idea for consideration, and not take too much time to pursue it, because it is one which I think could be pursued some way.

I would also like just to throw out for consideration in that context the idea that the obligation referred to, not to aggravate or extend an existing dispute, might be seen as a parallel to another well-known obligation, that not to defeat the object and purpose of a treaty during the stage between the signature of the treaty and its actual coming into force[37]; or the obligation, which the Court in the Nicaragua *v.* United States case recently dealt with at some length[38], even in respect of an existing treaty, not only to comply with

---

35 *P. C. I. J., Series A/B, No. 79*, 199.

36 *Ibid.*

37 Cf. Vienna Convention on the Law of Treaties, Article 18.

38 *Military and Paramilitary Activities in and against Nicaragua (Nicaragua* v. *United States of America) I. C. J. Reports 1986*, 135–138, paras. 270–276.

its terms, but also not to defeat the object and purpose of the treaty[39]. In both cases you have, as it were, a legal kernel of obligation or asserted obligation contained in the original dispute, or in the treaty, and you have in parallel to that an obligation or asserted obligation not to enlarge, spoil, or defeat the kernel of law. I am having to put it in those rather vague terms because of the fact that while in the case of the treaty there is an admitted obligation to observe the treaty, in the case of the dispute there is no admitted obligation, there is only an asserted obligation, and a denial of it on the other side.

Whichever view one takes of this function of provisional measures of preventing any step of any kind being taken which might aggravate or extend the dispute, a problem still remains: Is this a separate power or is this an aspect of the main power destined to preserve the rights of the parties? There has been some controversy on this, and the jurisprudence of the Court probably does not provide an answer; but I would draw attention to some of the decisions which may point one way or the other. As we have seen, in the *Electricity Company* case the non-aggravation provision was asserted in conjunction with the idea of prejudicial effect of the decision to be given, prejudicial, that is, to the rights claimed. The matter was raised again in the *Aegean Sea Continental Shelf* case, and the Court there left open the question whether there was any independent power to indicate provisional measures merely to prevent aggravation or extension of the dispute[40]. In the *Frontier Dispute* case between Burkina Faso and Mali, the matter was also raised, and I would like to draw attention to the text of the relevant Order, because I think the precise wording is of importance, against the background of the *Aegean Sea* case in which the Court had deliberately left the point open.

The Chamber – I would recall it was a chamber, not the full Court – said that

> "Considering that independently of the requests submitted by the Parties for the indiciation of provisional measures, the Court or, accordingly, the chamber possesses *by virtue of Article 41 of the Statute* the power to indicate provisional measures with a view to preventing the aggravation or extension of the dispute whenever it considers that circumstances so require"[41].

---

[39] Cf. the observations of the present writer, "The Law and Procedure of the International Court of Justice", Part Four, 63 *British Yearbook of International Law* 48–54 (1992).

[40] "Whereas, independently of its request regarding the preservation of its rights, Greece requested the Court during the public sittings to indicate interim measures of protection in order to prevent the aggravation or extension of the dispute; whereas, before this request could be entertained, the Court would have to determine whether, under Article 41 of the Statute, the Court has such an independent power to indicate interim measures having that object; whereas, however, for the reasons now to be explained, the Court does not find it necessary to examine this point;" (*I. C. J. Reports 1976*, 12, para. 36).

[41] *I. C. J. Reports 1986*, 9, para. 18.

'There is here apparently a clear assertion that that power does exist; but the opening phrase is rather odd, because one would expect it to say "independently of the power to protect rights or to preserve rights". It does not say that, it says "independently of the requests submitted by the parties for the indication of provisional measures", and that, of course, is totally uncontroversial. It is quite clear, and indeed laid down in the Rules of Court, that the Court or the Chamber can indicate measures independently of what the parties have asked for. There is nonetheless here an assertion of an independent power to indicate provisional measures merely to prevent the aggravation or extension of the dispute.

If however one looks at what the Chamber actually did, the operative clause of the Order begins by stating that the two Governments

> "should each of them ensure that no action of any kind is taken which might aggravate or extend the dispute ... or prejudice the right of the other Party to compliance with whatever judgment the Chamber may render in the case"[42].

Now while that is a slightly different wording, I would suggest it is clearly an indication not to "anticipate" the judgment, to use the *Fisheries Jurisdiction* term, the essential direction being that each party is not to prejudice the rights of the other party. In other words, although the Chamber asserted an independent power to indicate measures just to prevent the extension or aggravation of the dispute, it did not in fact use it, so that one is left with an assertion *in vacuo*, as it were, rather than an element establishing the practice of the Court.

The most recent cases before the International Court in which there has been a request for provisional measures are the two cases arising out of the Lockerbie incident, the proceedings brought by Libya against the United Kingdom and the United States. The result in those cases is most enlightening on the point now under consideration, not so much for what is in the Orders, but for what is *not* in the Orders. If you take the Lockerbie Orders, by which the Court refused the requests for provisional measures, and read first of all the dissenting opinions attached to them, you find that there was a very strong current of thought among the minority dissenting judges in favour of indicating measures addressed solely to preventing the aggravation or extension of the dispute[43]. The Order itself might therefore have been expected to touch on the point, and to indicate either that the Court was not satisfied that it had power to indicate measures for that sole purpose, or that

---

[42] *I. C. J. Reports 1986*, 11–12, para. 32 (1) (A).

[43] See dissenting opinion of Judge Bedjaoui, *I. C. J. Reports 1992*, 48–49, paras. 31–34; dissenting opinion of Judge Ranjeva, *ibid.*, 74–77; dissenting opinion of Judge Ajibola, *ibid.*, 89–90, 92–93; dissenting opinion of Judge *ad hoc* El-Kosheri, *ibid.*, 110–111, paras. 59–60. Judge Weeramantry dissented on different grounds.

it thought that it had such a power, thus accepting the view of the *Frontier Dispute* Chamber, but did not consider it appropriate to exercise it.

In fact, however, the matter is left totally uncommented on in the Order. The requests for provisional measures were refused, basically on the ground that the rights sought to be protected were, because of the events which had happened, no longer appropriate for protection[44]; the question of preservation of rights was thus settled quite clearly and definitively by the Court. The Court did not make any comment whatsoever on the possiblity that it might nonetheless have indicated measures designed to prevent aggravation or extension of the dispute. This, I suggest, points to a general feeling, at least, that either no independent power in that respect exists, or it is one which, if it exists, should be exercised very sparingly.

E. Preservation of evidence

One other purpose of provisional measures which I would like just to touch on in passing, since it is not of great importance, is the purely procedural justification, in the sense of measures designed to prevent, for example, destruction of evidence. This was mentioned in the PCIJ President's Order in the *Sino-Belgian* case[45]. Turkey in the *Aegean Sea* case made a remarkably bold attempt to argue that the steps it was taking, which Greece sought to prevent by seeking provisional measures, were in fact steps designed to secure evidence[46], thus hinting that not only should they not be forbidden, but they should be encouraged! The Court was not convinced.

The only other case in which the matter of preservation of evidence was raised was the *Frontier Dispute (Burkina Faso/Mali)* case, where the essential reason why provisional measures were sought was because hostilities had broken out, and one of the points mentioned by the Court in its Order was that there was a risk of destruction of evidence which might be material to the frontier dispute of which the Court was seized[47].

III. The conditions for the indication of provisional measures

I see that time is running short, so I will perhaps pass rather rapidly over some further points, but there is at least one which must be dealt with in

[44] *I. C. J. Reports 1992*, 15, para. 40.

[45] *Denunciation of the Treaty of 2 November 1985 between China and Belgium, P. C. I. J., Series A, No. 8.*

[46] *Aegean Sea Continental Shelf, Pleadings, Oral Arguments, Documents*, 75, para. 21.

[47] *Frontier Dispute, I. C. J. Reports 1986*, 9, para. 20.

some depth. The first condition for the indication of provisional measures is a very simple one. Measures are indicated in proceedings before the Court, so there must be an established case before the Court, already instituted. This is not necessarily as obvious as it might seem, because I believe there are tribunals which are not subject to that restriction[48].

Secondly, the rights which it is sought to protect by provisional measures must be, if not identical to, linked closely with the rights which the main case is destined to have declared or have protected. The *Arbitral Award* case between Guinea-Bissau and Senegal recently decided by the Court provides a textbook example on this point. Guinea-Bissau was seeking to have the Court declare the 1989 Arbitral Award void, non-existent or invalid, and it asked for provisional measures which were essentially destined to preserve the *status quo* in the maritime areas which were the subject of the Arbitral Award. The Court pointed out that the two concepts proposed were perfectly separate, and in particular that, if the Court were to give judgment in favour of Guinea-Bissau on the main case, that would have no effect whatsoever on the rights which Guinea-Bissau was trying to have protected by the provisional measures. The Court said:

> "whereas accordingly the alleged rights sought to be made the subject of provisional measures are not the subject of the proceedings before the Court on the merits of the case; and whereas any such measures could not be subsumed by the Court's judgment on the merits;
>
> Whereas moreover a decision of the Court that the award is inexistent or null and void would in no way entail any decision that the Applicant's claims in respect of the disputed maritime delimitation are well founded, in whole or in part; and whereas the dispute over those claims will therefore not be resolved by the Court's judgment"[49].

A. Existence of jurisdiction

I now turn to a more vital issue, the question of jurisdiction, which was already alluded to by our Chairman in connection with Judge Mosler's opinion in the 1976 *Aegean Sea* case. Jurisdiction in this context has given rise to a lot of confusion and a lot of argument: what I say now may perhaps be challenged in debate, in fact I hope it will!

---

[48] The Court of Justice of the European Communities distinguishes two classes of application for interim relief, one which is "admissible only if it is made by a party to a case before the Court and relates to that case" and the other which is "admissible only if the applicant is challenging [the measure the suspension of which is sought] in proceedings before the Court": Rules of Procedure, Article 83, paragraph 1. Sztucki (*op. cit.*, note 1 above, 13) mentions examples of Mixed Arbitral Tribunals which admit requests for interim protection prior to the filing of an application.

[49] *I. C. J. Reports 1990*, 70, paras. 26–27.

There is, I think, general agreement that there are two sorts of jurisdiction to be considered here, and that they have to be kept distinct[50]. In every case, the Court must have jurisdiction to take a decision in the matter, and until it is established that it has jurisdiction to take a decision, it should not even proceed to hear the case if the defendant objects. That is the basis of the whole preliminary objection system. The Court has, however, also jurisdiction to indicate provisional measures and that is a separate jurisdiction flowing from Article 41 of the Statute. These two sorts of jurisdiction have generally, and correctly, been distinguished; they are both based on consent, but the one is "consent to Statute" and the other is "consent to case". There are two useful German terms for them[51], but I will not inflict my German accent – or rather my English accent in German – upon you!

Two separate consents are involved: what then is the relation between them? Now of course at one extreme it would be possible to say that the Court has jurisdiction to indicate provisional measures only if it has jurisdiction to decide the case; and when we say it has "jurisdiction to decide the case", we mean either that there is no challenge to that jurisdiction, or that the Court has already found that it has jurisdiction to hear the case. But that of course would lead to a virtual denial of the possibility of provisional measures in any case where the jurisdictional question was of any complexity, and I do not think that that is defended now. At the other extreme, it would be possible to argue that jurisdiction over the merits is totally irrelevant to jurisdiction to indicate provisional measures, that all the Court needs to do is to look at Article 41, to note that it is given power to indicate provisional measures, and to exercise that power, because it considers that the circumstances so require. I think it would be generally agreed that that would be too much a cheapening of States' consent underlying jurisdiction in the case[52]; and it is not of course the position of the Court.

---

[50] For the contrary view, see the dissenting opinion of Judge Forster in the *Nuclear Test* cases, *I. C. J. Reports 1973*, 111 and 148.

[51] Fall-Zustimmung and Statut-Zustimmung: see Magiera, "Zur Bezeichnung vorsorglicher Maßnahmen durch den Internationalen Gerichtshof: Verfahrenseffektivität gegen staatliche Souveränität", 17 *Jahrbuch für Internationales Recht* 275 (1974).

[52] The position was well stated by Judge Hersch Lauterpacht in his separate opinion in the *Interhandel* case: "However, it is one thing to say that action of the Court under Article 41 of the Statute does not in any way prejudge the question of its competence on the merits and that the Court need not at that stage satisfy itself that it has jurisdiction on the merits or even that its jurisdiction is probable; it is another thing to affirm that the Court can act under Article 41 without any regard to the prospects of its jurisdiction on the merits and that the latter question does not arise at all in connection with a request for interim measures of protection ... Governments ought not to be discouraged from undertaking, or continuing to undertake, the obligations of judicial settlement as the result of any justifiable apprehension that by accepting them they may become exposed to the embarrassment, vexation and loss, possibly following upon interim measures, in cases in which there is no reasonable possibility, *prima facie* ascertained by the Court, of jurisdiction on the merits. Accord-

The confusion which at one time reigned as to the relevance in proceedings on a request for provisional measures of questions of jurisdiction does in fact seem now to have been dissipated. A clear distinction is drawn between the Court's jurisdiction to indicate provisional measures, and its jurisdiction to determine the merits in the case in the course of which the request for measures is made. There is no direct link of dependence of the one on the other. The jurisdiction to indicate provisional measures derives directly from Article 41 of the Statute and exists independently of jurisdiction over the merits, in the sense that it is not necessary to prove the existence of merits-jurisdiction as a precondition to the indication of measures. A form of jurisdiction derived directly from the Statute, like the jurisdiction to revise or interpret a judgment, or the jurisdiction to give an advisory opinion, is not exposed to jurisdictional objections designed to show that an asserted jurisdiction over the merits is non-existent or does not extend to the case brought. Probably only an objection that the Applicant was not a State entitled to appear before the Court[53], or that the proceedings had somehow not been validly instituted at all[54], could be considered as a possible bar to the very existence of jurisdiction under Article 41.

The probability or otherwise of the existence of jurisdiction over the merits is however a "circumstance" to be taken into account by the Court, on a prima facie basis, when considering whether to exercise its jurisdiction under Article 41. As Judge Shahabuddeen has put it:

> "in considering whether it has prima facie jurisdiction over the merits, the Court is not considering whether it has power to indicate interim measures (for this rests on another basis), but is rather considering whether the case is a fit and proper one for exercising that power"[55].

The parallel with the giving of an advisory opinion is a close one. The consent of a State involved in a dispute in relation to which an advisory opinion is requested of the Court is not necessary for the jurisdiction of the Court derives directly from the Charter and Statute. It is however material to the decision to be taken by the Court as to how to exercise its discretion to give or refuse an opinion; this was established

---

ingly, the Court cannot, in relation to a request for indication of interim measures, disregard altogether the question of its competence on the merits". (*I. C. J. Reports 1957*, 118).

53 A situation which arose – after this paper was delivered – in a case concerning *Application of the Convention on the Prevention and Punishment of the Crime of Genocide*: see *I. C. J. Reports 1993*, 12–14, paras. 15–19.

54 An interesting theoretical question is raised by Article 38, paragraph 5, of the 1978 Rules of Court concerning proceedings instituted with an admission by the Applicant of the absence of an existing title of jurisdiction, and an invitation to the Respondent to accept jurisdiction *ad hoc*. The Rule provides that, with the exception of the transmission of the application to the State named as respondent, no action is to be taken on it unless and until that State accepts jurisdiction. It was applied for the first time to an Application related to the Danube dam, later superseded by the Special Agreement between Hungary and Slovakia on the *Gabcikovo-Nagymaros Project case*: see ICJ Press Communiqué No. 92/17. Given that Article 41 jurisdiction does not depend on the existence of merits-jurisdiction, can the Court by a Rule exclude a party from asserting a right given by the Statute? In practice, of course, a request for provisional measures in such circumstances would inevitably be rejected on the grounds that there was no prospect of merits-jurisdiction: but could an applicant insist on the Court going through the motions of hearing its request (with consequent publicity!) and giving its decision in an Order?

55 *Passage through the Great Belt*, (separate opinion), *I. C. J. Reports 1991*, 30.

in the *Peace Treaties* and *Western Sahara* cases, and restated recently in the so-called "Mazilu" case:

> "While, however, the absence of the consent of Romania to the present proceedings can have no effect on the jurisdiction of the Court, it is a matter to be considered when examining the propriety of the Court giving an opinion"[56].

The underlying reason is of course different: while in the case of advisory opinions, it is necessary to avoid "circumventing the principle that a State is not obliged to allow its disputes to be submitted to judicial settlement without its consent"[57], in the case of provisional measures what has to be avoided is simply an order indicating measures made by a court which later proves to have lacked jurisdiction.

The Court has said in the Nicaragua *v.* United States case that jurisdiction over the merits is a point which is given "fullest consideration compatible with the requirements of urgency"[58]; and it is the point which, in all cases in which the question was examined, has been considered first. When the Court considers a request for provisional measures, you usually find in the Order giving or – in most cases – refusing provisional measures first of all a consideration of the question: does the Court have jurisdiction on the merits?

One view which has been brought forward in an opinion by Judge Jiménez de Aréchaga, and which is an attractive one, is that when the Statute talks of the circumstances which the Court has to consider before indicating provisional measures, one of those circumstances – and perhaps the most important – is the likelihood of establishing jurisdiction over the merits[59]. That is an attractive idea because it lends flexibility to the procedure which, I would suggest, is an essential element of it. However, it involves two difficulties. One is that Article 41 of the Statute says the Court may indicate measures if it considers that the circumstances so "require", and in no way you can say that the existence of jurisdiction *requires* the indication of measures. The second is that it puts jurisdiction on the same level as all the other circumstances which the Court may consider, and possibly therefore downgrades it a little too far.

I do not myself have a clear theory to offer to you on exactly how this relationship should be defined; it will be interesting to see whether one emerges in the course of today's discussion. All I can do is throw out some further ideas on this, and mention in particular a text to which the Chairman has already referred, Judge Mosler's opinion in the *Aegean Sea* case. Judge Mosler, as I understand him, does not accept the idea that jurisdiction is only one of the circumstances which the Court can examine. He says:

---

56 *Applicability of Article VI, Section 22, of the Convention on the Privileges and Immunities of the United Nations, I. C. J. Reports 1989*, 190–191.

57 *Western Sahara, I. C. J. Reports 1975*, 25, quoted in *I. C. J. Reports 1989*, 191.

58 *I. C. J. Reports 1984*, 179, para. 25.

59 *I. C. J. Reports 1973*, 107.

"I would add that provisional affirmation of jurisdiction is in my view not a 'circumstance' contributing to the necessity of provisional measures in the sense of Article 41, but a precondition of the examination whether such circumstances exist"[60].

In other words, there must be a two stage operation, as I understand the argument: the Court must first consider whether in its view there is a probability, possibility, quasi-certainty (just which remains to be seen) of jurisdiction on the merits. If that is so then it proceeds to the next stage: what are the circumstances and do they justify the indication? Now that is in fact more or less how the Court has worked. But it is the theoretical underpinning which is interesting. Judge Mosler's opinion continues:

"If the Court, however, as in the present Order, rejects the request because the circumstances are not considered to require interim measures, it examines the legal situation existing between the parties to the dispute and thus, to that extent, also assumes jurisdiction. But in this hypothesis the Court has only to satisfy itself that it does not manifestly lack jurisdiction, since the Order does nothing to interfere with the rights of the respondent party"[61].

That is, I take it, a reply to a possible objection based both on practice and theory. Supposing the Court is perfectly satisfied that it has jurisdiction on the merits, but finds that it is not a case for provisional measures, because circumstances do not justify them, does the classification of the jurisdictional question as a precondition mean that the Court has first of all to establish a possibility of jurisdiction – jurisdiction on the merits – before it can go on to the next stage of rejecting a request for provisional measures as unjustified? There is obviously a certain lack of procedural economy in so acting; but is it in fact a theoretically possible construct?

My suggestion – and here I am offering Judge Mosler the birthday present of a disagreement with his views, which is always more stimulating than agreement! My own suggestion is that one cannot treat the possible existence of jurisdiction over the merits as a precondition to the indication of provisional measures without confusing the two sorts of jurisdiction. If, as Judge Mosler says, when the Court rejects a request because the circumstances are not considered to require interim measures, "it examines the legal situation existing between the parties to the dispute and thus to that extent

[60] *I. C. J. Reports 1976*, 25.

[61] *I. C. J. Reports 1976*, 25. Judge Mosler's view is in fact intermediate between those judges who in the *Aegean Sea* case held that jurisdiction must in every case be examined first (Judge Lachs, *loc. cit.*, 19, Judge Morozov, *ibid.*, 21, Judge Ruda, *ibid.*, 22, and Judge Tarazi, *ibid.*, 32) and those who held that no examination of jurisdiction was required if there was an independent reason for rejecting the request for measures (Judge Jiménez de Aréchaga, *loc. cit.*, Judge Singh, *ibid.*, 17–18, and Judge Elias, *ibid.*, 27).

also assumes jurisdiction"[62], i.e., is exercising jurisdiction, one has to ask: what jurisdiction? My suggestion would be that in doing so it is exercising only its Article 41 jurisdiction, its distinct statutory jurisdiction; it is not using any part of its merits jurisdiction. If that is right, then there is no reason at all to justify taking the merits-jurisdiction question first.

In view of the shortage of time I must leave the particular argument there, and proceed just to mention another which I think has been defended by some authorities including President Pescatore[63] also. This is the idea that the jurisdiction of a Court to decide a dispute can be as it were broken up, sliced up, taken in stages, that if the Court has authority and jurisdiction to decide the merits of the dispute, it can exercise a scintilla, or some part, of that jurisdiction, at an early stage to indicate provisional measures. This is the view that, for the reasons which I hope I am making clear, I do not find easy to accept; it seems to me one has to treat the two jurisdictions as quite distinct.

With an eye on the clock, I shall pass rapidly over the problem of the extent to which jurisdiction over the merits must be established. There is an article of Professor Mendelson in the *British Yearbook* some twenty years ago[64] in which he gave a whole list, a whole spectrum of cases, jurisdiction certain, jurisdiction quasi-certain, evenly balanced, jurisdiction doubtful, jurisdiction impossible, and so on, and discussed the possible effect of each; but I think the only conclusion one can draw from such a discussion is that it is impossible to arrive at a water-tight definition. The Court must have some indication that it is going to be able to decide the case on the merits, but how sure of that it should be is probably impossible to define. In fact, the general trend seems to be towards a very low standard of proof. Judge Schwebel, in the Nicaragua *v.* United States case, suggested that "the nub of the matter" appears to be that "the Court gives the defendant the benefit of the doubt"; while Vice-President Oda in the recent Lockerbie cases suggested that in fact precedents indicate that it is sufficient if the lack of jurisdiction is not obvious[65], an approach that may not be acceptable for the whole Court, but cannot be far wrong.

---

[62] *Loc. cit.*: the French translation reads, correctly it is suggested, "... elle exerce effectivement *une* compétence", and not "la compétence" or "sa compétence".

[63] *"Les mesures conservatoires et les référés"*, *in La juridiction internationale permanente*, Société française pour le droit international, Colloque de Lyon (1987), 349–350.

[64] M. H. Mendelson, "Interim Measures of Protection in Cases of Contested Jurisdiction", 46 *British Yearbook of International Law* 259 et seq. (1972–1973). See also J. H. Merrills, "Interim Measures of Protection and the Substantive Jurisdiction of the International Court", 36 *Cambridge Law Journal* 86 et seq. (1977).

[65] Judge Schwebel: *I. C. J. Reports 1984*, 207. Vice-President Oda: "... through the Court's jurisprudence, it is established that, if the Court appears prima facie to possess jurisdiction, it may (if it thinks fit) indicate provisional measures, and this rule has always been interpreted most generously in favour of the applicant, lest a denial be needlessly prejudicial to the continuation of the case. Thus the possibility of

A curious sidelight on the question of the relevance of the probability of jurisdiction over the merits is afforded by a procedural incident in the Nicaragua *v.* United States case in June-July 1984. Provisional measures had been indicated in May 1984; it had been decided that questions of jurisdiction and admissibility would be pleaded first, and in fact the Court was to uphold its jurisdiction by a Judgment of 26 November 1984. On 25 June 1984, Nicaragua complained that the United States had failed to comply with the measures, and asked for fresh measures recording such non-compliance, and declaring that the United States was under "a particular legal duty to cease and desist" from activities inconsistent with the measures[66]. A letter from the President of the Court indicated rejection of the request by the Court. The President referred to the proceedings in the Security Council when the United Kingdom endeavoured to obtain a decision calling on Iran to carry out the measures indicated in the *Anglo-Iran Oil Co.* case, which proceedings were adjourned "until the International Court of Justice has ruled on its own competence in the matter"[67]. The President's letter continued:

> "The Court sees no reason to take a different position in regard to your present Request and would suggest that you await the outcome of the present proceedings on jurisdiction".

Apart from the reliance on a purely political decision in the Secrity Council as a precedent, this decision seems inconsistent with the generally-accepted position as to jurisdiction. If the Court were to find that it had no jurisdiction, the measures would lapse for the future[68]; but pending a decision on the merits-jurisdiction, the measures, indicated in exercise of the special statutory jurisdiction, were perfectly valid and effective, and capable of such enforcement as provisional measures in general – whatever that may be.

B. Existence of a prima facie case

The proceedings on the request of Finland for the indication of provisional measures in the case concerning Passage through the Great Belt raised the question whether or to what extent a State requesting measures must "be able to substantiate the right that it claims to a point where a reasonable prospect of success in the main case exists"[69]. Denmark argued that this was a requirement, and that "not even a prima facie case exists in favour of the Finnish contention", since it denied that there was "a right of free passage through the Danish Strait for structures up to 170 metres high"[70]. The Court's ruling did not in fact resolve the point directly:

---

indicating provisional measures may be denied *in limine* only in a case where the lack of jurisdiction is so obvious as to require no further examination of the existence of jurisdiction in a later phase". (*I. C. J. Reports 1993*, 18).

66 The Nicaraguan request and the President's letter in reply have not yet been published, but will appear in the volume of the Court's series of publications entitled *Pleadings, Oral Arguments, Documents* devoted to the case.

67 SCOR, 6th year, 563rd meeting, 17 October 1951, para. 10. See further Sztucki, (*op. cit.*, note 1 above), 44.

68 In the *Anglo-Iranian Oil Co.* case itself, the Court's Judgment of 22 July 1952 deciding that it had no jurisdiction specifically stated that the Order on provisional measures "ceases to be operative upon the delivery of this Judgment and ... the Provisional Measures lapse at the same time" (*I. C. J. Reports 1952*, 114).

69 *I. C. J. Reports 1991*, 17, para. 21.

70 *I. C. J. Reports 1991*, 17, para. 21.

"Whereas it is the purpose of provisional measures to preserve 'rights which are the subject of dispute in judicial proceedings' (*United States Diplomatic and Consular Staff in Tehran, I. C. J. Reports 1979*, 19, para. 36; see also *Frontier Dispute, I. C. J. Reports 1986*, 8, para. 13); whereas the Court notes that the existence of a right of Finland of passage through the Great Belt is not challenged, the dispute between the parties being over the nature and extent of that right, including its applicability to certain drill ships and oil rigs; whereas such a disputed right may be protected by the indication of provisional measures under Article 41 of the Statute if the Court 'considers that circumstances so require'"[71].

The implication seems to be that the problem whether there is a prima facie case on the merits does not arise if the existence of a right to be protected is admitted, the only question in dispute being whether it extends to the factual situation brought before the Court. This would thus differentiate the *Great Belt* case from, for example, the *Nuclear Test* cases, where the very existence of a right to redress for damage caused by fall-out from nuclear tests was disputed. The criterion chosen by the Court, while appropriate for the facts before it, does not lend itself for generalization: cases could be imagined in which a right well established in international law was relied on to claim relief in circumstances very far removed from the normal sphere of operation of that right; if there is any requirement that a prima facie case be made out as a condition of provisional measures, this must be so in principle even where what is asserted is an extension of a recognized right.

The Court's handling of the question did not satisfy Judge Shahabuddeen, who wrote a full separate opinion on the point[72]. On the basis of a thorough analysis of the question, and a survey of the relevant previous decisions of the Court, Judge Shahabuddeen concludes that

"a State requesting interim measures ... is required to establish the possible existence of the rights sought to be protected in the sense in which Judge Anzilotti spoke of the Court, by a *summaria cognitio*, taking 'into account the *possibility* of the right claimed ... and the *possibility* of the danger to which that right was exposed'"[73].

No attempt will be made here to summarize Judge Shahabuddeen's survey of the question, which demands to be read in its entirety, and with which the present writer respectfully, and whole-heartedly, agrees. One point of interest made in the opinion relates to the generally accepted requirement that some prima facie jurisdiction over the merits must be shown. Judge Shahabuddeen observes:

"But jurisdiction over the merits is merely one element which the applicant must establish in order to succeed in the substantive case which it has brought – a truth undiminished, in my view, by the importance of that element or by the fact that it may be argued as a preliminary issue. If the applicant cannot make out a prima facie case of substantive jurisdiction, this circumstance shows that it has no possibility of succeeding. Why should the applicant be limited to being required to show a prima facie case in respect of only one of the elements which it must establish if it is to succeed? ... It is not suggested that the requesting State should anticipate and meet each and every issue which could arise at the merits. How far it should do so in any particular case will depend on the nature and circumstances of the case.

---

[71] *I. C. J. Reports 1991*, 17, para. 22.

[72] *I. C. J. Reports 1991*, 28–36.

[73] *I. C. J. Reports 1991*, 36; the quotation is from Judge Anzilotti's dissenting opinion in the *Polish Agrarian Reform* case, *P. C. I. J., Series A/B, No. 58*, 181.

What is important is that enough material should be presented to demonstrate the possibility of existence of the right sought to be protected"[74].

The emphasis in the reported decisions on the jurisdictional element as requiring to be established prima facie is explicable, in the light of the fact that it is on this jurisdictional element that respondents have frequently concentrated attack when arguing against the granting of provisional measures. Furthermore, even when the distinction between jurisdiction on the merits, and jurisdiction under Article 41 to indicate provisional measures, has been clearly recognized, the urgent and proper concern of the Court not to overstep the bounds of its jurisdiction has probably led it to concentrate on this aspect. If, having indicated measures, the Court ultimately finds that it is without jurisdiction, that does not mean that it acted without jurisdiction when indicating them; nor even that it acted in breach of a condition to the exercise of that jurisdiction, provided it acted as appropriate to satisfy itself of a prima facie possibility of jurisdiction. Nevertheless, such a situation would produce an appearance of having acted without jurisdiction which should be avoided where possible. For this reason it is suggested that, *pace* Vice-President Oda[75] the degree of probability required for jurisdiction should be somewhat higher than that needed for the other elements of a prima facie case on the merits.

C. Urgency

The other conditions for the indication of measures I shall have to pass over quickly. One is that there must be urgency in the request for provisional measures; that was nicely demonstrated and defined in the *Great Belt* case, but I shall not dwell on that because I want to get on to the other main controversial question.

The definition of "urgency" in the *Great Belt* case is elegantly brief:

"Whereas provisional measures under Article 41 of the Statute are indicated 'pending the final decision' of the Court on the merits of the case, and are therefore only justified if there is urgency in the sense that action prejudicial to the rights of either party is likely to be taken before such final decision is given"[76];

At the outset of proceedings, the date on which the final decision will be given is fairly unforeseeable – increasingly so, with the current trend for more cases to be brought to the Court. There is however no fixed time in the course of the proceedings at which a request for provisional measures must be brought: on the contrary, Article 73, paragraph 1, of the Rules of Court specifically states that such a request may be made "at any time during the course of the proceedings in the case". Thus if a case drags on for longer than expected, and a threat to the Applicant's rights becomes urgent, a request for measures can be presented; and Article 75, paragraph 3, makes it clear that this is so even if an earlier request has been rejected, provided the second request is "based on new facts".

Furthermore, the Court in the *Great Belt* case also made it clear that the institution of proceedings itself will have protective effect on the rights claimed, in the sense that the date of proceedings will be a "critical date" after which action by a State cannot

---

[74] *I. C. J. Reports 1991*, 31.

[75] Opinion in the *Genocide Convention* case, quoted above, text and note 64.

[76] *I. C. J. Reports 1991*, 17, para. 23.

improve its position. Denmark had argued (rather unwisely) that 'if the Court ruled in favour of Finland on the merits, any claim by Finland could not be dealt with by an order for restitution, but could only be satisfied by damages inasmuch as restitution in kind would be excessively onerous". The Court's response to this was firm:

> "whereas the Court is not at present called upon to determine the character of any decision which it might make on the merits; whereas in principle however if it is established that the construction of works involves an infringement of a legal right, the possibility cannot and should not be excluded a priori of a judicial finding that such works must not be continued or must be modified or dismantled"[77].

It also made it clear that for a State to continue with operations claimed to infringe another State's rights would not strengthen the active State's position – rather the contrary:

> "Whereas no action taken *pendente lite* by a State engaged in a dispute before the Court with another State 'can have any effect whatever as regards the legal situation which the Court is called upon to define' (*Legal Status of the South-Eastern Territory of Greenland, P. C. I. J., Series A/B*, No. 48, 287), and such action cannot improve its legal position vis-à-vis that other State;
>
> Whereas it is for Denmark, which is informed of the nature of Finland's claim, to consider the impact which a judgment upholding it could have upon the implementation of the Great Belt project, and to decide whether or to what extent it should accordingly delay or modify that project"[78].

There is nothing novel or revolutionary about these statements, but they bring a welcome clarification of the position pending proceedings before the Court, which it is the whole purpose of provisional measures to regulate.

It appears from the *Passage through the Great Belt* decision, quoted above, that urgency is not an absolute, but may be a matter of degree; and indeed this is a matter of common sense. On the filing of a request for the indication of provisional measures, the purpose of the convening of the Court is so that it may proceed to a decision on the request as a "matter of urgency" (Rules, Article 74, paragraph 2). It is therefore presumably for the President, when fixing a date for hearing, to take into account, in a very provisional way, the degree of urgency indicated by the nature of the request, and to relate it to other material considerations. This is the explanation for the wide range of lapses of time between the filing of a request and the holding of a hearing: in the *Passage through the Great Belt* case, a hearing 40 days after the request was filed was found perfectly adequate to the degree of urgency involved, while in the Tehran Hostages cases, the Court was able to sit 10 days after the request was filed.

Among the other material considerations, one of the most important must be the application of the rule *audi alteram partem*: the Rules of Court require that the date of hearing be so fixed that the parties are afforded the opportunity of being represented at it (Article 74, paragraph 3). In many cases it may be this, rather than the time needed to assemble the full Court, which primarily determines the date, so that nothing would be gained by acting immediately on the basis of a bare quorum. A further consideration is that the respondent State cannot be deprived of its right under Article 31, paragraph 3, of the Statute to appoint a judge *ad hoc*, for which some time must be allowed.

The problem of irreparability of damage is one which we have already touched on. There was in the Lockerbie cases a very interesting suggestion

[77] *I. C. J. Reports 1991*, 19, para. 31.

[78] *I. C. J. Reports 1991*, 19, paras. 32–33.

by Professor Rosalyn Higgins, appearing for the United Kingdom[79], that irreparability could mean – I just quote her categories – first, irreparable prejudice to the potential judgment of the Court; secondly, irreparable harm to rights claimed (as we have seen that is a rather doubtful starter); and thirdly irreparable harm to persons and property, – and that bearing in mind the *United States Diplomatic and Consular Staff in Tehran* case, and the *Trial of Pakistani Prisoners of War* case, must undoubtedly be present in this discussion, even if it is difficult to define in statutory terms.

IV. The content of provisional measures: the "interim judgment"

A trend has been observed over the last 20 years or so for proceedings to be instituted before the Court in circumstances suggesting that the intention was less to obtain a judgment on the merits than to obtain the short-term tactical advantage of an order indicating provisional measures. Even if this *procès d'intention* is unjustified in the specific cases heard by the Court, it is evident that the fact that neither jurisdiction nor the claim itself have to be proved up to anywhere near the hilt for measures to be granted must offer a temptation where a case can be made for urgency even if the merits of the claim are shaky or the jurisdictional title dubious. In the circumstances, appeal might apparently be made by a respondent State to the Order of the Permanent Court in the *Chorzów* case in 1927 dismissing a request by Germany as not related to interim protection "but as designed to obtain an interim judgment in favour of part of the claim"[80].

This approach was adopted by Judge Gros in his dissenting opinion appended to the Order of 22 June 1973 on the requests for provisional measures in the *Nuclear Test* cases. Referring to the PCIJ dictum he said:

> "Here we have a condition of general scope for the interpretation of Article 41 of the Statute of the Permanent Court of International Justice, which was identical to the present Article 41, and the recognition of a procedural requirement operating in regard to interlocutory jurisdiction. For it would indeed, by definition, be contrary to the nature of interlocutory proceedings if they enabled the dispute of which they were only an accessory element to be disposed of"[81].

This for Judge Gros was an additional reason for rejecting the requests of Australia and New Zealand, which the Court dismissed on other grounds. The result of Judge Gros's argument, if a case were otherwise made out for the indication of measures, is curious. The measures requested must, it is well established, relate to the rights claimed in the Application. Could the Court refuse to indicate measures requiring the temporary cessation of nuclear tests merely because the claim was for a permanent cessation of such tests? Assuming that there was sufficient evidence of urgency and the prospect of irreparable damage, the mere coincidence of the request for measures with the terms of the claim would be a strange and artificial reason for refusal. It might be suspected in some cases (and this may well have been in Judge Gros's mind) that,

---

79 Verbatim record, sitting of 26 March 1992, CR 92/3, 53.
80 *P. C. I. J., Series A, No. 12*, 10.
81 *I. C. J. Reports 1973*, 123, 158.

having obtained an indication of measures, the party interested would be in no hurry to have the case heard in the merits; but that could be dealt with by a provision in the Court's Order for the measures to be reviewed after a time in the light of (*inter alia*) the progress of the proceedings on the merits[82].

The thinking behind the decision in the *Chorzów* case is, it is suggested, rather different. The German request was presented at a stage in those complex proceedings when Germany had obtained a judgment from the Court that Poland had committed breaches of the Geneva Convention of 15 May 1922, and a further judgment that the Court had jurisdiction to entertain a claim for reparation for those breaches. Accordingly, Germany contended that it was entitled to adequate compensation which "could not be less than a certain minimum; it is therefore in reality only the upper limit of the sum to be awarded which is in dispute"[83]. It alleged various economic circumstances whereby "unless payment be immediate, the amount of the damage and of the compensation would considerably increase" and "the prejudice caused by a further delay would be irreparable materially"[84].

In the Order of the Court, the passage cited above, and relied on by Judge Gros, was preceded by a recital recalling that while the Court had found that it had jurisdiction, the claims on the merits had been "reserved for judgment". In this context, the Court appears to have seen the German request as based on an unfounded assumption, namely that the payment of some compensation by Poland was a foregone conclusion, and that therefore a minimum amount should be paid at once. Thus the reference to "an interim judgment in favour of a part of the claim" does not relate to the fact that the request for measures and the merits claim were identical in seeking compensation, but to the basis of the German request. It was not so much asking for protection *pendente lite* of the rights asserted in the Application, as asking for immediate satisfaction of what it regarded as an indisputable part of the claim[85].

V. Binding or non-binding effect of provisional measures

Before closing I would like to turn to the other very controversial question in this field, and that is, to what extent, if at all, are provisional measures binding on the State to which they are directed? It may be said at once that the text of the Statute is rather against the thesis that measures are binding: you will remember that the Court merely "indicates" measures, it does not "order" them, and they are measures which "ought to be taken", not which "must be" taken or "are to be" taken. The *travaux préparatoires* of 1922 also rather point to an intention that measures should be not-binding[86]. The

---

[82] Cf. the Orders made the previous year in the *Fisheries Jurisdiction* cases.

[83] Request, set out in the Order of 21 November 1927, *P. C. I. J., Series A, No. 12*, 4.

[84] P. C. I. J., Series A, No. 12, 6. The original French text reads "matériellement irréparable"; the PCIJ translation is "would actually be irreparable" which does not seem to be correct.

[85] Cf. the treatment by the Court of a similar claim by Nicaragua at the merits stage of the Nicaragua *v.* United States case, *I. C. J. Reports 1986*, 143, para. 285.

[86] See the analysis in Sztucki, *op. cit.* (note 1 above) at 23–27, 263–265. Particularly to be noted is the substitution of the French verb "indiquer" for "ordonner", and the reference in the English version to "the measures *suggested*".

doctrine I think is divided, but there is quite a strong current of opinion in favour of the view that they are binding[87].

I see further difficulties in that view, and an indication of these will be a particular contribution I should like to offer to the debate on this point. I think it is essential to be sure what we mean by binding: binding in what way? Whenever a State enters into an arbitral or judicial procedure, the eventual judgment of the Court or of the tribunal is going to be binding as a matter of treaty-law, because the State has accepted in the *compromis*, or by accession to the Statute, that it shall be. So the binding nature of a judgment of the Court, I suggest, is, initially, purely a matter of treaty-law. Insofar as the judgment declares the rights of the parties under general international law, however it is backed by a separate obligation; States therefore comply with the judgment not solely as a matter of treaty-law, but as a matter of general international law which has been clarified or declared by the Court. There are thus two parallel obligations.

Now if we look at an Order for provisional measures, such an Order does not define the rights of the Parties under the general international law applicable to their relations. It *assumes* that certain rights exist and that the facts of the case are such that the rights need to be protected, but it in no way decides that those rights exist, so that that second obligatory character that we find in the case of a judgment is missing. Therefore, I suggest, a provisional measures Order can only be binding as a matter of treaty-law; the thesis that measures are binding rests solely on the premise that the Statute to which the States parties have acceded gives the Court power to indicate binding measures. If you once take that as your starting point, you can of course conclude that measures are binding; but because of the wording of the Statute and the *travaux préparatoires* it is very difficult to accept that premise that measures were intended by Statute to be binding.

A distinction is however here in order. The above discussion rests on the assumption that the provisional measures indicated direct the respondent State to refrain from doing something which it claims to be entitled to do, but which the applicant State considers to result in an infringement of its rights: examples of this are of course the *Nuclear Tests* cases, and the *Great Belt* case. Another possible situation is that in which the question is not whether the action complained of is lawful, but whether it is the respondent State which is responsible for it. In the Nicaragua *v.* United States case, there was no dispute that the mining of Nicaraguan ports was unlawful; the question was whether it was the United States which had done it. The measure directing the United States not to lay mines to endanger access to Nicaraguan ports[88] *was* thus parallelled by an obligation of general international law, independent of the provisional measures, binding on the United States. Were the United States to lay mines after the measures had been indicated, the question whether the measure which forbade mining was binding would be academic; the United States would in any event

87 See the very full discussion in Sztucki, *op. cit.* (note 1 above) at 280–287.

88 *I. C. J. Reports 1984*, 187, para. 41 (B) (1).

be acting unlawfully[89]. These considerations do not, however, it is suggested, detract from the essentially treaty-law basis for the effect of provisional measures.

It has however been suggested that provisional measures are binding as a result of a general principle of law[90]. This is an argument put forward particularly in a book by Professor Elkind[91] some years back. Reliance in this respect may be placed on the statement from the *Electricity Company* case which I quoted earlier[92]. That dictum however goes only so far as to accept that there is a universal principle that parties must abstain from measures capable of exercising a prejudicial effect in respect to the execution of the decision of the Court, which is rather different from saying that parties must accept the decision of a Court that certain measures should be abstained from. What is more, if one works on the basis that the matter is one governed by treaty, then can this general principle in fact operate in that field, bearing in mind the usual relationship between the various sources of law?

It has been suggested also by doctrinal authority that when the Charter and Statute[93] refer to compliance with a "decision" of the Court, this includes an Order on provisional measures, because such an Order is a "decision". There is no doubt about that, it is a decision; but it is a decision of a rather special nature. If the Court makes a decision, not on the merits, but of an interlocutory kind, that something is to be done, for example that a pleading should be filed within a certain time, then the State must comply with that decision. But what is *decided* by an Order indicating provisional measures is simply that the circumstances are such that it would be desirable

---

89 This is still more evident in the recent case of *Application of the Convention on the Prevention and Punishment of the Crime of Genocide (Bosnia and Herzegovina* v. *Yugoslavia (Serbia and Montenegro))*, where Yugoslavia was directed, by way of provisional measures, to take all measures within its power to prevent commission of the crime of genocide. See the addendum at the end of this paper.

90 One weakness of this argument is the fact that the European Convention on Human Rights does not contain a provision for the indication of provisional measures, and this omission was apparently deliberate: see the Court's Judgment in the Cruz Varas Case (referred to in the discussion, *infra*), Series A, Vol. 201, 34, paras. 94–95. If a court can be created without being given any power to order interim protection, then it must be possible to create a court which has power only to suggest the appropriateness of interim measures; cf. also the terms of Article 38 of the Rules of Procedure of the European Commission of Human Rights.

91 J. B. Elkind, *Interim Protection: A Functional Approach* 162 (Nijhoff, 1981): "It is the central theme of this book that the power to indicate interim measures is 'a general principle of law recognized by civilized nations' and that it is hence a principle of general international law under Article 38 (1) (c) of the Statute. As such a principle, interim measures indicated by the Court are binding".

92 *Supra*, text and note 14.

93 Specifically, Article 94, paragraph 1, of the Charter; Article 59 of the Statute is, as Dumbauld points out *op. cit.* (note 4 above) 289, less resorted to. Cf. however Judge Elias, "The International Court of Justice and the Indication of Provisional Measures of Protection", Gilberto Amado Memorial Lecture, 1978, 11, quoted in Elkind, *op. cit.* (note 43 above) 161.

that certain measures be taken, so that the only *decision* is not anything that can be complied with[94]. A State, in my submission, is entitled, having paid great respect to an Order indicating provisional measures, to say: "I accept your decision that this would be a good thing, but for other reasons I am not going to do it". Now whether or not it is internationally to be recommended or not, that is not a non-compliance with the decision.

Furthermore, if one accepts that the Order indicating provisional measures is binding, what happens if it is breached before the end of the case, but judgment is given for the Respondent? Is it open to the Court simultaneously to find that the Applicant has not made out the rights it claims, and to give judgment against the Applicant, but at the same time to find that the Order made to protect those rights has not been complied with, and that the Respondent is therefore condemned for not having complied with those measures? Can the Respondent be ordered to pay reparation for breach of a right which the Court in the same breath says does not exist?

If provisional measures were binding, it would be to be expected that in any case in which the Court, having indicated measures which had not been complied with, gave judgment in favour of the claim, it would in that judgment draw legal conclusions from the non-compliance. This situation arose in the case of *United States Diplomatic and Consular Staff in Tehran*, with the additional piquant feature that the Applicant itself had also acted in a way which could be regarded as a violation of the bilateral measure of "non-escalation" indicated by the Court[95]. The Court's approach to the situation is analyzed by Sztucki[96]; his conclusion, based not only on the Judgment in this case, but on pointers in earlier decisions is that

> "it would be difficult to find in the Court's texts any indication of its opinion that interim measures are formally binding in law"[97].

This conclusion is reinforced by the experience of the Nicaragua *v.* United States case. The Judgment on the merits in that case contains the following account of the procedural incident already discussed above in connection with the question of jurisdiction:

> "On 25 June 1984, the Government of Nicaragua addressed a communication to the Court referring to the Order indicating provisional measures, informing the Court of what Nicaragua regarded as 'the failure of the United States to comply with that Order', and requesting the indication of further measures. The action by the United States complained of consisted in the fact that the United States was continuing 'to sponsor and carry out military and paramilitary activities in and against Nicaragua'. By a letter of 16 July 1984, the President of the Court informed the Agent of Nicaragua that the Court considered that that request should await the outcome of the proceedings on jurisdiction which were then pending before the Court. The Government of Nicaragua has not reverted to the question"[98].

---

[94] The point is another expression of the limited terms of Article 41 of the Statute: the Court is called upon to indicate, and therefore to decide, what provisional measures "ought to be taken". It does not decide that measures shall be taken, or that there is a legal duty to take certain measures.

[95] *I. C. J. Reports 1979*, 21, para. 46 (1) (B).

[96] *Op. cit.* (note 1 above), 270–274.

[97] *Op. cit.* (note 1 above), 274.

[98] *I. C. J. Reports 1986*, 144, para. 287.

In its communication of 25 June 1984, Nicaragua stated that:

> "The purpose of this Request is to inform the Court, pursuant to paragraph 41 (C) of the Order [of 10 May 1984], of the failure of the United States to comply with that Order, and to request urgently, in accordance with Article 41 of the Statute of the Court, Articles 73, 76 and 78 of the Rules of Court, and paragraph 41 (C) of the Order of 10 May 1984, that the Court indicate measures to secure compliance with that Order".

There was thus no request for measures additional to or different from those already ordered (or those already requested, but not included in the Court's Order), but simply for reiteration or reinforcement of the measures ordered. It might be supposed that a fresh Order to this effect would have no more impact than the original Order; however, the real reason why Nicaragua presented its request is probably to be found in the third measure requested (paragraph 9 (c) of the request):

> "(c) That, until such time as the United States ceases and desists from all activities that do not comply with the Order of 10 May 1984, the facilities of the Court shall not be available to the United States for the purpose of rendering a decision in its favor in any other pending or future case, and the United States shall not be permitted to invoke the Court's aid in any matter".

Since the proceedings in the *Gulf of Maine* case were then in progress, an Order to this effect would have made considerable impact.

The reply by the President, which was expressed to convey the view of the Court, was an outright rejection of this request, as "not only unacceptable but also impermissible in that it unduly restricts the Court in the exercise of its normal function as a court"[99]. Thus not even a procedural sanction, within the control of the Court itself, could be imposed for breach of an order indicating provisional measures.

In its 1986 Judgment, however, the Court came as near as it ever has to defining its view on the binding or non-binding character of provisional measures. After alluding to the Nicaraguan approach in June 1984, the Court proceeded to re-emphasize, by quoting from its Order on provisional measures, the need for respect of Nicaragua's right to sovereignty and political independence, and then continued:

> "Furthermore, the Court would draw attention to the further measures indicated in its Order, namely that the Parties
>
> 'should each of them ensure that no action of any kind is taken which might aggravate or extend the dispute submitted to the Court'
>
> and
>
> 'should each of them ensure that no action is taken which might prejudice the rights of the other Party in respect of the carrying out of whatever decision the Court may render in the case'.
>
> When the Court finds that the situation requires that measures of this kind should be taken, it is incumbent on each party to take the Court's indications seriously into account, and not to direct its conduct solely by reference to what it believes to be its rights. Particularly is this so in a situation of armed conflict where no reparation can efface the results of conduct which the Court may rule to have been contrary to international law"[100].

Thus for the Court, the State to which measures – or at least measures "of this kind" – are addressed is not bound strictly to comply with them, but "to take the Court's

---

[99] A more cogent point is that the proposal would cause injustice to Canada, an innocent third party which was as much interested in a decision of the *Gulf of Maine* case as was the United States. This may have been what President Elias had in mind.

[100] *I. C. J. Report 1986*, 144, para. 289.

indications seriously into account". If measures have a binding character, this is the extent in the Court's view, of the obligation.

VI. The consequences of measures

One final point is the impact of an Order on the rights of the State against which measures are ordered. This was thrashed out in the *Great Belt* case recently in an extremely interesting discussion[101], but the question in fact did not find a place in the eventual Order. It was argued very strongly by Denmark that it was going to cost it a fortune to suspend operations on the Great Belt bridge and the fixed link[102], and that Finland, if it got its Order for provisional measures, would be under an obligation, or possibly would be bound to undertake an obligation, to indemnify Denmark for those expenses if the Court eventually ruled in favour of Denmark. The argument of Denmark was based largely on arguments from municipal law and general principles of law. Finland argued that there was no such principle, and that the Court had no power under the Statute and Rules to make an Order of this kind; it indicated that it was not ready to accept any such obligation.

My own suggestion on this is that if the Court had found measures necessary, it could have dealt with the problem[103] simply by imposing a condition on the measures, and saying that the measures would only come into effect, or could only be taken advantage of by Finland, provided it entered into an undertaking to indemnify Denmark in the event of a final judgment in favour of Denmark. No question of the extent of the Court's powers under Article 41, or of general principles of law would then arise; once again we are back to treaty-law obligations, since Finland would be given the option of accepting such an obligation on a treaty basis.

Mr. Chairman, I must apologize: the hands of the clock have gone round much further than I intended them to do while I was still on my feet, but that I think concludes what I have to say at this stage, and I thank you very much for your attention.

---

[101] See the verbatim records of the hearings, CR 91/10, 67–68 (Sinclair); CR 91/12, 24–32 (Magid); CR 91/13, 60–66 (Treves); CR 91/14, 35–37 (Magid).

[102] This was the unusual feature of the case, which probably accounted for the fact, stressed by Finland during the oral proceedings, that the request by Denmark for an "undertaking in damages" was unprecedented. In many cases, compliance with an order for provisional measures will cause the State addressed little more than inconvenience; in the Lockerbie cases, however, the Court mentioned as a material circumstance that "an indication of the measures requested by Libya would be likely to impair the rights which appear prima facie to be enjoyed by the [Applicants] by virtue of Security Council resolution 748 (1992)"; (*I. C. J. Reports 1992*, 15, para. 41).

[103] Specifically, the problem raised by Finland that the Court could not, under Article 41 of the Statute, make an Order directing Finland to pay compensation if judgment was given against it, or to enter into an undertaking to pay compensation in that event.

Addendum

Since the date of the Colloquium at which the above paper was presented, but before the present volume of Proceedings went to press, the International Court was seized of, and gave a decision on, two successive requests for provisional measures, in the case concerning *Application of the Convention on the Prevention and Punishment of the Crime of Genocide (Bosnia and Herzegovina* v. *Yugoslavia (Serbia and Montenegro))*. It is not proposed here to give a full account of the proceedings and decision, but simply to note the treatment in the Court's Order of 8 April 199[104] of some of the problems discussed at the Colloquium.

Jurisdiction

Generally the Court has its attention drawn, at the stage of provisional measures, to the question of its jurisdiction on the merits, because the Respondent disputes that such jurisdiction exists. In the *Genocide* case, the unusual situation arose that the Court raised *ex officio* a question of jurisdiction which the Respondent had apparently chosen (and with good reason) not to raise. The Republic of Yugoslavia (Serbia and Montenegro)[105] claimed to be the successor of the Socialist Federal Republic of Yugoslavia, and as such to be entitled to continue that State's membership in the United Nations. That claim had not been accepted by the Security Council and General Assembly; but "Yugoslavia" had continued to participate in the work of the Organization on terms which were confused, if not self-contradictory[106]. It was therefore apparent that it was questionable whether the Yugoslavia before the Court, though undoubtedly a State, was a State to which the Court was open, in accordance with Article 35 of the Statute, since unless it was a United Nations Member, it was not a party to the Statute. Bosnia and Herzegovina was not likely to raise this question, since to do so would undermine its case on jurisdiction; and Yugoslavia would not wish to prejudice its claim to United Nations membership as successor of the "old" Yugoslavia.

The solution found by the Court to this dilemma[107] is not here to the purpose; what is of interest is that the Court found it necessary to raise a jurisdictional issue

[104] *I. C. J. Reports 1993*, 3. Unfortunately, the Order of 13 September 1993 came too late to be included in this analysis.

[105] There was some confusion even as to the name of the Respondent State, which had appeared in different forms in different United Nations documents; the representatives of the State insisted that the name was simply "Republic of Yugoslavia", but the Court preferred the formula most used in United Nations circles: Republic of Yugoslavia (Serbia and Montenegro).

[106] See the outline in the Order of the procedure followed in New York, *I. C. J. Reports 1993*, 12–14, paras. 15–17; the Court observed warily that "the solution adopted [in New York] is not free from legal difficulties": *ibid.*, 14, para. 18.

[107] See *I. C. J. Reports 1993*, 14, para. 19.

itself at the provisional measure stage, introducing its examination of that issue in the Order with the classic formula as to the need for prima facie jurisdiction, but with two interesting variations[108]. The Court did not comment on the fact that neither Party had raised the jurisdictional issue; and this is natural since the jurisdictional defect (if defect it was) was one which could not be cured by *forum prorogatum*. This indeed is clearly the justification for the Court taking the point *ex officio*.

Relationship between measures, rights claimed, and jurisdiction

As was made clear in the case of the *Arbitral Award of 31 July 1989*, measures can only be indicated to protect the rights asserted in the Application, not other rights, however evident and however threatened. The *Genocide* case made clear that even the rights claimed in the Application cannot be protected by provisional measures unless they are rights in respect of which the Court would have jurisdiction under the title which the Court regards as prima facie established. Bosnia and Herzegovina based jurisdiction on the Genocide Convention; it then alleged a wider supplementary basis of jurisdiction, which the Court found unconvincing[109]. The measures which it requested, while corresponding to the claims made in the Application, went well beyond matters within the ambit of the Genocide Convention, as indeed did the claims. The Court defined the limits of its powers as follows:

> "Whereas the Court, having established the existence of a basis on which its jurisdiction might be founded, ought not to indicate measures for the protection of any disputed rights other than those which might ultimately form the basis of a judgment in the exercise of that jurisdiction; whereas accordingly the Court will confine its examination of the measures requested, and of the grounds asserted for the request for such measures, to those which fall within the scope of the Genocide Convention;"[110]

The possibility that the measures requested go beyond the jurisdictional title relied on is one which will normally be raised by the party to which the measures would be addressed, so that this is not necessarily a matter which the Court needs to examine *ex officio*. If the party concerned, while appearing in the proceedings, and raising other objections, did not raise the matter, an interesting problem would arise. The question is one of the extent of jurisdiction on the merits; but a failure to raise it in the context of indication of provisional measures can hardly be treated as *forum prorogatum* on the merits, so that that party would be debarred from objecting subsequently that the title of jurisdiction was not co-extensive with the claim.

---

[108] "Whereas on a request for provisional measures the Court need not, before deciding whether or not to indicate them, finally satisfy itself that it has jurisdiction on the merits of the case, yet it ought not to indicate such measures unless the provisions invoked by the Applicant or found in the Statute appear, prima facie, to afford a basis on which the jurisdiction of the Court might be established; whereas this consideration embraces jurisdiction both ratione personae and ratione materiae, even though, inasmuch as almost all States are today parties to the Statute of the Court, it is in general only the latter which requires to be considered". The variations are the inclusion of the words "or found in the Statute" (explained by paragraph 19 of the Order) and the last phrase concerning jurisdiction *ratione personae* and *ratione materiae*.

[109] *I. C. J. Reports 1993*, 18, para. 32.

[110] *I. C. J. Reports 1993*, 19, para. 35; cf. also para. 38.

Nature and effect of measures

The principal measure indicated by the Court was as follows:

> "The Government of the Federal Republic of Yugoslavia (Serbia and Montenegro) should immediately, in pursuance of its undertaking in the Convention on the Prevention and Punishment of the Crime of Genocide of 9 December 1948, take all measures within its power to prevent commission of the crime of genocide"[111].

The background to this was that there was evidence to suggest that acts forbidden by the Genocide Convention had been committed, but responsibility for them could not be attributed with any confidence; and that

> "in the view of the Court, in the circumstances brought to its attention ... in which there is a grave risk of acts of genocide being committed, Yugoslavia and Bosnia-Herzegovina, whether or not any such acts in the past may be legally imputable to them, are under a clear obligation to do all in their power to prevent the commission of any such acts in the future"[112].

The measure quoted thus called upon Yugoslavia to do what it has already undertaken to do, by becoming a party to the Genocide Convention, and to refrain from doing what that Convention forbade it to do. Even more clearly than in the Nicaragua *v.* United States case, therefore, there was an independent obligation of conduct which renders academic any question of a binding effect of the measures themselves.

---

[111] *I. C. J. Reports 1993*, 24, para. 52 (A) (1).
[112] *I. C. J. Reports 1993*, 24, para. 45.

Interim Measures in the Law and Practice of the Court of Justice of the European Communities

Francis G. Jacobs*

Introduction

The Court of Justice of the European Communities occupies, in the context of this publication, a distinctive position. In some respects its functions can be compared with those of an international court, especially where the issue of interim measures arises in the course of proceedings brought against Member States, particularly those brought by the Commission of the European Communities against Member States for failure to fulfil their Treaty obligations. In other respects, however, the Court of Justice can more appropriately be compared with a national court, especially a national administrative court, since one of its principal functions is to review the measures adopted by the other Community institutions, namely the Council, the Commission and the European Parliament; in these cases, the issue of interim measures calls for comparison with national administrative law, in particular the administrative law of the Member States of the European Communities. Moreover, in contrast with any international court, the Court of Justice is a court of automatic as well as compulsory jurisdiction.

In accordance with the sequence suggested by the editors of this publication, this contribution will consider interim measures before the Court of Justice[1] by reference to (I) the legal bases for the grant of interim measures, (II)

---

* The author is grateful to Jaqueline Suter, of the Research and Documentation Division of the Court of Justice, for her valuable assistance in the preparation of this paper.

[1] On this subject generally, see: G. Anselmi, *Rassegna di giurisprudenza comunitaria in tema di procedure «en référé»*, (1981) Diritto comunitario e degli scambi internazionali 295; G. Borchardt, *The Award of Interim Measures by the European Court of Justice*, (1985) 22 *CMLRev* 203; E. Grabitz and others, *Kommentar zum EWG-Vertrag* (1986)

the conditions for the grant of interim measures, (III) the permissible content of interim measures, (IV) the binding force and enforceability of interim measures and (V) the legal consequences of measures later found unjustified. Finally, the issue of (VI) interim measures in respect of Community provisions in the national courts will be examined[2].

I. Legal bases for the grant of interim measures

A. The founding Treaties

Reflecting the importance with which interim measures were evidently regarded, the main provisions governing such measures appear in the founding Treaties themselves rather than in the Statute of the Court (a separate Protocol attached to, and having the same force as, each of these Treaties) or in its Rules of Procedure. These provisions appear among those relating to the Court of Justice (Articles 164–188 of the EEC Treaty), which are confined to matters regarded as of fundamental importance. They concern the general function of the Court (Article 164), membership of the Court (Articles 165–168), the main heads of the Court's jurisdiction (Articles 169–184), interim measures (Articles 185 and 186), enforcement of judgments (Article 187) and provision for the Statute of the Court and the Rules of Procedure (Article 188).

The main provisions of the EEC Treaty governing interim measures are Articles 185 and 186, which reflect a distinction between the suspension of a measure (Article 185) and "any necessary interim measures" (Article 186)[3].

(commentary on Articles 185 and 186 by E. Grabitz); C. Gray, *Interim Measures of Protection in the European Court*, (1979) *ELRev* 80; H. von der Groeben, J. Thiesing and C-D. Ehlermann, *Kommentar zum EWG-Vertrag* (1991), p. 4672 (commentary on Articles 185 and 186 by H. Krück); R. Joliet, Protection juridictionnelle provisoire et droit communautaire, (1992) *Rivista di diritto europeo* 253; J. G. Huglo, Cour de justice, Le référé in *Juris-Classeurs Europe* (1992), fascicule 390/161-29; K. P. E. Lasok, *The European Court of Justice, Practice and Procedure* (1984), p. 145; J. Mégret, M. Waelbroeck, J-V. Louis, D. Vignes, J-L. Dewost, Le droit de la Communauté économique européenne, volume 10, *La Cour de justice. Les actes des institutions*, Tome 1 (1983), p. 365, by M. Waelbroeck, J-V. Louis et G. Vandersanden; B. Pastor and E. van Ginderachter, La procédure en référé (1989) *Revue trimestrielle de droit européen* 561; P. Pescatore, Les mesures conservatoires et les référés, in *La juridiction internationale permanente* (1987), p. 315; G. Tesauro, Les mesures provisoires dans le système Communautaire, in *Hacia un nuevo orden internacional y europeo*, ed. M. Pérez González and others (1993), p. 1241. See also the exceptionally wide-ranging survey by Lawrence Collins, Provisional and protective measures in international litigation, in *RCADI*, Volume 234 (1992-III).

[2] However, this paper does not cover the case-law of the Court on interim measures under the Brussels Convention on Jurisdiction and the Recognition and Enforcement of Judgments in Civil and Commercial Matters.

Additional provisions relating to the suspension of the enforcement either of judgments of the Court or of certain decisions of other institutions are contained in Articles 187 and 192.

Articles 185 and 186 maintain the substance of the provisions of the earlier European Coal and Steel Community Treaty, although in that Treaty the corresponding provisions were combined in a single article (Article 39). Provisions similar to Articles 187 and 192 of the EEC Treaty are contained in Articles 44 and 92 of the ECSC Treaty.

As is generally the case with the provisions concerning the Court, the Euratom Treaty follows the same pattern as the EEC Treaty in regard to the main provisions in Articles 157 and 158[4]. There is similar provision for the suspension of enforcement in Articles 159 and 164.

1. Article 185 of the EEC Treaty

The opening words of Article 185 of the EEC Treaty state what in many legal systems would go without saying, namely that "Actions brought before the Court of Justice shall not have suspensory effect." It is then added that the Court may, if it considers that circumstances so require, order that application of the contested act be suspended[5].

These provisions can be understood in the light of the differences in the national laws of the Member States concerning the suspensory effect of challenges to administrative action and the powers of national courts to suspend administrative measures[6]. Even with the original Member States of

[3] The provisions applicable in the European Communities can be contrasted with the position under the European Convention on Human Rights. In regard to the latter, the European Court of Human Rights has held that the Convention does not contain a specific provision empowering its institutions to order interim measures. Moreover, in the absence of a Convention provision, an "indication" under Rule 36 of the Rules of Procedure of the European Commission of Human Rights could not give rise to a binding obligation: Eur. Court H. R., case of Cruz Varaz and Others, decision of 29 August 1990, Series A No 201.

[4] However, see note 5 below.

[5] Article 39 of the ECSC Treaty and Article 157 of the Euratom Treaty are substantially the same. However, Article 157 of the Euratom Treaty (which corresponds to Article 185 of the EEC Treaty) opens with the words "Save as otherwise provided in this Treaty." These words refer to the second subparagraph of Article 83(2) which provides that, by way of derogation from Article 157, appeals brought before the Court of Justice against decisions of the Commission which impose any of the sanctions provided for in paragraph 1 (for infringement of the "safeguards" provisions of Title Two, Chapter VII of the Treaty) shall have suspensory effect; the Court of Justice may, however, on application by the Commission or by any Member State concerned, order that the decision be enforced forthwith. An application for immediate enforcement was granted in Case C-308/90 *Advanced Nuclear Fuels* v *Commission* [1990] ECR I-4499.

[6] M. Fromont, La protection provisoire des particuliers contre les décisions administratives dans les Etats Membres des Communautés européennes, (1984) *Revue internationale des sciences administratives* 309.

the Community, the national laws differed considerably: in German law, for example, suspension is the rule rather than the exception, the effect of legal proceedings often being automatically to suspend the measure challenged; while in French law, on the contrary, suspension is very much the exception, and the statutory provisions concerning the Conseil d'Etat expressly contained a provision corresponding to the first sentence of Article 185, namely that actions brought before the Conseil shall not have suspensory effect. Possibly those differences in national law reflect certain fundamental differences in the respective conceptions of the essential functions of administrative law, the main emphasis in French law being on the objective control of the administration while German law puts the emphasis above all on judicial protection of the individual.

2. Article 186 of the EEC Treaty

Article 186 of the EEC Treaty is very broadly drafted: the Court may in any cases before it prescribe any necessary interim measures. In accordance with the broad terms of Article 186, the Court has considered itself justified in ordering such measures even in proceedings against Member States (it has done so in several cases since the first applications by the Commission in 1977[7]), despite the fact that in its final judgment in such cases it can only grant a declaration.

Moreover, the Court has used the occasion of proceedings under Article 186 to spell out the Commission's powers to adopt interim measures in the course of its competition procedures. Notwithstanding the absence of any express provision for such powers in the basic Council regulation governing those procedures, Regulation No 17[8], the Court held in *Camera Care* v. *Commission*[9] that Article 3(1) of the Regulation affords the Commission the power to take interim measures which are "indispensable for the effective exercise of its functions and, in particular, for ensuring the effectiveness of any decisions requiring undertakings to bring to an end infringements which it has found to exist". It was for the Commission, not the Court, to decide whether there were grounds for adopting the interim measures sought. The Court's rôle consisted in undertaking the legal review of the action taken by the Commission[10].

---

[7] Cases 31/77 R and 53/77 R *Commission* v *United Kingdom* [1977] ECR 921 (proceedings under Article 93(2)); Case 61/77 R *Commission* v *Ireland* [1977] ECR 937 (no order was made but the Court plainly considered that it had the power to do so).

[8] OJ English Special Edition 1959–1962, p.87.

[9] Case 792/79 R [1980] ECR 119 at 131.

[10] Subsequently, the Commission indicated its attitude to interim measures in a statement to the parties in this case: see "Practice Note. Applications to the E. C. Commission for interim measures under Article 3 of Regulation 17", [1980] 2 CMLR 369. However, that statement must be read in the light of subsequent decisions:

3. Articles 187 and 192 of the EEC Treaty

Article 192 of the EEC Treaty deals with the enforcement in the Member States of decisions of the Council or of the Commission imposing a pecuniary obligation; under Article 187, judgments of the Court are enforceable under the same conditions. The second paragraph of Article 192 states that enforcement is governed by the rules of civil procedure in the State where it is carried out. However, under the fourth paragraph, enforcement may be suspended only by a decision of the Court of Justice. There is thus provision for suspension; but there appears to be no practice under these provisions.

B. The Statutes of the Court of Justice

Article 36 of the EEC Statute of the Court[11] contains three main elements. First, applications for suspension or for interim measures may be dealt with by the President of the Court or, if the President is prevented from acting, by another Judge[12]. Secondly, applications are to be dealt with by way of summary procedure. Thirdly, a decision of the President is provisional and "shall in no way prejudice the decision of the Court on the substance of the case."

Articles 49 to 54 of the EEC Statute[13] deal with appeals against decisions of the Court of First Instance. Since 1989 that Court has exercised, at first instance, jurisdiction in competition cases and in cases brought by Community servants; from 1 August 1993 it will have jurisdiction, at first instance,

---

C. Bellamy and G. D. Child, *Common Market Law of Competition* (1987), paragraphs 12-049 to 12-054. Thus, an application for interim measures will be entertained only when accompanied by or following a formal complaint alleging infringements of Articles 85 or 86 of the EEC Treaty, or when formal proceedings have already been opened by the Commission; and there must exist a reasonably strong prima facie case of infringement of Articles 85 or 86. The applicant is expected to specify the measures required and may be required to give a suitable bond or guarantee against loss resulting to the undertaking against whom measures are ordered if no infringement is subsequently established. Unreasonable delay on the part of the applicant may lead to the request being refused; and the applicant should consider whether relief might not more appropriately be obtained before the national courts. The Commission will consider a subsequent application for review of the decision on interim measures if circumstances have changed.

[11] Corresponding provisions are contained in Article 33 of the ECSC Statute and in Article 37 of the Euratom Statute.

[12] Under the conditions laid down in the Rules of Procedure of the Court of Justice of the European Communities of 19 June 1991 (OJ 1991 L 176, p. 7): see Article 85, second paragraph, and Article 11 of the Rules. Compare with Articles 106, second paragraph, and 9 of the Rules of Procedure of the Court of First Instance of the European Communities of 2 May 1991 (OJ 1991 L 136, p. 1).

[13] Similar provisions are contained in Articles 49–54 of the ECSC Statute and Articles 50–55 of the Euratom Statute.

in most direct actions by persons other than Member States and Community institutions[14]. Corresponding provisions on interim measures apply[15]. By virtue of the second paragraph of Article 50,[16] decisions on interim measures may be appealed to the Court of Justice. Article 53 preserves the right of a party to apply to the Court of Justice for interim measures in the course of a substantive appeal.

C. The Rules of Procedure of the Court of Justice

Although adopted by the Court, its Rules of Procedure require, under Article 188 of the EEC Treaty,[17] the unanimous approval of the Council. In this respect the position of the Court of Justice may be contrasted with that of the International Court of Justice, and of the European and American Courts of Human Rights. However, given the broad scope of the Treaty provisions on interim measures, that requirement has not had any restrictive effect on the jurisdiction of the Court of Justice in respect of such measures.

Articles 83 to 89 of the Rules of Procedure[18] contain more detailed provisions on applications for interim measures and the conditions for their adoption. Some of these provisions are considered further in subsequent parts of this contribution.

Under Article 85 of the Rules of Procedure[19], the President shall either decide on an application for interim measures himself or refer it to the Court. Where an application is referred to the Court, the Court must postpone all other cases and give a decision after hearing the Advocate General.

Since 1953 eighteen cases involving applications for interim measures have been considered by the full Court[20]; these cases mainly concerned

---

[14] See Council Decision of 8 June 1993 (OJ 1993 L 144 p. 21).

[15] Article 4, Council Decision of 24 October 1988 establishing a Court of First Instance of the European Communities (88/591/ECSC, EEC, Euratom), OJ 1988 L 319, p. 1 and 1989 L 241, p. 4 (corrigenda).

[16] Corresponding provisions are contained in Article 50 of the ECSC Statute and Article 51 of the Euratom Statute.

[17] Corresponding provisions are contained in Article 160 of the Euratom Treaty and in Article 55 of the ECSC Statute. Article 168a(4) of the EEC Treaty, Article 32d(4) of the ECSC Treaty and Article 140a(4) of the Euratom Treaty contain a similar requirement in relation to the Rules of Procedure of the Court of First Instance.

[18] Similar provisions are contained in Articles 104 to 110 of the Rules of Procedure of the Court of First Instance.

[19] Compare Article 106 of the Rules of Procedure of the Court of First Instance.

[20] The cases concerned are: Case 6/56 *S.à r.l. Merlini* v *High Authority* (not reported); Case 11/56 *Société d'exploitation minière Petrus Segen Steinkohlenbergbau* v *High Authority* (not reported); Case 18/57 *Nold* v *High Authority* [1957 and 1958] ECR 121; Case 19/59 *Geitling, Mausegatt, Präsident* v *High Authority* [1960] ECR 34; Case 50/69 R *Germany* v *Commission* [1969] ECR 449; Case 31/77 R and 53/77 R, *Commission* v

actions by the Commission against Member States under Article 169 of the EEC Treaty and particularly important cases introduced by Member States or undertakings. In such cases it used to be the practice for the Advocate General to deliver an Opinion in open Court in the same way as in an ordinary case. The practice now is for the Advocate General to retire with the Judges when they deliberate and for him to give his opinion in closed session then; in such cases it is not normally published.

Where, as is usually the case, the President hears the application himself without referring it to the Court, he is usually assisted by the Judge-Rapporteur and the Advocate General. In addition to his power to decide an application himself, the President plays an important rôle in the conduct of an application for interim measures. First, under Article 84(2) of the Rules of Procedure[21], he may order a preparatory inquiry. This is not the usual practice. However, in *Group of the European Right* v *Parliament*[22], the President sought specific information from the Parliament.

Again in the *Dundalk Water Supply* case[23], where an Irish local authority invited tenders for a new water supply scheme which required compliance with an Irish technical standard, the President made an *ex parte* order that, pending the outcome of the interim application, no award of the contract should be made; subsequently, however, the President considered, after hearing argument on the interim application *inter partes*, that the interim measure should not be continued, because, among other reasons, there was evidence that the water shortage created a fire hazard, and even a hazard to the health of the inhabitants of Dundalk[24].

Secondly, the President decides whether there will be an oral hearing. Of the 100 applications for interim measures brought in the Court between 1986 and 1992, there were oral hearings in 72 cases[25].

United Kingdom [1977] ECR 921; Case 61/77 R *Commission* v *Ireland* [1977] ECR 937; Case 61/77 R II *Commission* v *Ireland* [1977] ECR 1411; Case 792/79 R *Camera Care* v *Commission* [1980] ECR 119; Joined Cases 24 and 97/80 R *Commission* v *France* [1980] ECR 1319; Case 42/82 R *Commission* v *France* [1982] ECR 841; Case 171/83 *Commission* v *France* [1983] ECR 2621; Case 37/84 R *EISA* v *Commission* [1984] ECR 1749; Case 45/84 R *Association des aciéries européennes indépendantes* v *Commission* [1984] ECR 1759; Case 195/90 R *Commission* v *Germany* [1990] ECR I-3351; Cases C-66/91 and C-66/91 R *Emerald Meats* v *Commission* [1991] ECR I-1143; Case 280/93 R *Germany* v *Council* [1993] (Order of 29 June 1993). In addition in regard to cases which were, before the introduction of the Court of First Instance, assigned to Chambers of the Court (cases brought by Community servants), the President of the Chamber referred the decision on interim measures to the full Chamber in the following cases: Case 10/81 *Farrall* v *Commission* [1981] ECR 717; Cases 259/84 and 259/84 R *Strack* v *Parliament* [1985] ECR 453; Cases 264/88 and 264/88 R *Valle Fernandez* v *Commission* [1988] ECR 6341.

21 Compare Article 105(2) of the Rules of Procedure of the Court of First Instance.

22 Case 221/86 R [1986] ECR 2579.

23 Case 45/87 R *Commission* v *Ireland* [1987] ECR 783.

24 [1987] ECR 1369.

25 See Annex.

Thirdly, Article 84(2) of the Rules of Procedure[26] further states that the President may grant the application even before the observations of the opposite party have been submitted. An example of such an *ex parte* order is *Group of the European Right* v *Parliament*[27]. Having learned that, on the day of the lodging of the application for interim measures, the competent departments of the European Parliament had been authorized to carry out the payments of the appropriations under challenge, the President ordered the European Parliament to take all necessary steps to ensure that the political groups did not use the sums paid to them.

II. Conditions for the grant of interim measures

A. Conditions of admissibility of an application for interim measures

It is clear from the provisions on the conditions of admissibility not only that an application for interim measures can be made solely in the context of a main action but also that their grant depends on the object of that action. Here a distinction has again to be made between suspension and other interim measures.

Thus, an application to suspend the operation of any measure adopted by an institution is admissible, under Article 83(1) of the Rules of Procedure[28], only if the applicant is challenging that measure in proceedings before the Court. As to other interim measures, Article 186 of the EEC Treaty refers to the Court's power to prescribe such measures "in any cases before it" and Article 83(1) of the Rules of Procedure further states that an application for any other interim measure is admissible only if it is made by a party to a case before the Court and relates to that case.

It would seem that suspension of a measure can be sought only in the framework of an action for annulment and not, for example, in an action for damages, even if such an action puts in issue the legality of the measure in question.

However the Court granted, in a staff case[29], suspension of the operation of the vacancy notice for the post which the applicant had previously occupied, even though in the main action his application was for the annulment

[26] Compare Article 105(2) of the Rules of Procedure of the Court of First Instance.

[27] Case 221/86 R [1986] ECR 2579. See also: Case 107/82 R *AEG* v *Commission* [1982] ECR 1179; Case 229/82 R *Ford* v *Commission* [1982] ECR 2849; Case 293/82 R *De Compte* v *Parliament* [1982] ECR 4001; Case 214/86 R *Greece* v *Commission* [1986] ECR 2505; Case 194/88 R *Commission* v *Italy* [1988] ECR 4547.

[28] Compare Article 104(1) of the Rules of Procedure of the Court of First Instance.

[29] Case 18/65 R *Gutmann* v *Commission* [1966] ECR 134. For an earlier, more restrictive approach, see Joined Cases 35/62 and 16/63 R *Leroy* v *High Authority* [1963] ECR 134; this approach is criticised by Gray, p. 86. For a review of the early cases,

of a decision suspending him from his duties and transferring him to Brussels. The Court stated that it would be "excessively formalistic in an application for the adoption of an interim measure to compel the parties to enter multiple pleadings when the facts of the case show that the subject matter of the main application and of the application for the adoption of the interim measure are so linked as cause and effect that the second appears as the inevitable consequence of the first"[30]. Whilst it is clear that the Court can thus, on an application for interim measures, order the suspension of the operation of an act other than the act challenged in the main proceedings[31], it has also held, in *Nashua Corporation* v *Commission*[32], that it is necessary for both acts to emanate from the same institution and for that institution to be a party to the proceedings.

In contrast, the Court has not yet clearly defined the link between an application for other interim measures and the main action. However, in *B* v *Parliament*[33], the Court rejected as inadmissible an application by a Parliament official for an order in terms that the Parliament assist him in connection with a dispute with an insurer on the grounds that the application was, in effect, identical to that made by the main action and that it did not have the provisional character required by Article 83 of the Rules of Procedure.

From one perspective, the requirement that the application for interim measures can be made only in the context of proceedings already brought before the Court is understandable: normally the purpose of interim measures is precisely to protect the position of the applicant or of the parties pending the outcome of the proceedings. On the other hand, from another perspective, the requirement might seem incompatible with the need for interim protection: in a very urgent case, such an order might be necessary even before an applicant has started proceedings. That is recognized in, for example, English law, where applications for injunctions may be made before the main proceedings have been launched.

As to the form of application, Article 83(3) of the Rules of Procedure[34] states that an application for interim measures must be made by a separate document. It may be held inadmissible if made in the application commencing the action, rather than separately[35]. The application for interim measures

---

see also Borchardt, p. 208; Pastor and Van Ginderachter, p. 566 and Huglo, paragraph 23.

[30] Joined Cases 35/62 and 16/63 R [1966] ECR 134 at 137.

[31] Case 133/87 R *Nashua Corporation* v *Commission* [1987] ECR 2883 at 2887.

[32] Case 133/87 R [1987] 2883.

[33] Case 794/79 R [1979] ECR 3635.

[34] Compare Article 104(3) of the Rules of Procedure of the Court of First Instance. The application must comply with Article 104(2) as well as Articles 43 and 44 of these Rules.

[35] Case 108/63 *Merlini* v *High Authority* [1965] ECR 1; Case 32/64 *Italy* v *Commission* [1965] ECR 365; Case 81/83 *Busseni* v *Commission* [1984] ECR 2951 at 2966 (Advocate General Lenz).

must comply with Article 83(2) concerning the matters of substance required to be set out as well as Article 37 dealing with pleadings generally and Article 38 relating to applications commencing an action[36]. Accordingly, it must state the applicant's name and address, the designation of the defendant, the name and address of the person authorized and willing to accept service in Luxembourg; it must bear a date, be signed by the party's agent or lawyer, be lodged with the required number of copies and be accompanied by a list of the annexes.

The matters of substance to be set out are contained partly in Article 38 and partly in Article 83(2)[37]. They comprise: the subject matter of the proceedings; the circumstances giving rise to urgency; the pleas of fact and law establishing a prima facie case for the interim measures applied for; the form of order sought and the nature of any evidence offered in support.

Non-compliance with the requirements of form and of substance may lead to an application being rejected as inadmissible. In *B* v *European Parliament*[38], an application for interim measures was rejected as inadmissible on the grounds that the written documents in support did not in any way comply with the requirements of Article 38.

The applicant should also ask for his costs in his application for interim measures[39]. However, the normal order is for the question of costs to be decided in the final judgment[40]. While it is clear that an application for interim measures can be made only in the context of a main action, it is less clear whether the Court can make an order of its own motion in the absence of an application for interim measures. There is no provision for such an order in the texts. Moreover, such an order seems inconsistent with the texts as they stand. On the other hand, the interim measures adopted can differ from those requested by the applicant. An example is provided by *Raznoimport* v *Commission*[41], in which the applicant, a Soviet trading organization, sought the suspension of a Commission Regulation imposing a provisional anti-dumping duty on imports of nickel originating in the Soviet Union. Although it rejected the application for suspension, the Court ordered the

---

[36] As to the language of the case, see Article 29 of the Rules of Procedure of the Court of Justice and Article 35 of the Rules of Procedure of the Court of First Instance.

[37] Compare Articles 44 and 104(2) of the Rules of Procedure of the Court of First Instance.

[38] Case 731/79 R II [1980] ECR 829. On the scope for the applicant to put an application in order or to produce certain documents under Article 38(7) of the Rules of Procedure, see Pastor and Van Ginderachter, p. 573.

[39] Lasok, p. 173; Pastor and Van Ginderachter, p. 575.

[40] However, some Orders dismissing applications for interim measures have awarded costs against the applicant: Case 263/82 R II *Klöckner-Werke* v *Commission* [1982] ECR 4225; Case 121/86 R *Epichiriseon* v *Council and Commission* [1986] ECR 2063.

[41] Case 120/83 R [1983] ECR 2573.

Commission to monitor from day to day any changes in prices on the market of the product in order to determine whether it was necessary to maintain the duty or the rate thereof.

B. Conditions of substance concerning the grant of interim measures

It will be recalled that Article 83(2) of the Rules of Procedure requires the applicant to state the circumstances giving rise to urgency as well as the pleas of fact and law establishing a *prima facie* case for the interim measures applied for. To these two conditions, the Court has added a third[42]: the "balance of interests" between the interest of the applicant and the interest of the defendant, of third parties or of the Community in general. However, before examining these three conditions, consideration will be given to a preliminary problem which can arise in connection with an application for interim measures, namely that of the admissibility of the main action.

1. The admissibility of the main action

There are three conflicting lines of cases[43] concerning this problem. First, a number of orders invoke the manifestly inadmissible nature of the main action as the ground for rejecting the application for interim measures[44]. It is considered that where the applicant will manifestly be unable to succeed in the main action, there is no reason to seek to protect the effectiveness of the final judgment.

In contrast, in a second line of cases[45] orders have stated that the issue of admissibility of the main action could not be examined in proceedings relating to an application for interim measures.

In a third line of cases an intermediate position has been endorsed. Thus, in *Group of the European Right* v *Parliament*[46], the Court stated:

---

[42] As to the order (not always the same) in which the Court has considered these conditions, see Pastor and Van Ginderachter, p. 586.

[43] Huglo, paragraph 16; Pastor and Van Ginderachter, p. 588.

[44] Case 10/81 *Farrall* v *Commission* [1981] ECR 717; Case 50/84 R *Bensider* v *Commission* [1984] ECR 2247; Cases 259/84 and 259/84 R *Strack* v *Parliament* [1985] ECR 453; Cases 264/88 and 264/88 R *Valle Fernandez* v *Commission* [1988] ECR 6341.

[45] Case 25/62 R *Plaumann* v *Commission* [1963] ECR 126; Case 28/65 R *Fonzi* v *Commission* [1966] ECR 508; Case 75/72 R *Perinciolo* v *Council* [1972] ECR 1201; Case 186/80 R *Suss* v *Commission* [1980] ECR 3501; Case 23/86 R *United Kingdom* v *Parliament* [1986] ECR 1085; Case 351/85 R *Fabrique de fer de Charleroi* v *Commission* [1986] ECR 1307; Case 65/87 R *Pfizer* v *Commission* [1987] ECR 1691; Case C-257/90 R *Italsolar* v *Commission* [1990] ECR I-3841.

[46] Case 221/86 R [1986] ECR 2969 at 2975. See also Case 118/83 R *CMC* v *Commission* [1983] ECR 2583; Case 1/84 R *Ilford* v *Commission* [1984] ECR 423; Case

"It is true that the Court has already repeatedly stressed that in principle the issue of the admissibility of the main application should not be examined in proceedings relating to an application for interim measures. It should be reserved for the examination of the main application so as not to prejudge that application ... However, when, as in the present case, it is contended that the main application from which the application for interim measures is derived is manifestly inadmissible, it seems necessary to establish grounds for concluding *prima facie* that the admissibility of the main application cannot be completely ruled out."

In this third situation the Court may be led to consider whether "it cannot be excluded that a thorough examination"[47] leads to acceptance of the admissibility of the main action.

One writer[48] has stressed the considerable confusion surrounding the Court's case-law on the admissibility of the main action. With regard to the degree of certainty required, the Court is seen as having indicated its preference for a "possibilist" solution (namely, that it suffices that at first sight the admissibility of the main action appears possible) as against the "probabilist" approach (in other words, that admissibility must be likely or probable). In his view, the "possibilist" solution can be justified by the consideration that the application can lead only to the grant of interim measures, with all matters being open to reconsideration in the final judgment; it would thus be inappropriate to be too stringent when examining the issue of the admissibility of the main action.

Nevertheless it seems clear that, where the main action is manifestly inadmissible, the application for interim measures should be rejected. In such cases the very basis of interim measures – the need to protect the effectiveness of the final judgment – is absent.

2. The pleas of fact and law establishing a prima facie case for the interim measures applied for

The Court has used varying formulations in its interpretation of the requirement imposed by Article 83(2) of the Rules of Procedure relating to the pleas of fact and law establishing a *prima facie* case for interim measures. In *Lachmüller* v *Commission*[49], the Court considered that there should exist "a strong presumption that the application in the main action is well-founded

---

82/87 R *Autexpo* v *Commission* [1987] ECR 2131; Case 376/87 R *Distrivet* v *Council* [1988] ECR 209; Case 160/88 R *Fédération européenne de la santé animale and Others* v *Council* [1988] ECR 4121; Case C-117/91 R *Bosman* v *Commission* [1991] ECR I-3357.

[47] Case 118/83 R *CMC* v *Commission* [1983] ECR 2583 at 2597.

[48] Pescatore, p. 330.

[49] Joined Cases 43/59, 44/59 and 48/59 [1960] ECR 489 at 492.

(*fumus boni juris*)". In two other early cases[50] the Court stated that the main action should appear *prima facie* to be clearly well-founded.

Subsequently, in *Johnson and Firth Brown* v *Commission*[51] in 1975, the Court considered it sufficient for this requirement if "certain of the grounds on which the substantive application is made appear, on first examination, not to be manifestly without foundation". The most recent case-law appears to adopt this approach, even though differing formulations are used. Thus the Court has stated that "at the present interlocutory stage, the application does not appear to be devoid of all foundation"[52] or that "the pleas relied on - ... are, prima facie, not without proper foundation."[53] In another case[54] the Court considered it sufficient that the defendant institution had "adopted a decision which raises delicate questions as to the exact scope of Article 86 of the Treaty and of the Commission's powers under Regulation No 17."

Writers are divided on the extent of the Court's scrutiny, on an application for interim measures, of the factual and legal situation. According to one view[55], the Court is required, in so far as the condition of urgency is fulfilled, to consider the merits of the pleas of fact and law in support of the main action. In contrast, another writer[56] considers that the Rules of Procedure correctly deal with the problem by requiring the parties to put forward arguments justifying the measures sought; strong criticism is levelled at the extent to which reference is made in the Court's case-law to the term *fumus boni juris*, which is not mentioned in the Rules of Procedure and which is seen as tantamount to prejudging the outcome of the case. However, this criticism of the Court's approach is rejected by another writer[57] who, moreover, considers it unclear why the Rules of Procedure included the term *prima facie* if it were merely a question of justifying the measures sought as necessary and appropriate to avoid the threat of serious and irreparable harm.

In this debate, a number of points have to be borne in mind if the issues are to be properly understood.

First, much confusion seems to have been caused by the wording of Article 83(2), which refers to a "*prima facie* case for the interim measures applied for". What is required is, plainly, a *prima facie* case for the grant of interim measures; but the use of the term *prima facie* is somewhat strange in this context, and seems sometimes to have given rise to the idea that the

---

50 Joined Cases 19 and 65/63 *Prakash* v *Commission* [1965] ECR 576; Case 68/63 R *Luhleich* v *Commission* [1965] ECR 618.

51 Case 3/75 R [1975] ECR 1 at 6.

52 Case 56/89 R *Publishers Association* v *Commission* [1989] ECR 1693 at 1700.

53 Case C-345/90 P-R *Parliament* v *Hanning* [1991] ECR I-231 at 238.

54 Joined Cases 76, 77 and 91/89 R *RTE and Others* v *Commission* [1989] ECR 1141 at 1146.

55 Pastor and Van Ginderachter, p. 595. This view is shared by Borchardt, p. 210.

56 Pescatore, pp. 339–340.

57 Joliet, p. 269.

applicant must establish a *prima facie* case on the *merits*, a context in which the term *prima facie* case is more appropriate. Moreover the requirement of a *prima facie* case on the merits is found in some legal systems as a pre-condition for the grant of interim measures[58].

Secondly, the Court's own case-law is not free from confusion on this point. However, complete consistency should not be expected in this area of the law, where decisions have to be taken rapidly and where the outcome must depend in part on an overall appreciation of the case.

Thirdly, it may often be neither necessary nor appropriate to go into the merits of the case. However, one can easily see possible exceptions. If, to take an extreme example, it became apparent at the outset that the main application was wholly unfounded – as where for example the respondent could immediately demolish the case and the applicant clearly had no answer – then the application for interim measures should plainly be rejected. Where the main action is manifestly ill-founded, an application for interim measures should be rejected, just as where the main action is manifestly inadmissible, and for the same reason: where the applicant will manifestly be unable to succeed in the main action, there is no reason to seek to protect the effectiveness of the final judgment.

Less obviously, it is perhaps inevitable, even if it is not always acknowledged, that some preliminary assessment of the merits may influence the grant of interim measures. If, for example, there were an application for suspension of a measure where there appeared to be a flagrant illegality, suspension would be likely in practice to be more readily granted; conversely, if there were serious doubts about the merits of the main action, it would probably prove more difficult in practice to satisfy the conditions for the grant of interim measures.

Proceedings for interim measures are quintessentially proceedings in which pragmatic considerations are rightly taken into account.

Finally, it goes without saying that any such assessment of the merits of the main action at the stage of an application for interim measures is without prejudice to the final judgment[59], as indeed the Statute of the Court makes clear[60].

---

[58] This seems often to be the case in German law, and was also the case in English law prior to the decision of the House of Lords in *American Cyanamid Co.* v *Ethicon* [1975] AC 396, a decision which has not escaped criticism: see Collins, op. cit. n. 1, p. 27. Collins, comparing the different approaches in national legal systems, suggests that "the solution ranges from the current English test that there may merely be a serious question to be tried on the merits to the more stringent test in civil law countries that there must be a probable, or *prima facie*, prospect of success on the merits" (p. 224).

[59] As Advocate General Sir Gordon Slynn has emphasized: "The fact ... that the Court enquires as to whether the case put forward in the main action is prima facie sound, or arguable or even strongly arguable, and is so satisfied, does not mean that it has prejudged the ultimate decision. That the Court considers even that the case is

3. Urgency: the risk of serious and irreparable harm[61]

(a) The concept of urgency

The requirement of urgency, imposed by Article 83(2) of the Rules of Procedure, must be assessed, in accordance with the formulation currently used by the Court, "in relation to the necessity for an order granting interim relief in order to prevent serious and irreparable damage to the party requesting the suspension" (or interim measures)[62]. (As will be pointed out below, the requirement that the damage be to the applicant does not apply where the applicant is a Member State or a Community institution).

Writers are divided on the issue of whether urgency and the requirement of serious and irreparable harm are two separate conditions. Whilst some support such a distinction[63], others do not[64]. According to an intermediate opinion[65], the concept of irreparable harm does not exhaust the situations of urgency that can arise.

In regard to the terms "serious and irreparable", these have sometimes been considered to be synonymous. Referring to the case-law of the Court, Advocate General Capotorti considered it necessary that the applicant "should be exposed to serious, in the sense of 'irreparable', damage"[66]. In his view, the irreparable nature could be understood in two senses:

> "in the sense that the nature of the damage rules out any possibility of compensation or in the sense, which in my opinion is more precise, that the damage would be such as to make the ultimate judgment pointless, so that in the absence of interim measures there would be no purpose in the ultimate judgment".

Subsequently, a definition based on the case-law of the International Court of Justice was proposed by one writer[67], who considered that irreparable

---

strongly arguable at the stage of an application for interim measures is not incompatible with an ultimate finding that the case which is put forward fails. Such an interim conclusion does not in any way prejudge the merits of the issues in the main action.": Case 42/92 R *Commission* v *France* [1982] ECR 841 at 864.

60 See e.g. Article 36 of the EEC Statute; see further below, p. 59.

61 The sequence of headings used in this section largely draws on that followed by Huglo, paragraphs 43–77. See also Pastor and Van Ginderachter, pp. 597–610.

62 Case C-345/90 P-R *Parliament* v *Hanning* [1991] ECR I-231 at 237. See subsequently Case C-213/91 R *Abertal e.a.* v *Commission* [1991] ECR I-5109 at 5115 and Case C-225/91 R *Matra* v *Commission* [1991] ECR I-5823 at 5830.

63 G. Vandersanden and A. Barav, Contentieux communautaire (1977), pp. 440–442; Waelbroeck and others, in Mégret and others, p. 370.

64 Tizzano, p. 398. Pastor and Van Ginderachter, (pp. 597–598), also appear to endorse this approach.

65 Pescatore, p. 339.

66 Joined Cases 24 and 97/80 R *Commission* v *France* [1980] ECR 1319 at 1341–1342.

67 Pescatore, p. 339. The expression used is "un préjudice irréparable aux droits en litige".

harm should be understood as meaning irreparable harm to the rights being litigated. Supporting this approach, others[68] consider it helpful to add to this criterion the requirement that the act in respect of which interim measures are sought must substantially concern the rights being litigated, thereby taking account of the word "serious".

(b) The burden of proof

In principle, it is for the party which requests interim measures to show the existence of serious and irreparable harm[69]. However, in two dumping cases[70], the Court, in ordering the suspension of a provision, has stated that the defendant had not been able to demonstrate that the adoption of interim measures would cause it appreciable detriment. While this statement has been regarded[71] as a reversal of the burden of proof, it is perhaps preferable to regard the statement as falling within the scope of the "balance of interests" involved.

(c) The imminent nature of the harm

The timing of the application for interim measures can be relevant to the way in which the Court assesses the imminent nature of the harm. In *Europemballage and Continental Can* v *Commission*[72], the Court considered that there was no need to order suspension of a measure when it could rule on the main action before the probable occurrence of the harm. Conversely, if the effectiveness of the measure in respect of which suspension is sought has been exhausted, no urgency will be recognized. Thus, in *Simmenthal* v *Commission*[73], an application was refused for the suspension of a Commission decision fixing minimum prices in circumstances where the time-limit for submitting applications for import licences had already expired. In *Mogensen* v *Commission*[74], the Court refused an application for an injunction prohibiting the Commission from the making of any appointment to the post involved in circumstances where it had already made an appointment to that post. In *Fabius* v *Commission*[75], the Court refused an application for an order that the Commission authorize the applicant to take part in the remainder of a competition for the filling of vacant posts in circumstances where the tests had already taken place and a reserve list of suitable candidates had been drawn up.

Delay in introducing the main action can also result in the Court considering that the requirement of urgency is not met. For example, in *Geist* v

---

68 Pastor and Van Ginderachter, pp. 602–603.

69 Case 31/59 *Acciaieria di Brescia* v *High Authority* [1960] ECR 98 at 100.

70 Case 113/77 R and 113/77 R-Int. *NTN Toyo* v *Council* [1977] ECR 1721 at 1725; Case 121/77 R *Nachi Fujikoshi* v *Council* [1977] ECR 2107 at 2110.

71 Pastor and Van Ginderachter, p. 598.

72 Case 6/72 R [1972] ECR 157 at 159.

73 Case 92/78 R [1978] ECR 1129 at 1136.

74 Case 10/82 R [1982] ECR 325.

75 Case 39/83 R [1983] ECR 2147.

Commission[76], the applicant had brought an action for annulment on 30 June 1976 in respect of a decision which was dated 10 December 1975 and took effect on 1 March 1976.

In addition, the harm is not considered to be of an imminent nature when the judgment in the main action could, even in the absence of interim measures, fully satisfy the applicant. In *González Holguera* v *Parliament*[77], the Court stated that since the competition in question was organized not in order to establish a reserve list for future recruitment but with a view to appointing a single candidate to a given post, the annulment of the contested decision of the Selection Board refusing to allow the applicant to take part in the tests, would entail as a consequence the annulment, which was also sought by the applicant, of the decision appointing the successful candidate which might have been adopted in the meantime.

Moreover, in assessing the question of urgency, the Court may take note of an undertaking by the defendant Community institution not to apply the contested measure[78]. A similar approach was adopted in regard to an undertaking by a third party intervener given in addition to a declaration by the Commission[79]; however, in a second order in this case, the Court considered a formal undertaking given by the Commission as insufficient[80].

(d) The characteristics of the harm

(i) The requirement of harm to the applicant in person

The harm must be to the applicant in person; the latter cannot invoke, in support of an application for suspension of the operation of a Community measure, the harm which would be caused to another person in the event of refusal of the application[81]. Nevertheless, where the applicant is a professional body, it seems that it may invoke the imminent harm to certain of its members[82].

However, where the applicant is a Member State, it can invoke the damage caused to a sector of its industry or certain of its producers[83]. But it

---

[76] Case 61/76 R II [1976] ECR 2075.

[77] Case 171/89 R [1989] ECR 1705.

[78] Joined Cases 160 and 161/73 R *Miles Druce* v *Commission* [1973] ECR 1049; Joined Cases 161 and 162/80 R *Carbognani and Coda Zabetta* v *Commission* [1980] ECR 2655; Case 89/22 R *Wölker* v *Commission* [1982] ECR 1323; Case 45/84 R *EISA* v *Commission* [1984] ECR 1759.

[79] Joined Cases 160 and 161/73 R *Miles Druce* v *Commission* [1973] ECR 1049.

[80] Joined Cases 160, 161 and 170/73 R II *Miles Druce* v *Commission* [1974] ECR 281.

[81] Case 12/64 R *Ley* v *Commission* [1965] ECR 132.

[82] Joined Cases 209 to 215 and 218/78 R *Van Landewyck* v *Commission* [1978] ECR 2111.

[83] Case 166/78 R *Italy* v *Council* [1978] ECR 1745. See now the Order of 29 June 1993 in Case C-280/93 R *Germany* v *Commission* (Bananas), paragraph 27: "En ce qui concerne la nature des préjudices susceptibles d'être invoqués par la République fédérale d'Allemagne, il importe de relever que les Etats membres sont responsables

cannot invoke the damage which, in the event of the dismissal of its application for interim measures, a specific undertaking would suffer[84]; this principle has been applied in relation to applications to suspend the operation of Commission decisions requiring a Member State to recover a State aid incompatible with the common market from the undertaking which received the aid.

Similarly, undertakings in a Member State cannot invoke damage to the equilibrium of the balance of payments of that State[85].

Where a Community institution brings a main action against a Member State, the harm which it invokes in support of an application for interim measures can relate not only to that which it suffers as guardian of the Community interest but also that caused to certain third parties. In this connection, the Commission has invoked the harm suffered by: contractors whose tenders were not considered and their suppliers[86]; fishermen of other Member States[87]; parallel importers in one Member State, exporters from other Member States and the final consumer[88]; undertakings in the textile and clothing industries of certain Member States[89]; and individuals who were nationals of Member States other than the one in which they were following their studies[90].

(ii) Non-material harm

The position concerning non-material harm (*dommage moral*) is unclear. One case[91] suggests that the harm involved may be non-material. Whilst certain writers[92] share this view, the contrary opinion[93] has also been expressed. In regard to the Commission invoking "moral" harm in the context of a Member State's failure to fulfil its Treaty obligations, Advocate General Capotorti stated in *Commission* v *France*[94]:

---

des intérêts, notamment économiques et sociaux, considérés comme généraux sur le plan national, et ont, à ce titre, qualité pour agir en justice en vue d'en assurer la défense. En conséquence, ils peuvent faire état de préjudices affectant un secteur entier de leur économie, notamment lorsque la mesure communautaire contestée est susceptible d'entraîner des répercussions défavorables sur le niveau de l'emploi et le coût de la vie".

84 Case 142/87 R *Belgium* v *Commission* [1987] ECR 2589; Case C-356/90 R *Belgium* v *Commission* [1991] ECR I-2423.

85 Case 112/88 R *Crete Citron Producers Association* v *Commission* [1988] ECR 2597.

86 Case 45/87 R *Commission* v *Ireland* [1987] ECR 1369.

87 Case 61/77 R *Commission* v *Ireland* [1977] ECR 1411.

88 Case 154/85 R *Commission* v *Italy* [1985] ECR 1753.

89 Case 171/83 R *Commission* v *France* [1983] ECR 2621.

90 Case 293/85 R *Commission* v *Belgium* [1985] ECR 3521.

91 Case 206/81 R *Alvarez* v *Parliament* [1981] ECR 2187.

92 Vandersanden and Barav, p. 442; Gray, p. 102; Waelbroeck and others, in Mégret and others, p. 370; Pastor and Van Ginderachter, p. 599; Huglo, paragraph 60.

93 Lasok, p. 164.

94 Joined Cases 24 and 97/80 R *Commission* v *France* [1980] ECR 1319 at 1342.

"in the present case the Commission, or rather the Community which it represents, would suffer, so it is said, 'moral' damage from the continued failure to comply with a judgment of the Court; but that does not seem to me the kind of damage of a nature to justify interim measures. If it were thought otherwise it would be necessary to go as far as maintaining that any action brought by the Commission for infringement of Article 171 would automatically justify interim measures against the defendant State. This however, in my view, would distort the system of the Treaty both as regards the objective of interim measures and the position of Member States in default as against the Community".

(iii) Potential harm

Potential harm may not be sufficient to justify interim measures. In *Commission* v *Italy*[95], the Commission and the intervener argued that the refusal of the Italian authorities to authorize an airline company to operate a "fifth freedom" scheduled air service on a certain route would cause the company serious and irreparable damage in the form of a loss of potential profit calculated on the basis of the possible transfer to that company of part of the traffic then carried by two other airline companies. The Court merely stated that the business of airline companies involved was of such a magnitude that a loss of the sum in question could not be regarded as constituting sufficient damage to establish urgency.

However, in *Belgium* v *Commission*[96], the Court decided that indefinite future damage, such as the risk of being made liable to a company's creditors in court proceedings, could not in any event be regarded as serious and irreparable damage.

(iv) Financial harm

Where the damage alleged is of a financial nature, the Court has held that it is not in principle considered to be serious and irreparable unless it could not be wholly recouped if the applicant were to be successful in the main action[97]. This principle leads one writer[98] to conclude that pecuniary loss may not be serious and irreparable in the context of an action for damages or in proceedings where the Court has unlimited jurisdiction and can award damages even though the claim is only for annulment; on the other hand, in an action for annulment where the Court does not have unlimited jurisdiction, the loss may well be serious and irreparable unless it would be fully compensated by the annulment of the measure in question. It is considered, for example, that if the effect of annulment were the repayment of money withheld, plus interest thereon, there would have to be evidence that the payment of the

---

95 Case 352/88 R [1989] ECR 267.

96 Case 142/87 R [1987] ECR 2589.

97 Case C-358/90 R *Compagnia Italiana Alcool* v *Commission* [1990] ECR I-4887 at 4894.

98 Lasok, p. 166.

sum in question would cause damage which could not be compensated by payment of interest in order to show that there was risk of serious and irreparable damage. On the other hand, it is argued that where the damage consists, not simply of a pecuniary loss but of an injury to property rights, not even an award of damages may prevent this damage from being considered serious and irreparable[99].

However, account is also taken of the size of the undertaking and the repercussions that financial losses could have on its continued existence. Thus, in *Sofrimport* v *Commission*[100], the Court compared the amount of the transaction in question with the undertaking's annual turnover. In the case of a Member State[101], the Court has compared expenditure not recognized as chargeable to the European Agricultural Guidance and Guarantee Fund (and hence chargeable to the Member State) with the amount of the budget deficit of that State.

In the case of applications for the suspension of the operation of regulations imposing anti-dumping duties, the Court has required applicants to establish further matters. Thus, in *Technointorg* v *Council*[102], it was considered insufficient that in seeking to demonstrate the urgency of its application, the applicant confined itself to describing effects which were inherent in the imposition of anti-dumping duties, namely a rise in the price of its products and a consequent diminution of its market share. The Court added that it was clear from a consistent line of cases that the party requesting suspension must at least adduce evidence that, first, the damage suffered by it as a result of the imposition of the anti-dumping duty was special to it[103], and, secondly, the balance of the interests at stake pointed in its favour in the sense that the grant of interim measures requested would not cause appreciable injury to the Community industry[104].

4. The balance of interests

In considering the merits of an application for interim measures, the Court may also take into account the "balance of interests": an attempt may be made to weigh on the one hand the harm to the applicant if interim measures are not adopted and on the other hand the harm to the defendant, or even

---

[99] In this last connection, Case 232/81 R *Agricola Commerciale Olio* v *Commission* [1981] ECR 2193 is cited.

[100] Case 152/88 R [1988] ECR 2931. See also Case 352/88 R *Commission* v *Italy* [1989] ECR 267; Cases C-51/90 and C-59/90 R *Comos-Tank and Others* v *Commission* [1990] ECR I-2167.

[101] Case 32/89 R *Greece* v *Commission* [1989] ECR 985.

[102] Case 77/87 R [1987] ECR 1793.

[103] The Court referred to Case 258/84 R *Nippon Seiko* v *Council* [1984] ECR 4357.

[104] The Court referred to Case 250/85 R *Brother Industries* v *Council* [1985] ECR 3459.

the wider interest, if interim measures are adopted. The practice of the Court in relation to this condition, which is not specified in Article 83(2) of the Rules of Procedure, is consistent with the practice of the International Court of Justice and of the English courts[105].

As a former Member of the Court has written[106]:

> "Two recent cases show how interests have to be balanced. In one the Commission sought to prevent construction work in an area protected as the habitat of migratory birds. It was said that this construction work would cause the loss of the natural habitat. As an interim measure, relief was refused because the Commission had delayed and the remaining work was unlikely to cause serious harm to the birds[107].
>
> In the second case, an application was made to prevent the coming into effect of German legislation imposing a toll on lorry drivers using the motorways. This was said to be discriminatory because the road tax on German lorries was reduced by an amount approximately equal to the toll, so that only drivers from other States would pay an extra amount. Despite arguments that these tolls were urgently needed for environmental purposes, an interim order was made that the legislation should not be put into effect because of the likely serious damage to small road haulage contractors in other Member States[108]".

In cases between Community servants and institutions, the Court has often proceeded by balancing the interests of the applicant and the interests of the defendant institution[109], the latter having frequently prevailed.

The balancing of interests may make it difficult to obtain the suspension of anti-dumping measures[110]. Applications for the suspension of Commission regulations imposing provisional duties in the course of an anti-dumping investigation have been dismissed in several cases[111]. In one case, however, other interim measures were adopted to protect the applicant[112]. The position is rather similar with the regulations by which, at the end of the investigation, the Council takes a definitive decision on the need to impose anti-dumping duties. The provisions imposing definitive duties have never

---

105 Lasok, p. 168.

106 Gordon Slynn, *Introducing a European Legal Order* (1993), pp. 38–39. For a further recent example of the balancing of interests, see the Order of 29 June 1993, Case C-280/93 R *Germany* v *Commission* (Bananas), paragraphs 49–54.

107 Case C-57/89 R *Commission* v *Germany* [1989] ECR 2849.

108 Case C-195/90 R *Commission* v *Germany* [1990] ECR I-2715.

109 For example, Case 63/88 R *Maindiaux* v *ESC* [1988] ECR 1659 at 1666; Case C-345/90 P-R *Parliament* v *Hanning* [1991] ECR I-231 at 238.

110 Joliet, p. 266.

111 See e.g. Case 294/86 R *Technointorg* v *Commission* [1986] ECR 3979; Case 304/86 R *Enital* v *Council and Commission* [1987] ECR 267.

112 Case 120/83 R *Raznoimport* v *Commission* [1983] ECR 2573.

been suspended[113]. However, undertakings have obtained the suspension of provisions ordering the definitive collection of the provisional duties imposed by the Commission[114].

In anti-dumping cases it may be necessary to balance the likely harm to the Community industry if the measures are suspended against the likely harm to the applicants if suspension is refused; so the suspension of anti-dumping regulations may be refused if suspension would cause appreciable injury to the Community industry[115].

In a different area, the interests of the Community in disposing, on conditions considered appropriate by the Commission, of the very large quantities of alcohol held in intervention resulting from the distillation operations provided for under the Common Agricultural Policy and whose storage caused significant logistical problems, prevailed over the commercial interests of an undertaking[116].

In regard to the award of public works contracts, the Court has stated, in dismissing applications for interim measures, that "the blocking of the funds earmarked for the execution of the project, with the grave consequences which such a measure would entail for all the parties concerned, would be a disproportionate response to the doubts which the facts alleged by the applicants have raised concerning the regularity of the tender procedures"[117] and, in the *Dundalk Water Supply* case already mentioned, that delay in the award of the contract at issue would aggravate the existing health and safety hazards for the inhabitants of an area in such a way as to tilt the balance of interests in favour of the defendant[118].

However, in *Commission* v *Denmark*, the application was more successful. Although the Commission withdrew its application for interim measures[119], it did so only after the Danish government made a declaration in which it

[113] Case 240/84 R *NTN Toyo* v *Council* [1984] ECR 4093; Case 258/84 R *Nippon Seiko* v *Commission* [1984] ECR 4357; Case 250/85 R *Brother Industries* v *Council* [1985] ECR 3459; Case 260/85 R *TEC* v *Council* [1985] ECR 3467; Case 273/85 R *Silver Seiko* v *Council* [1985] ECR 3475; Case 297/85 R *Towa Sankiden* v *Council* [1985] ECR 3483; Joined Cases 277 and 300/85 R *Canon Inc.* v *Council* [1985] ECR 3491; Case 77/87 R *Technointorg* v *Council* [1987] ECR 1793; Case 133/87 R *Nashua Corporation* v *Commission* [1987] ECR 2883; Case 69/89 R *Nakajima All Precision* v *Council* [1989] ECR 1689; Case C-358/89 R *Extramet Industrie* v *Council* [1990] ECR I-431.

[114] Cases 113/77 R and 113/77 R-Int. *NTN Toyo* v *Council* [1977] ECR 1721; Case 119/77 R *Nippon Seiko* v *Council and Commission* [1977] ECR 1867; Case 121/77 R *Nachi Fujikoshi* v *Council* [1977] ECR 2107.

[115] See ante Case 77/87 R *Technointorg* v *Council* [1987] ECR 1793; Case 250/85 R *Brother Industries* v *Council* [1985] ECR 3459.

[116] Case C-358/90 R *Compagnia Italiana Alcool* v *Commission* [1990] ECR I-4887 at 4895.

[117] Case 118/83 R *CMC* v *Commission* [1983] ECR 2583 at 2601.

[118] Case 45/87 R *Commission* v *Ireland* [1987] ECR 1369 at 1378.

[119] Case C-243/89 R, Order of the Court of 22 September 1989, not published in the Reports of Cases before the Court.

recognized that a clause inviting tenders to use Danish labour and material as much as possible constituted a breach of the principle of non-discrimination. The Danish government also undertook to avoid discriminatory clauses or practices in future public works or supply contracts, to compensate undertakings which had submitted tenders where those claims were justified in Danish law and to reimburse the fees they had incurred[120].

In addition the various interests involved may lead the Court to determine the most appropriate interim measure for the purpose of safeguarding both the interests of third parties and those of the applicant. Thus, in *Johnson and Firth Brown* v *Commission*[121], the Court suspended only part of the Commission decision and ordered an intervener not to exercise the voting rights attached to any shares which it might acquire in the applicant.

III. Permissible content of interim measures

There appear to be few limitations on the content of interim measures. Article 86(1) states that the decision on the application must take the form of a reasoned order[122], from which no appeal shall lie[123]. It will also be recalled that, under Article 36 of the EEC Statute, the ruling of the President "shall in no way prejudice the decision of the Court on the substance of the case"[124]. In addition, Article 186 of the Treaty is extremely general in its terms, referring to "any necessary interim measures".

As regards the wide range of measures which may be adopted, examples have already been given in the cases of *Group of the European Right* v *Parliament*[125] and of *Raznoimport* v *Commission*[126]; reference has also been made to the fact that the interim measures adopted are not confined to those requested by the applicant. In *Commission* v *France*[127], which concerned restrictions imposed on the import of Italian wine, consisting of customs delays and chemical analysis of the wine, the Court laid down in great detail the limita-

---

[120] For a résumé of the terms of the settlement, see Opinion of Advocate General Tesauro of 17 November 1992 in Case C-243/89 (not yet published in the Reports of the Cases before the Court). See also L. La Marca, Sospensione cautelare dell'appalto già aggiudicato e conciliazione giudiziale: il caso Storebaelt (1990) *Rivista di diritto europeo* 803.

[121] Case 3/75 R [1975] ECR 1.

[122] Compare Article 107(1) of the Rules of Procedure of the Court of First Instance.

[123] It will be recalled, however, that decisions on interim measures of the Court of First Instance may be appealed to the Court of Justice; see above, p. 42.

[124] See above p. 41. For the rationale, see the Opinion of Advocate General Capotorti in Cases 24 and 97/80 R *Commission* v *France* [1980] ECR 1319 at 1337-8.

[125] Case 221/86 R [1986] ECR 2579; see above p. 44.

[126] Case 120/83 R [1983] ECR 2573; see above p. 46.

[127] Case 42/82 R [1982] ECR 841.

tions on the French controls which were to be observed pending judgment in the main action.

A further illustration of the permissible content of interim measures is afforded by *United Kingdom* v *Parliament*[128], in which the Parliament was alleged to have exceeded its powers in adopting the Community budget for 1986 by breaching the limits on the increase in non-compulsory expenditure. On an application for interim measures by the United Kingdom, the Court ordered the Commission to implement the budget provisionally with the effect that it was provisionally re-written so as to exclude the contested increases. The relevant parts of the Order were as follows:

(1) The Commission shall implement, until 10 July 1986 or until the date on which the Court delivers its judgment in Case 34/86, *Council* v *European Parliament*, whichever date shall be the earlier, the budget for the financial year 1986, as regards both payment appropriations and credit appropriations, on the basis of the draft budget established by the Council at its second reading on 27 November 1985, subject to those amendments decided by the Parliament on 12 December 1985 which do not have the effect of increasing non-compulsory expenditure, that is to say the amendments by way of transfer from budget line B 660 to the new lines B 6615, 6616 and 6617 and to line 6632 and from budget line B 944 to line A 1 100.

(2) In the first call which it makes, following this order, on the United Kingdom for funds relating to the 1986 budget, the Commission shall reduce the amount claimed, on the basis of the budget established by the Council at its second reading, by the amount of any overpayments made by the United Kingdom prior to this order on the basis of the budget declared by the President of the European Parliament on 18 December 1985.

A distinctive feature of this Order is that it was directed to the Commission rather than to the defendant Parliament. In this connection, the Commission had indicated that it accepted the procedure[129]. Moreover, it seems unquestionably correct that an order could be made against the Commission, even though it was not the defendant in the proceedings; an interim measure against the Council suspending operation of a Council regulation might similarly entail an obligation for the Commission to take the necessary steps.

IV. Binding force and enforceability of interim measures

It is clear that the measures are mandatory: this follows from the use of the terms (i) in Article 185 of the EEC Treaty, that the Court may *order* that the

[128] Case 23/86 R [1986] ECR 1085.
[129] [1986] ECR 1085 at 1093.

application of the contested act be suspended, (ii) in Article 186 of the EEC Treaty, that the Court may *prescribe* any necessary interim measures and (iii) in Article 86(1) of the Rules of Procedure, that the decision on the application shall take the form of a reasoned *order*.

However, it may be useful to distinguish, as regards enforceability, between suspension and other interim measures. An order suspending a measure adopted by a Community institution will of itself, it seems, automatically suspend the operation of the measure so that it will no longer be applicable either by the Community institutions or by the national authorities or the national courts. On the other hand, questions may arise as to the effect of suspension of national measures, for example, in Article 169 proceedings brought by the Commission against Member States. This cannot be regarded as suspension under Article 185, which is designed for challenge to Community measures; rather an order to suspend the application of national measures is to be regarded as falling within Article 186. In the context of challenges to the United Kingdom's legislation on fisheries, proceedings were brought by the Commission under Article 169 and on references from the English courts under Article 177. The Article 177 proceedings gave rise, *inter alia*, to the *Factortame*[130] judgment, in which the Court held that national courts must protect, by interim measures, putative Community rights claimed in the national courts, even if national law precludes such interim relief; the national court is obliged to set aside any rule of national law which would prevent the grant of interim relief in those circumstances. In the Article 169 action by the Commission, the Court[131] ordered the United Kingdom, pending delivery of the judgment in the main proceedings, to suspend the application of the nationality requirements laid down in section 14(1)(a) and (c) of the Merchant Shipping Act 1988, read in conjunction with paragraphs (2) and (7) of that section, as regards the nationals of other Member States and in respect of fishing vessels which, until 31 March 1989, were pursuing a fishing activity under the British flag and under a British fishing licence. The Order gave rise to some consideration, it seems, as to whether it should be treated as having direct effect (or as being self-executing) or whether it required implementing measures in the United Kingdom; in the event, however, the United Kingdom Government adopted its own specific measures to give effect to the suspension.

The case raises two interesting questions. First, in the absence of any implementing measures, what would be the effect in the national court of an order of the Court requiring the suspension of national legislation? In particular, would the national court be obliged not to apply such measures? It can certainly be argued, especially in the light of the Court's case-law on the

---

130 Case C-213/89 *Factortame and Others* [1990] ECR I-2433; this judgment is discussed in more detail at p. 46.

131 Case 246/89 R *Commission* v *United Kingdom* [1989] ECR 3125.

duties of national courts under Article 5 of the EEC Treaty, that the national courts would be obliged to treat the order of the Court as having the effect of suspending the national measures. Secondly, would there be any sanctions if a Member State failed to comply with such an order? It will be recalled that provision for sanctions against Member States is included in the Maastricht Treaty[132]. They will apply in any event in relation to judgments which the Court has given in Article 169 proceedings where Member States do not comply with the judgment. However, it remains to be seen whether they will apply to failure to comply with an interim order, made in such proceedings.

V. Legal consequences of measures later found unjustified

If in the course of the proceedings it is found that an order needs to be varied or cancelled on account of a change in circumstances, Article 87 of the Rules of Procedure[133] makes express provision for that eventuality. Similarly, under Article 88 of the Rules of Procedure[134], where the application for an interim measure has been rejected, the applicant is not barred from making a further application on the basis of new facts.

Moreover, by virtue of Article 86(3) of the Rules of Procedure[135], the measure lapses on final judgment, unless the order fixes the date on which the interim measure is to lapse.

The position of the party against which interim measures have been ordered can also be protected by the provision of security. Under Article 86(2) of the Rules of Procedure[136], enforcement of the order may be made conditional on the lodging by the applicant of security; the amount and nature of the security are to be fixed in the light of the circumstances. In particular, the Court has used this power in relation to Community measures under which applicants have been required to pay sums of money, such as regulations instituting anti-dumping duties[137] or decisions imposing fines for breach of competition rules[138]. But the Court has refused to order security in

---

[132] Treaty on European Union, Article G amending Article 171 of the EEC Treaty.

[133] Compare Article 108 of the Rules of Procedure of the Court of First Instance.

[134] Compare Article 109 of the Rules of Procedure of the Court of First Instance.

[135] Compare Article 107(3) of the Rules of Procedure of the Court of First Instance.

[136] Compare Article 107(2) of the Rules of Procedure of the Court of First Instance.

[137] For example, Cases 113/77 R and 113/77 R-Int. *NTN Toyo* v *Council* [1977] ECR 1721; Case 119/77 R *Nippon Seiko* v *Council and Commission* [1977] ECR 1867; Case 121/77 R *Nachi Fujikoshi* v *Council* [1977] ECR 2107.

[138] For example, Case 107/82 R *AEG* v *Commission* [1982] ECR 1549; Case 86/82 R *Hasselblad* v *Commission* [1982] ECR 1555.

the case of an undertaking which, because of its small size, might find difficulties in obtaining the necessary credit and where, having regard to the fact that it operated exclusively as a subcontractor, the amount of the fine might represent a heavier burden for it than for an undertaking which realized on its own behalf all the added value of the production concerned[139]. In addition, the lodging of security can be contemplated only if the party against which it is ordered is liable for the sums which the security is intended to cover and there is a risk of that party's insolvency[140].

Thus in *Commission* v *Germany* (lorry tax) the German Government claimed that the Commission should be ordered to provide a security of some DM 500 million to cover payment of the taxes for which carriers of other Member States would be liable pending the proceedings and which the Federal Republic of Germany would not be able to recover subsequently even if it were successful in its submissions. The Court rejected the claim, observing that the lodging of security pursuant to Article 86(2) of the Rules of Procedure could be contemplated only if the party against which it is ordered is liable for the sums which the security is intended to cover and there is a risk of that party being insolvent. That was not so in the present case since in any event there were no grounds for believing that the Community would not be able to meet any award of damages which might be made against it. There was therefore no ground for making the grant of the interim measure subject to the lodging by the Commission of security of DM 500 million[141].

VI. Interim measures in respect of Community provisions in the national courts

Although Articles 185 and 186 give the Court wide powers to grant interim measures in a direct action, they do not extend to proceedings before the Court in the form of a request for a preliminary ruling under Article 177 of the EEC Treaty. In these cases, as in other proceedings pending before national courts and involving questions of Community law, interim measures can be granted only by national courts. However, the Court has established certain principles in relation to the grant of interim measures by national courts.

---

139 Case 234/82 R *Ferriere di Roè Volciano* v *Commission* [1983] ECR 725. For examples of cases in which requests not to have to provide a bank guarantee were rejected, see Case 392/85 R *Finsider* v *Commission* [1986] ECR 959 and Case 213/86 R *Montedipe SpA* v *Commission* [1986] ECR 2623.

140 Case C-195/90 R *Commission* v *Germany* [1990] ECR I-3351.

141 *Ibid.*

A. Interim measures in national courts to protect Community rights

The Court has made it clear that the principle of effective judicial protection may require national courts to grant interim relief, notwithstanding the existence of a national rule prohibiting such an application being granted. This was decided in *Factortame and Others*[142]. The statutory system governing the registration of British fishing vessels was radically altered by Part II of the Merchant Shipping Act 1988 and the Merchant Shipping (Registration of Fishing Vessels) Regulations 198[143]. The purpose was to stop the practice known as "quota hopping" whereby, according to the United Kingdom, its fishing quotas were "plundered" by vessels flying the British flag but lacking any genuine link with the United Kingdom. Factortame and other companies owned or operated 95 fishing vessels which failed to satisfy the conditions for registration under section 14(1) of the 1988 Act. Since those vessels were to be deprived of the right to engage in fishing as from 1 April 1989, the companies in question, by means of an application for judicial review, challenged the compatibility of the relevant provisions of the 1988 Act with Community law. They also applied for the grant of interim relief pending final judgment.

The High Court[144] decided to request a preliminary ruling on the issues of Community law raised in the proceedings and ordered that, by way of interim relief, the application of Part II of the 1988 Act and the 1988 Regulations should be suspended as regards the applicants. On the Secretary of State's appeal against the order granting interim relief, the Court of Appeal[145] held that under national law the Court had no power to suspend, by way of interim relief, the application of Acts of Parliament. On further appeal, the House of Lords[146] held that, under national law, the English courts had no power to grant interim relief in a case such as the one before it. More specifically, it held that the grant of such relief was precluded by the old common law rule that an interim injunction could not be granted against the Crown, in conjunction with the presumption that an Act of Parliament was in conformity with Community law until such time as a decision on its compatibility with that law had been given. The House of Lords sought a preliminary ruling on, inter alia, whether Community law obliged or empowered the national court to grant interim protection in circumstances where a request for a preliminary ruling on a point of Community law had been made.

---

142 Case C-213/89 [1990] ECR I-2433.
143 Statutory Instrument 1988, No. 1926.
144 [1989] 2 CMLR 353.
145 [1989] 2 CMLR 392.
146 [1989] 2 WLR 997.

Replying in the affirmative, the Court stated:

> "... it is for the national courts, in application of the principle of cooperation laid down in Article 5 of the EEC Treaty, to ensure the legal protection which persons derive from the direct effect of provisions of Community law ...
>
> ... any provision of a national legal system and any legislative, administrative or judicial practice which might impair the effectiveness of Community law by withholding from the national court having jurisdiction to apply such law the power to do everything necessary at the moment of its application to set aside national legislative provisions which might prevent, even temporarily, Community rules from having full force and effect are incompatible with those requirements, which are the very essence of Community law ...
>
> ... the full effectiveness of Community law would be just as much impaired if a rule of national law could prevent a court seised of a dispute governed by Community law from granting interim relief in order to ensure the full effectiveness of the judgment to be given on the existence of the rights claimed under Community law. It follows that a court which in those circumstances would grant interim relief, if it were not for a rule of national law, is obliged to set aside that rule.
>
> That interpretation is reinforced by the system established by Article 177 of the EEC Treaty whose effectiveness would be impaired if a national court, having stayed proceedings pending the reply by the Court of Justice to the question referred to it for a preliminary ruling, were not able to grant interim relief until it delivered its judgment following the reply given by the Court of Justice"[147].

Accordingly, it remains the position that, as a matter of English domestic law, an interim injunction cannot be granted against the Crown. In contrast, if a dispute concerns rights under Community law, such an injunction may be granted. In his judgment in the decision of the English Court of Appeal in *M* v *Home Office*[148], Lord Donaldson MR criticized the position as "anomalous and wrong in principle".

B. Interim measures in national courts to suspend national measures implementing Community regulations

National rules on interim measures may also have to be qualified in the event of a national court being asked to suspend a national measure implementing a Community regulation. In *Foto-Frost*[149], a customs notice, based on a

[147] [1990] ECR I-2433 at 2473-2474.

[148] [1992] 4 All ER 97 at 141.

[149] Case 314/85 *Foto-Frost* v *Hauptzollamt Lübeck-Ost* [1987] ECR 4199.

Commission decision, was challenged in a German court, thus raising the question of the validity of the Commission decision. On a reference under Article 177, the Court held that national courts do not have the power to declare acts of the Community institutions invalid. Among other very compelling reasons, that would jeopardise the unity of the Community legal order and detract from the fundamental requirement of legal certainty. However, the Court added that the rule that national courts may not themselves declare Community acts invalid might have to be qualified in certain circumstances where the validity of a Community act was contested before a national court in proceedings relating to an application for interim measures. That question did not arise in *Foto-Frost*, but arose subsequently in another reference from a German court, *Zuckerfabrik Süderdithmarschen*[150]. Here the Court accepted that national courts should also be able to suspend enforcement of a national administrative measure adopted on the basis of a Community regulation. But the exercise of that power was subject to strict conditions. First, the national court must have serious doubts as to the validity of the Community regulation on which the contested administrative measure is based. Secondly, the national court must refer the question of validity to the Court if the question is not already before it. Thirdly, the granting of relief must be subject to uniform conditions in all the Member States. Thus, suspension could only be granted if there is urgency in the sense of a threat of serious and irreparable damage to the applicant and if the national court takes due account of the Community interests. The ruling of the Court was criticized[151] as limiting the scope of provisional judicial protection in German law; however, it seems clear that some limitations on procedural rules may be necessary to guarantee the uniform application of Community law in all the Member States.

C. Interim measures in national courts and the duty to adopt coercive measures required by Community law

The Court has also rejected an attempt by a Member State to justify its failure to comply with its Community obligations by reference to either the impossibility, in view of the requirements of national law, of adopting coercive measures required by Community law, or to the foreseeable refusal of courts to confirm such measures. This was decided in *Commission* v *Germany*[152]. Under the relevant Community regulations the Commission was required, in certain circumstances, to order the compulsory distillation of table wine in

[150] Joined Cases C-143/88 and C-92/89 *Zuckerfabrik Süderdithmarschen and Zuckerfabrik Soest* [1991] ECR 415.

[151] W. Dänzer-Vanotti, Der Gerichtshof der Europäischen Gemeinschaften beschränkt vorläufigen Rechtsschutz (1991) *Betriebs-Berater* 1015.

[152] Case C-217/88 [1990] ECR I-2879.

the event of a surplus. Wine-growers who did not comply with the obligation to distil were excluded from the benefits of the intervention measures provided for. Under Article 4(1) of Regulation No 337/79[153], Member States were to take all necessary measures to ensure compliance with Community provisions in the wine sector. The Commission ordered the distillation of 12,000,000 hl of table wine, of which 68,322 were to be distilled by German wine-growers. The German authorities issued notices to 614 German wine-growers informing them of the quantity that they were required to distil. Of these, 506 lodged appeals, arguing essentially that the criteria used by the Community regulations to determine the amount to be distilled by each wine-grower were discriminatory. Under German law, an appeal against an administrative decision has automatic suspensory effect. However, the administrative authorities may order the immediate enforcement of a decision if the public interest so requires. Such an order may itself be appealed against, in which event the administrative courts may again suspend the decision. The German authorities decided against ordering the immediate enforcement of the 506 notices against which appeals had been lodged. In the event, of the 68,322 hl of wine that should have been distilled in Germany, only 9,140 were in fact distilled. Taking the view that Germany's failure to take any further action to force the German wine-growers to participate in the scheme for compulsory distillation constituted a breach of Article 64(1) of Regulation No 337/79 and of Article 5 of the EEC Treaty, the Commission brought proceedings against Germany under Article 169 of that Treaty.

The Court held that a Member State may not plead provisions, practices or circumstances existing in its internal legal system in order to justify a failure to comply with its obligations under Community law. It could not therefore rely on the fact that the conditions laid down by its national law for the implementation of such measures were not satisfied in order to justify its own failure to resort to coercive measures against certain producers, as Community law required it to do. It also could not justify its inaction by contending that, had such measures been adopted, their application would probably have been suspended by the courts in view of serious doubts about the validity of the Community legislation which imposed them, since, in the first place, a Member State could not rely on the possible or probable attitude of its national courts in order to justify its own failure and, secondly, those courts have available to them the procedure under Article 177 if they are uncertain about the validity of Community legislation.

---

[153] OJ 1979 L 54, p. 1.

Concluding remarks

The powers of the Court of Justice to grant interim measures constitute an essential element of the Community legal order because from the litigant's point of view, they seek to ensure that the judgment in the main action retains its usefulness. As Advocate General Tesauro has expressed it, "the purpose of interim protection is to achieve that fundamental objective of every legal system, the effectiveness of judicial protection"[154].

In general, the Court's powers have been construed broadly; but it must be emphasized that interim measures have been granted in only a small proportion of the cases where they have been sought[155].

The Court's case-law on interim measures in respect of Community provisions in national courts has further underlined the importance of interim measures in the Community legal order. However, in contrast to the case-law on interim measures before the Court of Justice, this case-law is still in its infancy.

---

[154] Case C-213/89 *Factortame and Others* [1990] I-2433 at paragraph 18.

[155] See Annex.

Interim Measures in the Inter-American Court of Human Rights

THOMAS BUERGENTHAL

Introduction

The American Convention on Human Rights[1] is the only international human rights treaty to provide for judicially enforceable interim or provisional measures. The jurisdiction to grant these measures is conferred on the Inter-American Court of Human Rights[2] by Article 63(2) of the Convention, which reads as follows:

> "In cases of extreme gravity and urgency, and when necessary to avoid irreparable damage to persons, the Court shall adopt such provisional measures as it deems pertinent in matters it has under consideration. With respect to a case not yet submitted to the Court, it may act at the request of the [Inter-American] Commission [on Human Rights]".

As this provision indicates, the Court has the power to grant provisional measures in cases pending before it and in those not as yet referred to it. In

---

[1] The authoritative texts of the American Convention on Human Rights (English, Spanish, French and Portuguese) are reproduced in OAS Official Documents, OEA/Ser. A/16 (SEPF) (1970). All citations to these texts are to this document.

[2] On the Inter-American Court of Human Rights in general, see S. Davidson, *The Inter-American Court of Human Rights* (1992); C. Cerna, "The Inter-American Court of Human Rights", M. Janis (ed.), *International Courts for the Twenty-First Century* 117 (1992); Instituto Interamericano de Derechos Humanos, *La Corte Interamericana de Derechos Humanos: Estudios y Documentos* (1978); T. Buergenthal, "The Inter-American Court of Human Rights," 76 *A. J. I. L.* 231 (1982). See also, R. Nieto-Navia, *Introducción al sistema interamericano de protección a los derechos humanos* 74–158 (1993); C. Medina-Quiroga, *The Battle of Human Rights: Gross, Systematic Violations and the Inter-American System* 161–184 (1988); J. Kokott, *Das interamerikanische System zum Schutze der Menschenrechte* 151 (1987); A. Cancado-Trindade, "The Evolution of the Organization of American States (OAS) System of Human Rights Protection," 25 *Germ. YB. Int'l L.* 498, 505 (1982).

the latter category of cases, the request for the provisional measures can come only from the Commission. No such restrictions apply to the first type. Here, pursuant to Article 24 of the Court's Rules of Procedure[3], it can act on its own motion or on the request of the parties to the case, that is to say, at the request of the Commission and/or any of the States Parties to the case. Article 24, which regulates the procedures applicable to provisional measures, reads as follows:

> "1. At any stage of the proceeding involving cases of extreme gravity and urgency and when necessary to avoid irreparable damage to persons, the Court may, at the request of a party or on its own motion, order whatever provisional measures it deems appropriate, pursuant to Article 63(2) of the Convention.
>
> 2. With respect to matters not yet submitted to it, the Court may act at the request of the Commission.
>
> 3. Such request may be presented to the President, to any judge of the Court or to the Secretariat, by any means of communication. The recipient of the request shall immediately bring it to the attention of the President.
>
> 4. If the Court is not sitting, the President shall convoke it immediately. Pending the meeting of the Court, the President, in consultation with the Permanent Commission and, if possible, with the other judges, shall call upon the government concerned to adopt the necessary urgent measures and to act so as to permit any provisional measures subsequently ordered by the Court to have the requisite effect.
>
> 5. In its Annual Report to the General Assembly, the Court shall include a statement regarding the provisional measures ordered during the period covered by the report. If such measures have not been duly executed, the Court shall make whatever recommendations it deems appropriate".

Since its establishment in 1979, the Court has had the opportunity to interpret and apply Article 63(2) of the Convention and Article 24 of the Statute a number of times. It has done so in cases pending before it[4] and in those not yet submitted to it[5]. This jurisprudence and various other issues relating to

---

[3] For the most recent version of the Statute of the Inter-American Court of Human Rights, see *Basic Documents Pertaining to Human Rights in the Inter-American System,* OAS doc. OEA/Ser. L. V/II.82, doc. 6, rev. 1 (1992), p.145.

[4] To date the Court entered provisional measures in cases already before it only in the three Honduran Disappearance Cases, that is, in the Velasquez Rodriguez Case; the Godinez Cruz Case; and the Fairen Garbi and Solis Corrales Case. See Decisions of the Inter-American Court of Human Rights of January 15 and January 19, 1988, [1988] *Annual Report of the Inter-American Court of Human Rights* [hereinafter *Annual Report*], at 25 and 27, respectively (1988).

[5] To date, provisional measures have been granted by the Court in two cases which at the time were still pending before the Commission. See: (1) Bustíos-Rojas Case (Peru), Decision of August 8, 1990, [1990] *Annual Report* 33 (1991); and Decision

the interpretation and application of Article 63(2) will be analyzed in the pages that follow.

The subject of interim measures has a special importance within the Inter-American system for the protection of human rights. That is so because the system applies to a region where unlawful governmental action or inaction causing "irreparable damage to persons" is not an uncommon occurrence. The Article 63(2) remedy must thus be seen as a procedural and normative innovation that is not only capable of saving lives, but one that has already saved lives.

I. Jurisdictional Issues

The power of the Inter-American Court of Human Rights to grant provisional measures depends, in the first place, on a preliminary determination that the State against which such measures are sought has in one form or another accepted the Court's jurisdiction and that no other, readily apparent, fatal jurisdictional defects exist. That is to say, before this remedy may be granted there must be, at the very least, a *prima facie* finding of jurisdiction as far as the parties to the case are concerned[6]. This determination will always have to be made in those instances where the Commission seeks provisional measures in cases that have not as yet been submitted to the Court. It may also come up, however, in cases already referred to the Court. This would be so where the provisional measures are requested by one of the parties simultaneously with the filing of the case or in those situations where the request is made before the Court has had an opportunity to pass on the question of jurisdiction of a case pending before it.

To understand the preliminary jurisdictional issues the Court will have to address before examining the question whether a request for preliminary

---

of January 17, 1991, [1991] *Annual Report* 15 (1992). (These decisions were preceded by an Order of Urgent Measures, dated June 5, 1990, adopted by the President of the Court, [1990] *Annual Report* 28 (1991).); (2) Chunima Case (Guatemala), Decision of August 1, 1991, [1991] *Annual Report* 69 (1991), preceded by the President's Order of Urgent Measures, dated 15 July 1991, *ibid.*, at 61. The provisional measures ordered by the Court came to an end on December 3, 1991. See Letter of the President of the Court to the Government of Guatemala, dated December 3, 1991, *ibid.*,at 163.

The Court refused the Commission's request for provisional measures in two other cases. See: (1) Peruvian Prisons Case (Peru), Decision of January 27, 1993 (mimeo). (This decision was preceded by the President's Order, dated December 14, 1993, denying the request for urgent measures,[1992] *Annual Report* 101.); Chipoco Case (Peru), Decision of January 27, 1993 (mimeo). This decision was preceded by the Order of the President of the Court, dated December 14, 1992, denying the request for urgent measures. [1992] *Annual Report* 97 (1993). See also, Reggiardo Toloso Case (Argentina), Order of the President, dated November 19, 1993 (mimeo), granting urgent measures.

[6] See Buergenthal *supra* note 2, at 241; Kokott, *supra* note 2, at 129.

measures should be granted, it is useful to focus for a moment on the subject Court's jurisdiction in general[7]. The contentious jurisdiction of the Inter-American Court is spelled out in Article 62 of the American Convention. While the first two paragraphs of this provision regulate the manner in which States Parties may subject themselves to jurisdiction, the third paragraph defines the Court's powers. It reads as follows:

> "The jurisdiction of the Court shall comprise all cases concerning the interpretation and application of the provisions of this Convention that are submitted to it, provided that the States Parties to the case recognize or have recognized such jurisdiction, whether by special declaration pursuant to the preceding paragraphs, or by a special agreement".

Article 62(2) permits the States Parties to subject themselves to the Court's jurisdiction "unconditionally, on the condition of reciprocity, for a specific period, or for specific cases".

Once a State has accepted the Court's jurisdiction, another State Party or the Inter-American Commission on Human Rights may refer the case to it[8]. But, as Article 62(3) indicates, a State Party may only refer a case to the Court if it and the Respondent State have recognized the Court's jurisdiction; the Commission may only do so if the Respondent is subject to that jurisdiction. Individuals have no standing to take a case to the Court[9].

The Court has thus far not had to pass on the question whether a case brought to the Commission by a State not subject to the tribunal's jurisdiction may thereafter be referred to it by the Commission when the Respondent State has accepted that jurisdiction. This question is further complicated by the fact that the Convention, as we have seen, permits States to accept the Court's jurisdiction on condition of reciprocity, which some States have done.

The starting point for an analysis of this question must be the language of Article 62(3). It conditions the Court's jurisdiction to consider a case on the proviso that "the States Parties to the case recognize or have recognized such jurisdiction". The meaning of this phrase depends, in the first place, on how the word "case" is to be interpreted. If by "case" is meant the entire proceeding, starting with the institution before the Commission of the inter-State communication and ending with the proceedings before the Court,

---

[7] On this subject generally, see H. Gros-Espiell, "Contentious Proceedings Before the Inter-American Court of Human Rights," 1 *Emory J. Int'l Disp. Res.* 175, at 180 (1987); R. Piza-Escalante, "La jurisdicción contenciosa del Tribunal Interamericano de Derechos Humanos," Instituto Interamericano de Derechos Humanos, *La Corte Interamericana de Derechos Humanos* 155 (1987). See also, T. Buergenthal, C. Grossman & P. Nikken, *Manual Internacional de Derechos Humanos* 106 (1990).

[8] American Convention of Human Rights [hereinafter Convention], Arts. 51(1) and 61(1).

[9] See Convention, Art. 61(1).

then it would follow that a case originally filed by a State not subject to the Court's jurisdiction may not be accepted by the Court, even if it is the Commission rather than the State that is trying to take it to the tribunal. On the other hand, if by "case" is meant the case that is being referred to the Court, then it would follow that the "States Parties to the case," as that phrase is used in Article 62(3), refers only to those States that have standing to be parties to the case before the Court. This would exclude the State which filed the inter-State communication if it has not recognized the Court's jurisdiction, leaving only the Commission and the Respondent State as the proper parties in the proceedings before the Court. With regard to them, the Court clearly would have jurisdiction to consider the case.

Only if the original Applicant State were to be characterized as an indispensable party to the case would it follow that the Court would be debarred from hearing such a case despite the fact that the Respondent State had accepted its jurisdiction. But that argument is devoid of substance in the context of a human rights treaty such as the Convention. Here the real or potential victims of the human rights violation alleged in an inter-State communication are individuals. In that sense, there is no difference in the inter-American system between inter-State communications and individual petitions. Individuals are the "real parties in interest" in these cases, whether or not they originated as inter-State communications or individual petitions. Moreover, unlike the European Convention of Human Rights, which gives preferred treatment to inter-State communications at the admissibility stage and permits only victims of human rights violations to file individual petitions, the American Convention contains no such restrictions or differentiations. That is, the American Convention does not give more favorable treatment at the admissibility stage to inter-State communications[10] and it permits private petitions to be filed by individuals and private groups whether or not they are victims[11].

The fact that a case originated with an inter-State communication by a State which has not accepted the Court's jurisdiction should not deprive the Commission of the power the Convention confers upon it to refer the case to the Court, provided only that the Respondent State has accepted such jurisdiction. The Commission has that power with regard to individual petitions directed against States that have recognized the Court's jurisdiction. This power does not depend upon the nationality of the individual claimant or the fact that his/her State of nationality may not have recognized the Court's jurisdiction. Given this jurisdictional framework, it is difficult to see why the Commission should lose that power merely because the case originated as an inter-State communication.

---

[10] See Convention, Arts. 44–47.

[11] Convention, Art. 44.

Unlike other human rights treaties, the American Convention conditions the right to file inter-State communications on the specific acceptance by the Respondent and Applicant States of the right of the Commission to receive such communications[12]. However, the Commission has jurisdiction to deal with individual petitions as soon as the Respondent State has ratified the Convention[13]. The underlying rationale for permitting inter-State communications only when both States have accepted that right has its basis in the desire of the framers of the Convention to allow States to protect themselves against politically-motivated State meddling or interventions. That interest is served by the conditions the Convention imposes on the right to file inter-State communications. But once an inter-State communication is properly before the Commission, that body should be able to act on it the same way as it deals with individual petitions, and be able to refer it to the Court. Although the Convention established two separate requirements – one for the filing of inter-State communications, and one for the reference of a case to the Court[14] – it does not seem to make one depend on the other in limiting the Commission's independent decision to take or not to take a case to the Court, provided always that the Respondent State has accepted the Court's jurisdiction.

The question under consideration appears to be more difficult if the Respondent State has accepted the Court's jurisdiction on condition of reciprocity and the Applicant State, which has filed the inter-State communication with the Commission, has not subjected itself to jurisdiction. Here it could be argued that the reciprocity reservation prevents not only the Applicant State but also the Commission from referring the case to the Court. It is difficult to see, however, how the concept of reciprocity can be applied to the Commission, which has no reciprocal rights to grant or extend. Reciprocity makes sense only in the context of State-to-State relations[15]. Hence,

---

12 Convention, Art.45(2).

13 Convention, Art. 44.

14 Compare Convention, Art. 45 with Convention, Art.62(3).

15 On that subject, see The Effect of Reservations on the Entry into Force of the American Convention on Human Rights (Arts.74 and 75), Advisory Opinion OC-2/82 of September 24, 1982, I-A. C. H. R., *Series A: Judgments and Opinions* (1982), where the Court said:

"[M]odern human rights treaties in general, and the American Convention in particular, are not multilateral treaties of the traditional type concluded to accomplish the reciprocal exchange of rights for the mutual benefit of the contracting States. Their object and purpose is the protection of individual human rights irrespective of their nationality, both against the State of their nationality and all other contracting States. In concluding these human rights treaties, the States can be deemed to submit themselves to a legal order within which they, for the common good, assume various obligations, not in relation to other States, but towards all individuals within their jurisdiction" *(ibid.*, para.29).

See also, *ibid.*, para. 33, where the Court concluded that "... the Convention must be seen for what in reality it is: a multilateral instrument or framework enabling States

a reciprocity reservation can be meaningfully applied only to limit the rights of States – here their right to take the case to the Court – but not the powers of the Commission to do so.

It would appear, therefore, that the power of the Commission to refer a case to the Court, be it one that originated either as a private petition or an inter-State communication, should depend only on whether or not the Respondent State has accepted the tribunal's jurisdiction. Whether that State has done so unconditionally or on condition of reciprocity should be irrelevant. Thus, in determining whether the jurisdictional requirements for granting provisional measures have been met when such measures are requested by the Commission, the Court should have to ascertain merely whether the State against which they are sought has accepted the Court's jurisdiction.

The Convention does not expressly address the question whether a State is free to accept the jurisdiction of the Court during the proceedings before the Commission. Article 62(2) does, however, permit States to do so "for specific cases". It is clear, therefore, that a State against which a case has been filed in the Commission may at any time during these proceedings accept the Court's jurisdiction to hear that case. That is why Article 52 of the Regulations of the Commission, which is entitled "Referral of the Case to the Court", authorizes the Commission in its paragraph 3 "to call upon that State to make use of the option referred to in Article 62, paragraph 2 of the Convention to recognize the Court's jurisdiction in the specific case that is the subject of the [Commission's] report". It should be asked, therefore, whether the Commission may seek provisional measures against a State which has not accepted the jurisdiction of the Court while at the same time inviting it to do so in this particular case[16]. One part of the answer would appear to be that the Commission is certainly entitled to make an effort to get the State's agreement to the Court's jurisdiction. It is also clear that until the State has acted affirmatively, the Court cannot consider the case. It is an open question, however, whether it is proper for the Commission to request the measures from the Court without having previously obtained the State's decision accepting the Court's jurisdiction. Here it could be argued that to do so without knowing how the State will react has no purpose other than to embarrass the State or to pressure it unduly. It is certainly debatable

---

to make binding unilateral commitments not to violate the human rights if individuals within their jurisdiction".

16 Here it is interesting to note that Article 50(3) of the Regulations of the Inter-American Commission on Human Rights provides that, if the Commission concludes that a case should be referred to the Court where the Respondent State has not accepted the Court's jurisdiction, "... the Commission may call upon that State to make use of the option referred to in Article 62, paragraph 2 of the Convention to recognize the Court's jurisdiction in the specific case that is the subject of the [Commission's] report". For the text of the Regulations of the Commission, see *Basic Documents Pertaining to Human Rights in the Inter-American System*, *supra* note 3, at 103.

whether the need to act expeditiously to save human lives, which is the purpose of the provisional measures, legitimates such pressures.

When a request for provisional measures is made in cases that have already been referred to the Court or when the Court decides on its own motion to consider ordering such measures, the Court will only have to address the issue of *prima facie* jurisdiction if the question of jurisdiction was not resolved at an earlier stage of the proceedings. Here it is important not to confuse jurisdictional issues with questions bearing on the admissibility of a case. A case referred to the Court may not be admissible, for example, because domestic remedies have not been exhausted even though the States Parties to the case have accepted the Court's jurisdiction. The fact that a case might at some stage of the proceedings be determined by the Court to be inadmissible will not affect its power to grant provisional measures so long as it has jurisdiction over the parties. If that were not so, it would make no sense whatsoever to authorize the Court to issue provisional measures in cases not yet referred to it which, at that stage, would *ipso facto* be inadmissible under Article 61(2) of the Convention[17]. Moreover, the Court has already had occasion to grant provisional measures in three cases prior to deciding all outstanding issues of admissibility. Thus, in the so-called *Honduran Disappearance* Cases[18], the Court issued three separate orders in each one of the three cases[19] being examined by it, even though it had not yet decided whether domestic remedies had been exhausted in these cases. In its judgments of July 26, 1987, the Court disposed of various preliminary objections interposed by Honduras and decided to join the objection relating to the non-exhaustion of domestic remedies to the merits of the cases[20]. On January 15, 16 and 19, 1988, six months before it rendered its judgment on

---

[17] Article 61(2) of the Convention reads as follows: "In order for the Court to hear a case, it is necessary that the procedures set forth in Articles 48 to 50 shall have been completed". These provisions relate to the proceedings before the Commission. See generally, T. Buergenthal, "The Inter-American System for the Protection of Human Rights," T. Meron (ed.), *Human Rights in International Law: Legal and Policy Issues* 438, at 452 (1984).

[18] See generally, C. Grossman, "Disappearances in Honduras: The Need for Direct Victim Representation in Human Rights Litigation", 15 *Hastings Int'l & Comp. L. Rev.* 363 (1992); C. Cerna, *supra* note 2, at 131; D. Shelton, "Judicial Review of State Action by International Courts", and "Private Violence Public Wrongs, and the Responsibility of States", 12 *Fordham Int'l L. J.* 361 (1989), and 13 *ibid.* at 1 (1989–90). See also, T. Buergenthal, "Judicial Fact-Finding: Inter-American Court of Human Rights," R. Lillich (ed), *Fact-Finding Before International Tribunals* 261 (1992).

[19] See Decisions of the Court, dated of January 15, 16, and 19, 1988, *supra* note 4.

[20] Velasquez Rodriguez Case (Honduras), Preliminary Objections, Judgment of June 26, 1987, I-A. C. H. R., *Series C: Decisions and Judgments*, No.1 (1987); Fairen Garbi and Solis Corrales Case (Honduras), Preliminary Objections, Judgment of June 26, 1987, *ibid.*, No. 2 (1987); Godinez Cruz Case (Honduras), Preliminary Objections, Judgment of June 26,1987, *ibid.*, No.3 (1987).

the merits in the first of these cases and rejected the domestic remedies objection[21], the Court adopted provisional measures ordering Honduras to protect the lives of various individuals and to investigate the killing of two witnesses[22]. Here the Court never even so much as addressed the question whether it had the power to order the provisional measures before the admissibility of the case was resolved.

II. The Scope of Article 63(2)

Article 63(2) indicates that the remedy it establishes is to be granted only in exceptional circumstances. This conclusion is readily apparent from the dramatic language it uses: "in cases of extreme gravity and urgency, and when necessary to avoid irreparable damage to persons ...". The wording and the legislative history of the provision make clear that its sole purpose is to protect human beings against the loss of life or extreme physical or mental abuse when there is a very strong likelihood that they are in imminent danger and there exists a corresponding urgency for protective action. Here it is interesting to note that the Draft American Convention on Human Rights, which served as the principal working paper of the San José Conference, where the Convention was adopted, did not provide for provisional measures[23]. Costa Rica sought to remedy this situation by proposing the following addition to the Convention:

> "The Court shall be able to take provisional measures that it considers pertinent, in urgent situations and when there is sufficient cause to justify it, for the protection of the right allegedly violated".

This amendment, which would have permitted the use of provisional measures to protect any rights proclaimed in the Convention and was thus more liberal than the current text of Article 63(2), was defeated in Committee II[24].

---

[21] Velasquez Rodriguez Case (Honduras), Judgment of July 29, 1988, I-A. C. H. R., *Series C: Decisions and Judgments*, No.4 (1988). Thereafter the Court decided the two remaining cases on the merits: Godinez Cruz Case (Honduras), Judgment of January 20, 1989, *ibid.*, No. 5 (1989); and Fairen Garbi and Solis Corrales Case (Honduras), Judgment of March 15, 1989, *ibid.*, No.6 (1989).

[22] See *supra* note 4.

[23] For the text of the Draft Inter-American Convention on Protection of Human Rights, see [1968] *Inter-American Yearbook of Human Rights* 389 (1973). The Spanish text appears on p. 388, *ibid.*

[24] See San José Conference, Committee II, Sixth Session. The debates of the San José Conference, where the Convention was drafted, are reproduced in *Conferencia Especializada Interamericana sobre Derechos Humanos: Actas y Documentos* [hereinafter cited as *Conferencia Especializada*], San José, Costa Rica, 7–22 de noviembre de 1969, OEA/Ser. K/XVI/1.2 (1978). No official English text exists of this volume. For an English translation of these and other relevant materials relating to the legislative

It received one vote in favor, none against, and 16 abstentions. But Costa Rica persisted and introduced a revised version of its amendment – the current Article 63(2) – at one of the last plenary meetings of the San José Conference[25]. Here it was adopted without any objections or discussion.

This legislative history suggests that Article 63(2) is to be narrowly interpreted and its application limited to protection against situations involving an imminent threat to life and serious physical or mental harm. The here relevant provisions of the Convention are Article 4, which guarantees the right to life[26], and Article 5, which protects a person's right to physical, mental and moral integrity and, *inter alia*, prohibits torture, cruel, inhuman or degrading treatment and punishment[27]. Until recently, the Court had to deal only with requests for provisional measures involving allegations of imminent threats to life or other serious physical harm. The *Reggiardo Toloso* Case marks a departure from this practice. Here the Commission requested provisional measures in a case involving two children of persons who were "disappeared" in Argentina in the 1970's. As soon as they were born, the children were removed from their mother by an Argentine police official and

---

history of the Convention, see T. Buergenthal & R. Norris, *Human Rights: The Inter-American System*, Binder 2 (loose leave). All English-language references are to the Buergenthal & Norris translation.

[25] San José Conference, Third Plenary Session, *ibid.*

[26] Article 4 of the Convention reads as follows:
"1. Every person has the right to have his life respected. This right shall be protected by law and, in general, from the moment of conception. No one shall be arbitrarily deprived of his life.

2. In countries that have not abolished the death penalty, it may be imposed only for the most serious crimes and pursuant to a final judgment rendered by a competent court and in accordance with a law establishing such punishment, enacted prior to the commission of the crime. The application of such punishment shall not be extended to crimes to which it does not presently apply.

3. The death penalty shall not be reestablished in states that have abolished it.

4. In no case shall capital punishment be inflicted for political crimes or related common crimes.

5. Capital punishment shall not be imposed upon persons who, at the time the crime was committed, were under 18 years of age or over 70 years of age; nor shall it be applied to pregnant women.

6. Every person condemned to death shall have the right to apply for amnesty, pardon, or commutation of sentence, which may be granted in all cases. Capital punishment shall not be imposed while such a petition is pending decision by the competent authority".

[27] Article 5 of the Convention reads, in the here relevant parts, as follows:
"1. Every person has the right to have his physical, mental, and moral integrity protected.

2. No one shall be subjected to torture or to cruel, inhuman, or degrading punishment or treatment...

5. Minors while subject to criminal proceedings shall be separated from adults and brought before specialized tribunals, as speedingly as possible, so that they may be treated in accordance with their status as minors ...".

declared by him and his wife to be their children. They were subsequently taken by the couple to Paraguay. After their return to Argentina in the late 1980's, an organization of grandmothers of disappeared persons instituted proceedings to have the children removed from the couple. This litigation languished in the Argentinian courts for a number of years. Eventually the courts ordered the children to be placed with foster parents until the proceedings had been concluded, but this order has not been executed. The case was eventually brought to the Commission. In October 1993, the Commission filed a request for provisional measures with the Court seeking a decision ordering Argentina to remove the children, who are now teenagers, from the couple here in question. In November, the acting President of the Court issued an order of urgent measures, requiring Argentina "to adopt, without further delay, all necessary measures to protect the mental integrity of the minors ... [in order to] avoid causing them irreparable damage ..."[28].

It remains to be seen whether the Court will go along with this interpretation of Article 63(2). There is no doubt, of course, that the mental harm being caused here falls within the scope of the article. The more difficult issue, however, is whether, given all the time that has already elapsed, the Commission should not first have decided the claim and then referred the entire case to the Court instead of invoking the Article 63(2) procedure.

The most extensive analysis thus far of the scope of Article 63(2) can be found in the *Chunima* Case[29], where the Commission sought provisional measures against the Government of Guatemala in a case not yet submitted to the Court. Here the Court indicated that the proof the Commission must adduce to demonstrate the need for provisional measures does not have to be conclusive, but it had to provide the Court with a reasonable or sound factual basis, not adequately refuted by the Government, justifying the conclusion, at that stage of the proceedings, that the allegations are true[30]. The Court emphasized, moreover, that the language of Article 63(2) shows that the remedy it creates is "an extraordinary instrument, necessary in exceptional circumstances"[31].

Although the Court concluded in the *Chunima* Case that the evidence adduced by the Commission did not satisfy the requirements of Article 63(2), it nevertheless issued the requisite order because the additional facts brought to its attention by the Government at the public hearing strengthened the Commission's allegations. In two recent cases, however, the Court rejected the Commission's request for provisional measures against Peru on the ground that the Commission had failed to meet the strict standards of proof

---

28 Reggiardo Toloso Case (Argentina), Order of the President of the Court, dated November 19, 1993 (mimeo). The order was entered by Judge Sonia Picado, Vice President of the Court, after the President recused himself from hearing the case.

29 Chunima Case (Guatemala), Decision of August 1, 1991, *supra* note 5.

30 Chunima Case, *supra*, para. 6(a).

31 Chunima Case, *supra*, para. 6(b).

required by Article 63(2). Thus, in the *Chipoco* Case, the Court concluded that the Commission had failed to submit facts "sufficient to support the adoption of such measures"[32]. In its view the Commission had an obligation to present "preliminary evidence to support a presumption of the truth of the allegations" and of the existence of a situation "whose grave seriousness and urgency could cause irreparable harm to persons"[33]. The Court reached a similar conclusion in the *Peruvian Prisons* Case[34]. By contrast, the Commission encountered no such difficulties in an earlier case, the *Bustíos-Rojas* Case[35], also involving Peru. Here extensive provisional measures were granted by the Court to protect witnesses to an assassination, one of whom was murdered prior to the Commission's request for this remedy.

Although the Court's refusal to grant provisional measures in the *Chipoco* Case and the *Peruvian Prisons* Cases may have been justified, it can be argued that the Court misconceived the legal basis for its decisions in these cases. In the latter case, the Commission appears to have sought provisional measures to aid its investigation in the proceedings pending before it. The Government of Peru had been obstructing this investigation by refusing the Commission access to certain prisons where, the Commission alleged, prisoners were being killed and tortured. The Commission asked the Court, therefore, to order Peru to permit the Commission to carry out the very investigation the Commission would have to undertake in order to be able to establish the requisite *prima facie* case for provisional measures. The Commission thus found itself in a "Catch-22" situation: to qualify for the Article 63(2) remedy, it needed to obtain at least some credible evidence about conditions in these prisons, but it could get that evidence only by means of an investigation which the Government of Peru refused to permit in the proceedings pending before the Commission. Moreover, while the Commission might have been able to gather the requisite evidence from witnesses and other sources, it no doubt feared that the long time needed to accomplish this result would greatly increase the probable threat to the lives of the inmates of those prisons. By the same token, it is clear that the Court lacks the power to issue provisional measures in aid of an investigation by the Commission to establish the facts that might justify granting such a remedy. In the *Chipoco* Case, which was decided on the same day as the *Prisons* Case, it can also be argued that the denial of the remedy was justified, but not on the grounds stated by the Court. While Mr. Chipoco faced a real and undisputed threat of being arrested on his return to Peru, which the Commission fully substantiated, such a threat alone provides no valid basis for the remedy it sought. Of

---

32 Chipoco Case (Peru), Decision of January 27, 1993, para. 3 ("whereas" clauses).

33 *Ibid.*

34 Peruvian Prisons Cases (Peru), Decision of January 27, 1993, *supra* note 5.

35 The Court adopted two Decisions ordering provisional measures in the *Bustíos-Rojas Case* (Peru). See Decisions of August 8, 1990 and January 17, 1991, *supra* note 5.

course, what the Commission could also not prove in this case without the investigation it had been prevented by Peru from carrying out in the *Peruvian Prisons* Case, was that Chipoco would be subjected to inhuman conditions in the Peruvian prisons. Here again the real difficulty is that the Court has no powers under Article 63(2) to order such an investigation to establish the *prima facie* case.

These two cases point out the real dilemma the Court and Commission face because the Article 63(2) remedy is so narrowly drawn and because the Commission is limited in the powers it has to adduce the requisite evidence, and to do so in the short period of time often needed to save lives. It can be argued, however, that in situations where a Government obstructs all legitimate efforts by the Commission to gather evidence relating to allegations of violations of the right to life or physical or mental integrity, the Court might be justified in holding the Commission to a burden of proof that is less stringent than might be the case ordinarily[36].

At the very least, there should be a public hearing on the subject. In the two aforementioned cases the Commission was denied this opportunity, despite the fact that in the past such hearings have usually been held[37]. The hearing would have the advantage of allowing the Court to hear witnesses and force the Government to address the allegations of the Commission, which might in turn produce more evidence. The concerns for the protection of human life must here be balanced against the interests of a State which prevents the Commission from discharging its fact-finding responsibilities under the Convention.

III. The Nature of Provisional Measures

We turn now to the nature of the powers the Court has under Article 63(2). That provision, as already indicated, permits the issuance of provisional measures only to protect the lives and physical or mental integrity of individuals. The question to be addressed here has to do with the specific measures

---

36 The Court would find support for such an approach in its holding in the Velasquez Rodriguez Case, Judgment of July 29, 1988, I-A. C. H. R., *Series C: Decisions and Judgments*, No. 4 (1988), where it declared that "in proceedings to determine human rights violations the State cannot rely on the defense that the complainant has failed to present evidence when it cannot be obtained without the State's cooperation". *Ibid*, para. 135. The Court expressed the same view in the Godinez Cruz Case, Judgment of January 20, 1989, I-A. C. H. R., *Series C: Decisions and Judgments*, No. 5, para. 141 (1989). The Court's approach in these two cases of necessity presupposes the existence of at least some evidence to support the Commission's contentions concerning the need for provisional measures.

37 Such hearings were held in the Honduran Disappearance Cases, in the Bustíos-Rojas Case (Peru), and in the Chunima Case (Guatemala), *supra* notes 4 and 5.

the Court may order in furtherance of this objective. As an abstract proposition, it would appear that the Court has the power to order all measures reasonably calculated to achieve this purpose. Of course, it may not impose burdens on the States Parties that are totally disproportionate to the obligations they assumed by ratifying the Convention.

None of the provisional measures the Court has ordered in the past appear to have exceeded its authority under Article 63(2), despite the fact that it imposed strong and far-reaching measures in some cases. Thus, for example, in the *Honduran Disappearance* Cases, the Court not only ordered the Government to take all necessary measures to prevent additional killings of witnesses, to undertake a thorough investigation of the earlier murders, and to inform the Court of its actions in this regard[38]. Here the Court also ordered the Government, among other things, to make it known that "the appearance of an individual before the Inter-American Commission or Court of Human Rights ... is a right enjoyed by every individual and is recognized as such by Honduras as a party to the Convention"[39]. This part of the order was prompted by allegations that statements by some Government officials, accusing individuals appearing before the Court of being traitors to their country, served to encourage certain extremist groups to use violence against these witnesses.

In the *Bustíos-Rojas* Case, the Court first ordered the Government of Peru to take all necessary measures to protect certain witnesses to the killing of a Peruvian journalist[40]. After the Government complied with that order and informed the Court that it had established a system of military liaisons whom the protected persons could contact if they felt threatened, the Court ordered Peru to supplement it in three Peruvian localities with a comparable civilian liaison system[41]. This part of the order can be traced to the concern expressed by the Commission that the persons to be protected, some of whom were in hiding, accused various military officers of having been the killers. The witnesses might therefore have had a justified fear of military liaison officers affiliated with the very units that could have been involved in the murder and attempted coverup.

It is worth noting, in this connection, that in two of the cases in which provisional measures were sought by the Commission under Article 63(2) before they had been referred to the Court, it not only issued the requisite orders but also retained jurisdiction to ensure itself that the order was being complied with[42]. Here the assumption may have been that the Court would

[38] Honduran Disappearance Cases, Decision of January 15, 1988, *supra* note 4.

[39] Honduran Disappearance Cases, Decision of January 19, 1988, operative para. 2, *supra* note 4, at 28.

[40] Bustíos-Rojas Case (Peru), Decision of August 8, 1990, *supra* note 5, at 33.

[41] Bustíos-Rojas Case (Peru), Decision of January 17, 1991, *supra* note 5, at 17.

[42] Chunima Case (Guatemala), Decision of August 1, 1991, *supra* note 5, at 69; Bustíos-Rojas Case (Peru), Decision of August 8, 1990, *supra* note 5, at 33.

lose jurisdiction once the order was issued since the cases were still pending before the Commission. While an overabundance of caution may have prompted this action, it must be assumed that the Court retains jurisdiction to supervise compliance with its provisional measures unless it decides expressly to relinquish it. In the *Bustíos-Rojas* Case, after itself attempting to monitor compliance and encountering various practical problems in doing so, the Court returned the case to the Commission and charged it with that task[43]. This approach probably makes more sense anyway in cases that are still being examined by the Commission. Besides, the Commission can presumably come back to the Court at any time and seek new or additional measures if required by the circumstances.

IV. Inherent Powers

It might now be asked whether the Court has inherent powers to order some provisional measures other than those provided for by Article 63(2). On the one hand, the legislative history of this provision clearly indicates that the drafters of the Convention were not willing to give the Court the broad power to order provisional measures to protect all the rights the treaty guarantees. On the other hand, it is by no means equally clear that by adopting this position they necessarily wished to deprive the Court of those inherent, but more limited, powers judicial institutions may be deemed to have in order to properly exercise their functions and preserve their authority. Thus, for example, Article 40(2) of the Court's Rules of Procedure reads, in part, as follows: "States shall not institute proceedings nor take reprisals against any persons on account of their testimony before Court". It would appear that if the Court has the power to adopt this rule, which it no doubt has, then it must be deemed to have the power to order a State not to take these reprisals, even if they do not involve threats to life or other serious damage within the scope of Article 63(2), particularly when the reprisals interfere with the exercise of the Court's functions in an ongoing proceeding. There may be other such examples that might be cited. It is relevant to note, in this connection, that in entering provisional measures in the *Honduran Disappearance* Cases, the Court expressly recognized the existence of inherent powers without, however, spelling them out in any detail. In the orders it issued in these cases on January 19, 1988, the Court invoked the following legal provisions and principles to justify the grant of the provisional measures: "Articles 63(2), 33, and 62(3) of the ... Convention, ... Article 1 and 2 of the Statute and Article 23 of the Rules of Procedure of the Court, the judicial character of the Court and the powers which derive therefrom"[44].

[43] Bustíos-Rojas Case (Peru), Decision of January 17, 1991, *supra* note 5, at 17.
[44] Honduran Disappearance Cases, Decision of January 19, 1988, *supra* note 4, at 27.

Article 63(2), as we know, deals with provisional measures; Article 33 specifies merely that the Commission and Court "have competence with respect to matters relating to the fulfillment of the commitments made by the States Parties" to the Convention; and Article 62(3) concerns the Court's jurisdictions. Article 1 of the Statute[45] declares, in part, that the Court is "an autonomous judicial institution whose purpose is the application and interpretation" of the Convention, whereas Article 2 deals with the Court's jurisdiction. The here relevant stipulation is Article 2(1), which states that the Court's "adjudicatory jurisdiction shall be governed by the provisions of Articles 61, 62 and 63 of the Convention". Finally, Article 23 of the Court's Rules of Procedure, now Article 24, sets out the procedural rules applicable to "interim [provisional] measures".

The Court's enumeration of these provisions in their particular context, followed by the specific reference to inherent powers, suggests that it believes these powers to derive from the cited articles and, possibly, also to be functionally related to the application of provisional measures. If this analysis of the Court's approach is sound, it could be argued that the Court relied on its inherent powers when it ordered Honduras in the *Disappearance* Cases to make known to the country that an individual appearing before the Court is exercising "a right enjoyed by every individual and ... recognized as such by Honduras as a party to the Convention"[46]. Of course, the matter is not entirely free from doubt since this part of the order can also be deemed to fall within the scope of Article 63(2). If so, it is tantalizing to speculate why the Court felt compelled to make reference to its powers as a judicial institution and cite a number of articles in addition to Article 63(2) of the Convention and Article 23 (now 24) of its Rules of Procedure, which would have sufficed for that purpose.

V. Legal Effect of Provisional Measures

We turn now to the question whether decisions ordering provisional measures pursuant to Article 63(2) are binding on the addressees thereof. The answer to this question depends in part on an analysis of the differences in wording between the English text of the Convention, on the one hand, and the Spanish, Portuguese and French texts, on the other, all four being equally authentic.

---

[45] Statute of the Inter-American Court of Human Rights, *Basic Documents Pertaining to Human Rights in the Inter-American System*, *supra* note 3, at 133.

[46] Honduran Disappearance Cases, Decision of January 19, 1988, *supra* note 4, at 29.

The English text of Article 67 of the Convention declares that "the judgment of the Court shall be final and not subject to appeal", and its Article 68(1) specifies that "the States Parties to the Convention undertake to comply with the judgment of the Court in any case to which they are parties". By contrast, the Spanish text of Article 68(1) the Convention reads as follows: "Los Estados Partes en la Convención se comprometen a cumplir la decisión de la Corte en todo caso en que sean partes". While the Spanish "decisión" may be translated as "judgment", it is a more inclusive term and, as such, also embraces decisions and orders issued by a tribunal. This is not true of the word "fallo," which is used in the Spanish text of Article 67 of the Convention ("el fallo de la Corte será definitivo e inapelable") and which is the more precise and technically correct rendering of the English "judgment". The two remaining authentic texts of the Convention conform to the Spanish rather than English text. Thus, the Portuguese text uses "sentença" in Article 67 and "decisao" in Article 68(1), whereas the French text speaks of "arrêt" in Article 67 and "décision" in Article 68(1). It should also be noted that the Spanish, Portuguese and French texts of Article 68(2) use "fallo," "sentença," and "arrêt" in what appears to be a conscious effort to distinguish the meaning of that paragraph from paragraph 1 of Article 68, which uses the equivalent of the English "decision". The English text of Article 68(2) reads as follows: "That part of the judgment that stipulates compensatory damages may be executed in the country concerned in accordance with domestic procedure governing the execution of judgments against the state". Here the word "judgment" is clearly the correct technical term, and the Spanish, Portuguese and French texts render it accordingly.

The English text of Article 68(1) would make it very difficult to assert that the provisional measures the Court may order under Article 63(2) are binding on the State Party to which it is addressed. Clearly, such measures are not "judgments" in the sense in which that term is used in Articles 67 and 68(2); they are decisions. On the other hand, the Spanish, Portuguese and French texts support the opposite conclusion and suggest that Article 63(2) decisions are binding on the States to which they are addressed.

The legislative history of Article 63(2) does not provide any clues as to its binding character. The records of the San José Conference contain no debate on this provision. The participating States apparently merely voted on the proposal introduced by Costa Rica, defeating one version in committee and adopting another in plenary[47]. But there exists some interesting

[47] For the official text of the debates and documents of the San José Conference, see *Conferencia Especializada Interamericana sobre Derechos Humanos: Actas y Documentos* [hereinafter cited as *Conferencia Especializada*], San Jose, Costa Rica, 7–22 de noviembre de 1969, OEA/ Ser. K/XVI/1.2 (1978). For an English translation of this volume and other here relevant documents, see T. Buergenthal & R. Norris, *Human Rights: The Inter-American System*, Binder 2 (loose-leaf).

legislative history regarding the English text of Article 68(1). Article 56 of the Draft Convention[48] – the working document of the San José Conference – reads as follows: "The States Parties undertake to abide by the decision of the Court in any case to which they are parties". The Spanish text of the same article provided: "Los Estados Partes se comprometen a cumplir la decisión de la Corte en todo litigio en que sean partes"[49]. Note that here the English text uses "decision" as does the Spanish text. The latter text became Article 68(1) of the Spanish version of the Convention, except that it uses the word "caso" instead of "litigio", which would be translated as "proceedings". There is no explanation for this change, which was apparently made in the Style Committee. In the English version, "case" is employed both in draft Article 56 and in Article 68(1) of the Convention. Moreover, it also appears that the use of "decision" in the English text of draft Article 56 and its substitution by "judgment" was made in the Style Committee. Here, too, no explanation is to be found in the proceedings.

It is possible to conclude, therefore, that the word "decision" in the Spanish version of Article 68(1) of the Convention and of the comparable expression in the French and Portuguese texts was mistranslated as "judgment" in the English text. It would also appear that no substantive significance can be attached to the substitution of "litigio" for "caso" in the Spanish version. Here it is worth noting, moreover, that the French version of Article 68(1) of the Convention, unlike the three other authentic texts of this article, retains the French equivalent of the Spanish "litigio" when it speaks of "litige". The only real conclusion that can be drawn from the drafting history of these provisions and their effect on Article 63(2) is that they throw little light on the subject. This is so because by the time Article 63(2) was adopted, the other here relevant provisions had already been approved in committee without being reexamined in the plenary meeting.

The foregoing analysis indicates that neither the language of the Convention nor its drafting history is opposed to the proposition that the Court's decisions ordering interim measures under Article 63(2) are binding on the States Parties to the case. Moreover, the purpose this provision is intended to perform would appear to require that these decisions be deemed to be obligatory. Unlike the stipulations found in some other international instruments on the subject that are designed merely to maintain the *status quo* while a case is being litigated[50], Article 63(2) of the Convention applies only under exceptional circumstances to avoid "irreparable damage to persons". Given this function and the fact that the Convention is a human rights treaty, it is

---

[48] For the text of the Draft Inter-American Convention on Protection of Human Rights, see [1968] *Inter-American Yearbook of Human Rights* 389 (1973). This text is also reproduced in Buergenthal & Norris, *supra.*

[49] For the Spanish text of the Draft Convention, see *Yearbook*, *supra*, at 388.

[50] See, *e.g.*, Statute of the International Court of Justice, Art. 41.

difficult to support the proposition that Article 63(2) decisions should not be deemed to be legally binding. The sole purpose of such a decision, after all, is to ensure that the States Parties to a case refrain from causing irreparable physical or mental harm to persons subject to their jurisdiction until the Court or Commission has had an opportunity to examine the merits of the case. It is clear, of course, that by issuing the order under Article 63(2) the Court accepts, albeit only temporarily and on a *prima facie* basis, the allegation that the Respondent State is not discharging its obligation under the Convention to protect an endangered individual. In that sense the order amounts to an implicit judicial condemnation of the affected State. But that consequence can have no bearing on the question whether the Article 63(2) order is binding, because it would be the same whether or not the decision is obligatory.

Once the interest of the potential victim is balanced against the interest of the State not to be temporarily restrained in the exercise of its governmental functions, which is what is ultimately at issue here, it is apparent that the balance weighs very heavily in favor of the former. This consideration is an important factor in the interpretation of a human rights treaty. It would not tip the balance sufficiently, however, if the language of the Convention prevented an interpretation making decisions ordering provisional measures legally binding. In fact, the Convention not only permits, but also supports, the conclusion that Article 63(2) decisions are legally binding. As we have seen, the Spanish, French and Portuguese texts of the Convention require the States Parties to comply with the Court's "decisions" rather than only with its "judgments". Moreover, the use of the term "judgment" in the English text of Article 68(1) appears to have been a mistranslation to which no legal significance can be attached. Thus, the language of the Convention makes clear that decisions of the Court, and not only judgments that are final and nonappealable, can be legally binding on the States Parties to a case. This fact and the policy considerations discussed above compel the conclusion that Article 63(2) decisions fall into this category.

The only remaining issue to be discussed in this section concerns the legal effect of the temporary interim orders or so-called "urgent measures," which the President of the Court is authorized to enter pursuant to Article 24(4) of its Rules of Procedure. These orders may be emitted by the President when the Court is not in session at the time the request for provisional measures is made. They are designed to "permit any provisional measures subsequently ordered by the Court to have the requisite effect". The Convention itself is silent on the issue of the legal effect of these orders, and it contains no provision expressly authorizing the President to enter them. It is not possible to contend, therefore, that these orders are legally binding as Article 63(2) decisions, which they are not. They are procedural or interlocutory measures that the President must be deemed to have the inherent power to adopt when the Court is not sitting. But they cannot have the same legal status as decisions of the Court under Article 63(2), because nothing in the Convention permits the Court to delegate to the President its powers to adopt these decisions. Hence, although the States Parties to the Convention can reasonably be expected to comply with these Presidential orders, they are not under a formal legal obligation to do so.

The question whether the "urgent measures" the President may adopt are legally binding as such should be distinguished from the question whether a State Party would violate the Convention by not taking the protective measures the President indicated should be adopted. Thus, for example, if the President orders a State Party to take specific action to protect the life of an individual, and the person is killed because the State failed to provide the requisite protection, the State may well have violated the Convention. The violation results not from the failure to comply with the order, but from the State's failure to discharge its obligations under Article 1(1) of the Convention read in conjunction with Article 4[51]. Article 4 guarantees the right to life, while Article 1(1) requires the States Parties "to ensure to all persons subject to their jurisdiction the free and full exercise", *inter alia*, of the right to life. In the past, the Presidents of the Court have relied on these provisions to reinforce the normative character of their orders[52]. Thus, for example, in calling on Peru to adopt all measures necessary to protect the lives of certain individuals who had witnessed the killing of a journalist, the President invoked Article 1(1) of the Convention and declared that Peru is "obligated" to adopt these measures "to protect the lives ... of the persons whose rights may be threatened"[53].

Of course, not every failure by a State Party to comply with a Presidential decree ordering urgent measures will give rise to a violation of the Convention. Here much will depend upon the nature of the State's action or inaction and on the circumstances of the particular case. That must be so because noncompliance with the President's order is not *ipso facto* a violation of the Convention; the violation results, if at all, from the State's failure to discharge its obligation to protect a specific right guaranteed by the Convention. The opposite is true when a State Party refuses to comply with a decision of the Court imposing interim measures: here noncompliance alone is a violation of the State's obligations under Article 63(2) read in conjunction with Article 68(1). In addition, of course, the noncompliance may also constitute a breach of the specific rights the State is bound to protect as a party to the Convention.

---

[51] Velasquez Rodriguez Case (Honduras), Judgment of July 29,1988, *supra* note 21, at paras. 159 *et seq.*

[52] For the most recent order of the President of the Court following this practice, see Reggiardo Tolosa Case (Argentina), Order of November 19, 1993 (mimeo). The Court in plenum has not yet dealt with the matter.

[53] Bustíos-Rojas Case (Peru), Order of the President of June 5, 1990, *supra* note 5.

VI. Procedural Issues

The procedures that apply to the provisional measures provided for in Article 63(2) differ depending upon the manner in which the Court is seized of the matter. Here one has to distinguish between cases that are already pending before the Court and those that have not as yet been submitted to it. With regard to the first category of cases, Article 24(1) of the Court's Rules of Procedure provides that "at any stage of the proceeding ... the Court may, at the request of a party or on its own motion, order whatever provisional measures it deems appropriate, pursuant to Article 63(2) of the Convention". To date the Court has ordered provisional measures on "its own motion" and at the request of the Commission[54]. As a matter of fact, the first provisional measures the Court entered were adopted on its own motion[55]. Thus far, it has not been requested by any State Party to a case to order provisional measures.

Here it should be recalled that the private petitioner who files a case with the Commission that is subsequently referred to the Court has no standing as such to request provisional measures. Only the States Parties and the Commission are deemed to be "parties" within the meaning of the Court's Rules of Procedure[56]. This does not mean, however, that the Court is precluded from informally receiving information from interested private individuals who have acquired some procedural "standing" under its new Rules of Procedure[57]. This might be its only source of information in some of those cases where the Court decides on very short notice to issue provisional measures on its own motion.

When a case has not as yet been referred to the Court, provisional measures may only be issued at the request of the Commission. Here the Court may not act on its own motion, for it has no jurisdiction over cases still under consideration by the Commission, except for the powers conferred on it in the last sentence of Article 63(2). That clause permits the Court to act in these cases only at the request of the Commission. However, once the Court has been seized by the Commission of such a case, it must be deemed to have acquired jurisdiction to enter whatever order it deems appropriate under Article 63(2) and to retain jurisdiction for that purpose regardless of the wishes of the Commission. That jurisdiction would probably lapse once the Commission has dismissed the case, concluded a friendly settlement or made a formal determination, under Articles 50 and 51 of the Convention, not to refer the case to the Court.

---

[54] See *supra* notes 4 and 5 for a listing of these decisions.

[55] Honduran Disappearance Cases, Decision of January 15, 1988, *supra* note 4, at 25.

[56] See Rules of Procedure of the Court, Arts. 26–28.

[57] See, *e.g.*,the Court's Rules of Procedure, Arts. 28(1) and 31(1).

Under Article 24(3) of the Court's Rules of Procedure, requests for provisional measures may be presented to "the President, to any judge of the Court or to the Secretariat, by means of any communication". The recipient of such a request must immediately bring it to the attention of the President. Article 24(4) provides that if the Court is not sitting when the request has been received, the President "shall convene it immediately". That paragraph further stipulates that:

> "Pending the meeting of the Court, the President, in consultation with the Permanent Commission and, if possible, with the other judges, shall call upon the government concerned to adopt the necessary urgent measures and to act so as to permit any provisional measures subsequently ordered by the Court to have the requisite effect".

Although this provision is drafted in mandatory terms, it cannot be read to compel the President to order urgent measures whether or not he deems the request to be well-founded. The President must, of course, convene a meeting of the Court to deal with the request for provisional measures. Under the Convention, only the Court has the power to decide that issue. As far as urgent measures are concerned, however, they are for the President to adopt following the consultations required by Article 24(4)[58]. He must therefore be deemed to have discretion to decide whether they are required, and that is how the President has to date interpreted his powers under Article 24(4) of the Rules[59].

Article 24(5) of the Court's Rules requires the Court to include in its Annual Report to the OAS General Assembly "a statement regarding the provisional measures ordered during the period covered by the report". Moreover, "if such measures have not been duly executed, the Court shall make whatever recommendations it deems appropriate". Here it should be noted that Article 65 of the Convention, which establishes the Court's reporting requirement, speaks only of non-compliance with "judgments" of

---

58 As a rule, the President consults not only the Permanent Commission of the Court but usually also all other judges that can be reached. Although the President is free to disregard the views of the Permanent Commission or that of the other judges, he is unlikely to do so. The composition and functions of the Permanent Commission of the Court are described as follows in Article 6(1) of the Rules of Procedure of the Court:
"The Permanent Commission is composed of the President, the Vice-President and a third judge appointed by the President. The President may appoint a fourth judge for specific cases or on a permanent basis. The Permanent Commission assists the President in the exercise of his functions".

59 The President has denied requests for urgent measures in two recent cases. See Peruvian Prisons Case (Peru), Order of the President of December 14, 1992, *supra* note 5, at 101; and Chipoco Case (Peru), Order of the President of December 14, 1992, *supra* note 5, at 97. The Court subsequently affirmed the President's orders in these two cases. See *supra* note 5.

the Court[60]. The old Rules of Procedure of the Court did not contain any provision comparable to Article 24(5) of the current Rules. Its adoption suggests that the Court believes that a State's non-compliance with provisional measures falls within the jurisdiction of the OAS General Assembly to the same extent as non-compliance with its judgments. That would appear to be a sound conclusion given the binding character of the Court's decisions decreeing provisional measures.

With one exception, the practice of the Court until recently has been to hold a hearing on the request for provisional measures. It did not do so before it issued its first decision on the subject[61]. It then ordered a hearing and strengthened the original decision after the hearing[62]. The Court adopted the first decision on its own motion without a hearing after learning that a witness, who had earlier appeared in the pending *Honduran Disappearance* Cases, was murdered and that other witnesses had received death threats. Given these facts, the first decision resembled the "urgent measures" the President would have issued had the Court not been in session.

The Court departed from its earlier practice in two recent cases involving Peru, even though the Commission here asked for the hearings. In both cases, the President first denied the Commission's request for urgent measures. Thereafter, the Court upheld his ruling and rejected the petition for provisional measures ostensibly on the grounds that the Commission had failed to establish the requisite *prima facie* case[63]. Although the Court treated both cases in the same manner and used almost identical language to reject the requests, the *Peruvian Prisons* Case, unlike its companion *Chipoco* Case, raised very serious and urgent issues relating to the protection of the lives of numerous individuals. In that case the hearing should have been granted to enable the Commission, consistent with the Court's earlier practice, to produce testimony on the seriousness of the allegations and the urgency of the situation. Without that opportunity, and given the pressure of time, the Commission will often find it difficult to make the strongest case possible for provisional measures. Moreover, by depriving itself of the opportunity of hearing the arguments of the Respondent State, the Court is greatly limiting its own appreciation of the evidence.

If these two cases reflect a conscious decision by the Court to depart from its earlier practice, the protective value of preliminary measures will be substantially diminished. In the past, moreover, the mere threat of a hearing

---

[60] Article 65 of the Convention requires the Court to present an annual report on its activities to the OAS General Assembly. In it, the Court "shall specify, in particular, the cases in which a state has not complied with its judgments, making any pertinent recommendations".

[61] Honduran Disappearance Cases, Decision of January 15, 1988, *supra* note 4, at 25.

[62] Honduran Disappearance Cases, Decision of January 19, 1988, *supra* note 4, at 27.

[63] Peruvian Prisons Cases (Peru), Decision of January 27, 1993, *supra* note 5; Chipoco Case (Peru), Decision of January 27, 1993, *supra* note 5.

tended to make the State concerned more willing to adopt on its own certain protective measures it was previously unwilling to consider[64]. While it is obvious that the Court lacks the power to order provisional measures unless the requisite *prima facie* case has been established, there is certainly nothing wrong with the practice of giving the Commission an opportunity to be heard on the subject and requiring the State to participate in the hearing, provided only that the Commission's request is supported by credible evidence capable of being supplemented at the hearing.

The fact that Article 63(2) permits the Court to order provisional measures at the request of the Commission in cases that have not as yet been referred to the Court has produced an unanticipated problem relating to the supervision of compliance by the affected State. In these situations, the case is usually still being investigated by the Commission which, as a result, is in a much better position than the Court to know on a day-to-day basis what measures the State is taking. The Commission can keep the Court informed, of course, but the latter cannot really act on the information received unless it is sitting. To deal with this problem, the Court in one case assigned to its own Permanent Commission the task of monitoring compliance[65]. The Commission then began to transmit to the Court, without comment or analysis, all communications it received from the attorneys in the case relating to the provisional measures, forcing the Court to conclude that it was being asked to perform functions it was not legally competent to perform under the Convention. As a result, the Court returned the matter to the Commission for further monitoring[66]. The matter was never resubmitted to the Court.

In another case, the Court entered provisional measures against the Government of Guatemala by confirming the President's order of urgent measures and extending its duration to December 3, 1991[67]. Thereafter the Government informed the Court that it had complied with the Court's orders, specifying the various measures it had adopted. The Court transmitted this information to the Commission. When the Commission failed to comment thereon, the Court authorized its President to advise the Government that the provisional measures would expire on the date specified in the Court's original order[68].

The Court's experience in supervising provisional measures in cases not yet referred to it suggests the wisdom of fixing an expiration date in such

---

[64] For a telling example of this effect, see Chunima Case (Guatemala), Decision of August 1, 1991, *supra* note 5, at 69.

[65] Bustíos-Rojas Case (Peru), Decision of August 8, 1990, *supra*, note 5, at 33.

[66] Bustíos-Rojas Case (Peru), Decision of January 17, 1991, *supra* note 5, at 15.

[67] Chunima Case (Guatemala), Decision of the Court of August 1, 1991, *supra* note 5, at 69.

[68] Note of the President addressed to the Government of Guatemala, dated December 3, 1991, [1991] *Annual Report of the Inter-American Court of Human Rights*, OAS/Ser. L./V/III. 25, doc. 7, at 163 (1992).

cases. This approach avoids the problem the Court encountered in the *Bustíos-Rojas* Case, where the Commission simply referred to the Court all communications received from the petitioners without providing the Court with its own analysis of the facts. Moreover, by fixing an expiration date the Court is in fact giving the Commission an opportunity to ask for another hearing prior to the deadline if it has reason to believe that the order is either not being fully complied with or needs to be prolonged. As a practical matter, this practice also assigns the day-to-day task of monitoring compliance to the Commission. That makes a great deal of sense. For when a case is still before the Commission, that body is in a much better position than the Court to monitor compliance and to make an initial assessment of any new information it may have received from the private petitioners. In these cases it would make sense for the Commission to set up a special monitoring mechanism to keep the Court informed of compliance problems.

Conclusion

It is quite clear that the power of the Court to grant provisional measures has proved to be a very useful enforcement tool in the inter-American system. In a region of the world where serious violations of human rights are by no means a thing of the past, provisional measures can save lives, and they have done so on a number of occasions. As a matter of fact, I would argue that every international human rights court should have powers comparable to those Article 63(2) confers on the Inter-American Court. I also believe that such provisions should make explicit what is implicit in the American Convention, namely, that decisions ordering provisional measures are legally binding on their addressees.

The effectiveness of decisions by international human rights tribunals ordering provisional measures depends, in large measure, on their judicious use. They are exceptional measures and should be reserved for exceptional and urgent situations. Most of the time that means that they should be granted very sparingly. Such orders are likely to be disregarded or not fully complied with by States if they are permitted to be transformed from an exceptional remedy into one more procedural tool to be used against a recalcitrant State. Their effectiveness depends on their exceptional character precisely because that is how they preserve their shock value and corresponding effect on public opinion. Here it must never be forgotten that, in the final analysis, public opinion will determine whether or not the State will comply with the decision.

If this conclusion is sound, it would follow that the Inter-American Commission on Human Rights should ask for provisional measures in cases not yet referred to the Court only in exceptional circumstances. This means that it should come to the Court for this remedy only when it has a very strong *prima facie* case. The Commission should also have a very clear idea how compliance with the requested provisional measures should be monitored, and it should make its ideas on this subject known to the Court or establish its own mechanism. The remedy sought, moreover, should be very specific and narrow in scope; the broader the request the more difficult it will be for the Commission or the Court to monitor compliance.

At this time, the Court's Rules of Procedure do not provide for hearings on the request for provisional measures. It would make a great deal of sense to amend the Rules to require such hearings before a final order is entered. The Court or its President should, of course, be free to order temporary or urgent measures in particularly urgent situations without a prior hearing, but the final order should as a rule not be granted or rejected without it. The hearing, besides calling public attention to the case, gives the provisional measures procedure a solemnity that enhanced the chances of compliance and enables the Court to better assess the need for such measures. In the past the Court usually held hearings before deciding whether to order provisional measures. As we have seen, recently it has begun to depart from this practice. The inter-American system for the protection of human rights would be better served if the Court reverted to its earlier practice.

Interim Measures of Protection under the European Convention on Human Rights

Rudolf Bernhardt

Introduction

The European Convention on Human Rights, signed in 1950 and in force since 1953, provides for a control machinery which has functioned now for several decades, and the number of cases scrutinized by this machinery increases year by year. In 1993, more than 2000 individual applications were registered by the European Commission of Human Rights, and 60 judgments have been pronounced by the European Court of Human Rights[1]. The Council of Europe, the parent organization of this regional human rights system, comprised by the end of the year 1993 32 Member States, of which 28 ratified the Convention and accepted the right of individual petition to the Commission and the jurisdiction of the Court; the remaining 4 States (and other candidates for membership in the Council) have promised to follow soon.

It can hardly be doubted that a system instituted for the protection of human rights requires, in order to be effective, certain safeguards for ensuring that a final decision is not rendered ineffective because irreparable damage has already occurred. Several years can pass between the instituting of proceedings and the binding decision of the European Court of Human Rights and, at least in exceptional cases, it cannot be excluded that the final decision is only of theoretical interest and of no relevance for the individual whose rights have been violated.

---

[1] From 1955 to 1992, 21077 applications were registered by the European Commission, and it has taken 18820 decisions in this period, cf. Mark E. Villinger, *Handbuch der Europäischen Menschenrechtskonvention*, 1993, p. 413. For the European Court see the statistics in the "*Survey of Activities*" published anually by the Registry of the Court.

Unlike the American Convention on Human Rights[2], the European Convention does not contain any provision which empowers the institutions to grant interim measures of protection[3]. The best explanation for this lacuna is probably the reluctance of States and their representatives in 1949/50 to introduce a control machinery without at the same time protecting to a certain extent also the sovereign rights of the States.

In later years several protocols were added to the European Convention, but the original omission of a clause for interim measures was never rectified. When a new additional protocol was prepared in 1993, providing for profound changes in the control system with a single European Court of Human Rights, replacing the present organs (Commission and Court), it again proved impossible to introduce an express provision for interim measures of protection[4]. The result is that the Convention as an international agreement is and will remain silent on the problem discussed during this colloquium.

It is tempting to raise at the outset the question whether there is not a general principle of law that judicial bodies have the right to grant interim measures of protection in urgent cases, with binding force for the parties concerned, including the State as party and potential violator of human rights[5]. But it is premature to raise this question before considering more closely the actual practices and the basic problems involved.

Interim protection of rights can basically be granted in two different ways which we find especially in national administrative law: Either the beginning of formal review proceedings automatically suspends the enforceability of the decision which is challenged as illegal, or the judicial body responsible for the review can order the suspension of the decision of the administrative authority. Both ways could also be considered for an international human rights system, but the problems involved hardly permit in reality the automatic suspension of State acts challenged on the international plane. If a prison sentence, a police order or a taxation measure were automatically unenforceable at the moment when an international procedure commenced, the number of petitions would in all probability increase drastically and the

---

[2] See the report of Thomas Buergenthal, *supra* p. 69 ss. The originally presented version of the present report contained, in view of the absence of Professor Buergenthal at the colloquium, some remarks on the practice of the Inter-American Court which have now been omitted.

[3] A Draft Statute of the European Court of Human Rights prepared by the International Juridical Section of the European Movement contained in Art. 35 an express provision, see *Collected Edition of the "Travaux préparatoires"*, Vol. I, 1975, p. 314.

[4] When the present text was finalized in early 1994 a draft protocol no. 11 was being discussed in different bodies in the Council of Europe but no provision on interim measures was included in spite of suggestions made in this respect.

[5] See now the comprehensive article by Lawrence Collins, Provisional and Protective Measures in International Litigation, Recueil des Cours, Vol. 234 (1992-III), p. 13–238, esp. p. 216.

proper administration of justice and public order could be damaged, at least as long as no speedy and effective control of all petitions is possible. Therefore the only reasonable interim measure of protection on the international plane seems to be the power of an organ to grant protection in urgent and exceptional cases. We will now see how the problem is solved or at least approached under the European Convention on Human Rights[6].

I. Texts and Practices under the European Convention

As already mentioned, neither the original Convention nor the later additioned protocols contain any provision on interim measures of protection. But the need for such protection was felt a few years after the European Commission had begun its work. Under the Convention system, all proceedings start before the Commission; the Court comes into the picture much later, and it acts only in a relatively small number of cases. It is therefore clear that the need for interim measures of protection arises in the first instance during the procedure before the Commission.

It is interesting to note that right from the beginning a certain category of cases played the main role in the area of interim measures: persons present in one of the States parties to the Convention were in danger of being extradited or expelled to a third State and they feared torture or inhuman treatment or punishment, prohibited by Art. 3 of the Convention, in the target State. Such a case arose already in 1960, and it gave the Commission the opportunity to approach the Member State. In this case and in many similar cases thereafter, it seemed to be the practice of the Commission to

---

[6] Literature discussing the matter under the European System: C. A. Nørgaard and H. C. Krüger, Interim and Conservatory Measures under the European System of Protection of Human Rights, in: *Progress in the Spirit of Human Rights*, Festschrift für Felix Ermacora, 1988, p. 109–117; Dean Spielmann, Les mesures provisoires et les organes de protection prévus par la Convention Européenne des Droits de l'Homme, in: *Présence du Droit Public et des Droits de l'Homme*, Mélanges offerts à Jacques Velu. Tome deuxième. Bruylant, Bruxelles, 1992, p. 1293–1317. K. Oellers-Frahm, Zur Verbindlichkeit einstweiliger Anordnungen der Europäischen Kommission für Menschenrechte/Anmerkung zum Urteil des EGMR im Fall Cruz Varas gegen Schweden, EuGRZ 18 (1991), 197; K. Oellers-Frahm, *Die einstweilige Anordnung in der internationalen Gerichtsbarkeit*, 1975, p. 122 ss; K. Rogge, Einstweilige Maßnahmen im Verfahren vor der Europäischen Kommission für Menschenrechte, NJW 1977, 1570; M.-A. Eissen, Les mesures provisoires dans la Convention européenne des droits de l'homme, Revue des droits de l'homme 2 (1969), 526; G. Cohen-Jonathan, La Convention européenne des droits de l'homme, Revue Universelle des droits de l'homme (RUDH) 1991, 205; R. St. J. Macdonald, Interim Measures in International Law, with Special Reference to the European System for the Protection of Human Rights, Zeitschrift für ausländisches öffentliches Recht und Völkerrecht, Vol. 52 (1992), pp. 703–740.
See also Frowein/Peukert, *EMRK-Kommentar*, 1985, p. 360.

contact the government concerned, "and to ask that no measures be taken pending the examination of the application by the Commission"[7]. According to the available information, governments normally respected the Commission's wishes and waited with the extradition or expulsion until the Commission had taken the necessary steps and decisions. It can be assumed that the question was not yet formally raised and discussed whether the Government had a legal duty to act according to the Commission's request; it is more likely that a spirit of cooperation was more important than legal considerations. In any event, interim measures were recommended by the Commission and adopted by Governments at first without a legal text as basis. Such a basis was invented some years later; competent authors have given the following explanation: "The positive reaction by Member States encouraged the Commission to formalize this practice in the sense that, in October 1974, it introduced a new Rule in its Rules of Procedure"[8]. This new Rule 36 of the Commission's Rules of Procedure provides:

> "The Commission, or when it is not in session, the President may indicate to the parties any interim measure the adoption of which seems desirable in the interest of the parties or the proper conduct of the proceedings before it".

As concerns the Court, already the original text (Rule 34) of the Rules of the European Court of Human Rights, adopted in 1959, contained a provision on interim measures. The provision was later amended and reads now as follows:

> " Rule 36
> (Interim measures)
> 1. Before the constitution of a Chamber, the President of the Court may, at the request of a Party, of the Commission, of the applicant or of any other person concerned, or *proprio motu*, indicate to any Party and, where appropriate, the applicant, any interim measure which is advisable for them to adopt. The Chamber when constituted or, if the Chamber is not in session, its President shall have the same power.
> 2. Where the Commission, pursuant to Rule 36 of its Rules of Procedure, has indicated an interim measure as desirable, its adoption or maintenance shall remain recommended to the Parties and, when appropriate, the applicant after the case has been brought before the Court, unless and until the President or the Chamber otherwise decides or until paragraph 1 of this Rule is applied"[9].

---

[7] Nørgaard/Krüger, ibid., p. 111.
[8] Nørgaard/Krüger, ibid., p. 111.
[9] The amendments since 1959 to the first paragraph of this provision have been of secondary importance. The second paragraph of the present text was inserted only in 1989.

This provision has not yet played a great role; in one case the President of the Court expressed the wish that the State authorities "should consider the possibility of suspending execution" of a fine, although he denied the danger of irreparable damage[10].

In 1991, the Court summarized the practice of the Commission on the basis of the information given by it as follows:

> "... until October 1989 the Commission had been seised of 182 requests for interim measures in expulsion (as opposed to extradition) cases. In 31 of these cases an indication under Rule 36 [of the Commission's Rules] was given and complied with by the Contracting Parties concerned. In several cases concerning extradition the State has failed to comply with a Rule 36 indication"[11].

It is clear that extradition and expulsion are the most serious cases in which provisional protection can become necessary. But it is obvious that other constellations and Convention articles can also play a role. It is not possible to investigate here closer the practice of the European Commission of Human Rights. The available information is limited. Nørgaard and Krüger mention, besides expulsion and extradition, two situations in which interim measures have been indicated: It can be advisable to secure evidence; for this purpose a prison was visited in 1977. In other cases, the health conditions of detained persons required precautionary measures. It is also mentioned that interim measures may be ordered or indicated vis-à-vis an applicant, for instance in the case of a hunger strike. A great variety and number of other situations can be imagined in which interim measures may be useful or required. In many cases contacts and informal understandings with governments can make formal indications of interim measures unnecessary. Flexibility is of outstanding importance in this area, and the practice has to respond to changing conditions and different challenges.

One remark should be added: The Commission seems never to indicate interim measures when expulsion or extradition towards another State Party to the Convention is imminent, if this State has also accepted the control machinery[12]. The underlying reason is that the necessary protection can also be found in and from the target State. This assumption is probably reasonable under the normal circumstances, but one can imagine situations where protective measures are necessary before expulsion or extradition takes place even towards another Member State.

The Committee of Ministers of the Council of Europe adopted in 1980 a Recommendation concerning extradition to States not Party to the Conven-

---

10 *Bönisch* Case, Publications of the European Court of Human Rights, Series A Vol. 92, at pp. 65.

11 Case of *Cruz Varas and Others v. Sweden*, Series A Vol. 201, at p. 25.

12 See Nørgaard/Krüger, ibid., p. 113.

tion asking Member States "to comply with an interim measure which the European Commission of Human Rights might indicate under Rule 36 of its Rules of Procedure, as, for instance, a request to stay extradition proceedings pending a decision on the matter"[13]. This underlines the apparent consensus that irreparable damage should be avoided by interim measures preceding the final decisions of the Convention's organs.

II. The Case of Cruz Varas and the Obligation of States to Adopt Interim Measures of Protection

It was for the first time in 1990/91 that the European Commission and the European Court of Human Rights formally and extensively discussed the question whether a State may legally be obliged to respect a request of the Commission to take interim measures of protection. The factual situation, as far as here of interest, was rather simple: Mr. Hector Cruz Varas, his wife and his son, Chilean citizens, asked in Sweden for political asylum. The granting of asylum finally was denied by the Swedish authorities, and Mr. Cruz Varas was forced to leave the country on 6 October 1989. One day before, he had lodged an application against Sweden with the Commission under Art. 25 of the Convention. On 6 October at 9.00 hours, the Commission approached the Swedish Government under Rule 36 of its Rules of Procedure with the following request:

> "The Commission ... decided ... to indicate to the Government of Sweden ... that it was desirable in the interest of the Parties and the proper conduct of the proceedings before the Commission not to deport the applicants to Chile until the Commission had had an opportunity to examine the application during its forthcoming session from 6 to 10 November 1989".

The competent Swedish authorities decided not to stay the enforcement of the expulsion, and Mr. Cruz Varas had to leave the country on the same day at 16.40 hours[14].

Commission and Court had to answer the question whether the expulsion violated Art. 3 and Art. 25 of the Convention. A "violation" of Rule 36 of the Commission's Rules of Procedure alone could probably not be challenged, since a petition under Art. 25 of the Convention must allege "a violation ... of the rights set forth in this Convention ...". Court and Commission discussed the question whether the expulsion of Mr. Cruz Varas violated the last sentence of the first paragraph of Art. 25, worded as follows:

---

[13] Recommendation No. R (80) 9.

[14] All facts taken from the judgment of the Court, see *supra* note 11.

"Those of the High Contracting Parties who have made such a declaration undertake not to hinder in any way the effective exercise of this right". The two Convention organs come to different results: The Commission concluded by twelve votes to one that Art. 25 § 1 of the Convention had been violated, the Court held by ten votes to nine that there had been no violation of this provision. Instead of summarizing here the main arguments *pro* and *contra* and in view of the fact that the author of this report was one of the dissenting judges in the Court, extracts of the majority and the minority opinions are added as an appendix to the present report.

Interim measures in expulsion as well as in extradition matters presuppose that the Convention is also applicable if torture, inhuman or degrading treatment and punishment may occur not in the country where the applicant actually lives, but in the country into which the applicant may be expelled or extradited. This is in fact recognized by all Convention organs. The "extraterritorial" effect of the Convention has been extensively discussed by the Court in the *Soering* judgment[15]. It should be underlined that the prohibition of torture and similar treatment concerns most fundamental human rights, and any extraterritorial effects of Convention provisions of lesser importance may require different considerations and arguments. It may finally be added that one cannot exclude collisions between obligations arising out of the European Convention on Human Rights and extradition treaties concluded by a Member State with third countries; this problem can here only be mentioned, it was not relevant in the *Soering* Case since the extradition treaty between the United Kingdom and the United States of America contained relevant exceptions to the duty to extradite. These remarks are not of direct importance for the problem of interim measures of protection, but they may show that other intricate questions are connected herewith.

III. General Problems of Interim Measures in Human Rights Matters

International Conventions on Human Rights like the European Convention guarantee certain basic rights of individuals and oblige States and their organs to respect these rights. As far as control institutions exist, they normally step in when the alleged violation has already taken place. They have to see whether a certain event in the past was compatible with the Convention; only in a minority of cases may an alleged violation which has commenced in the past continue in the present, like the imprisonment of a person without sound legal basis. In expulsion and extradition cases, no violation of rights has already occurred: it is the danger of future violations which requires measures excluding this danger.

15 Judgment of 7 July 1989, Series A Vol. 161.

These considerations lead to the statement that interim measures of protection in human rights matters must, on the international plane, remain the exception. They can hardly be adequate if exclusively a violation of human rights in the past is alleged, without continuing effect into the present. It is true that we find in the internal legal order of States interim measures which go further and make, for instance, certain interim payments obligatory; but this can hardly be applied on the international level without a sound legal (conventional) basis. Such a basis for precautionary measures can be found in other treaties like the European Convention against torture which empowers a Committee to visit prisons without prior allegations of human rights violations, but that is different from our problem.

Other, more practical, considerations underline that interim measures must remain the exception in the area here under discussion. Human Rights Conventions normally require – like Art. 26 of the European Convention – the exhaustion of local remedies before petition to an international organ is permitted. The underlying idea is that States should have the possibility to redress eventual violations before being subjected to an international procedure. It must also be kept in mind that in the practice under the European system 90 per cent or even more of all registered applications to the European Commission are declared inadmissible. And applications declared admissible may be found unjustified after a lengthy procedure before the Convention organs. If interim measures were ordered in a greater number of cases it could not be excluded that valid interests of the State and society would suffer.

On the other hand, the effective protection of human rights may absolutely require interim measures of protection. Expulsion and extradition cases are here of outstanding importance. If, at the moment when the indication of interim measures is asked for, imminent and grave human rights violations cannot be excluded, interim protection is the only means to avoid irreparable damage. But also other situations may require interim measures: The continuing imprisonment of a person in spite of critical health conditions, or the separation of young children from their parents without adequate procedural safeguards. The decisive aspect probably is always the danger of irreparable damage if no interim measures are taken. It is the human being which is protected by the Human Rights Convention, and this protection must insofar be effective as the final result of the international procedure must have some practical relevance for the person concerned.

Opinions remain divided whether interim measures indicated by the European Commission and the European Court of Human Rights are obligatory for the State concerned. The silence of the Convention is often invoked for the denial of any binding force. It must also be admitted that the text of the relevant Rules of Procedure of both organs are drafted in a cautious manner. Interim measures may be *indicated* where their adoption *seems desir-*

able or *advisable*[16]. It is also true that in the actual practice of the Convention organs carefully drafted formulae are used, namely that an interim measure is desirable or that the authorities should consider certain measures. It is nevertheless the opinion of the author of this report that States are obliged to adopt interim measures of protection if these are indicated by the Convention organs in exceptional cases and if these measures are indispensible for the effective protection of rights guaranteed by the Convention. Whether such measures are indispensible must be decided on the basis of the knowledge available at the moment when the decision is required; later information is only insofar relevant as it might be necessary to change the original decision.

The legal basis for our opinion that interim measures may be obligatory under international law is twofold: A teleological interpretation of the Convention requires an effective protection of the rights guaranteed. Secondly, general principles of law as found in the internal legal system of States support this conclusion[17].

We have not yet discussed a special category of interim measures which have been relevant under the American Convention on Human Rights and which have occasionally been taken into account under the European Convention. The procedure before international organs may require proper and effective measures like the preservation of evidence. The Inter-American Court of Human Rights tried to protect potential witnesses. Also under the European system procedural steps may appear necessary or advisable. Such measures can be taken under the relevant rules for interim measures, but they may require different and additional considerations than is the case where the rights of the applicant need direct and immediate protection. Procedural measures fall also and undoubtedly under other provisions of the Convention: Under Art. 28 of the European Convention, the Commission has to ascertain the facts, to examine the petition and to investigate the matter. The Court's jurisdiction extends "to all cases concerning the interpretation and application of the present Convention ..." (Art. 45). It can hardly be doubted that interim measures which are necessary for the proper conduct of the procedure before the Convention organs are permitted by the provisions of the Convention and they are also obligatory for the parties concerned.

---

16 See the texts quoted *supra* p. 98.

17 See Collins, *supra* note 5. It is admitted that an extensive comparative study is not available, but there are good reasons for the assumption that nearly all legal systems provide for some interim protection.

Annex: Extracts from the Statements in the Case of Cruz Varas

1. (a) Opinion of the Commission of 7 June 1990

106. The government submit that the indication under Rule 36 is a non-binding recommendation; the Convention does not oblige the respondent State to follow such an indication given by the Commission. Further the language of the indication shows that it is not binding. The fact that such indications have been complied with in the past does not make the indication mandatory. Finally, the Government were unable under Swedish law to act in accordance with the indication.

107. Article 36 of the Convention authorises the Commission to draw up its rules of procedure. In the Rules of Procedure which have been adopted on the basis of this Article, a provision dealing with interim measures was included in Rule 36. It has not been alleged that the Commission, when including this provision, acted outside its competence under Article 36 of the Convention. Moreover, it should be noted that the European Court of Human Rights has acted in a similar way by including in Rule 36 of the Rules of Court a provision which gives the Court and its President competence to indicate to a party or an applicant any interim measure which is advisable for them to adopt.

108. In these circumstances, there is no doubt that the Commission has power to indicate interim measures under Rule 36. This view also finds support in the Court's judgment in the Soering case (Eur. Court H. R., Soering judgment of 7 July 1989, Series A no. 161, pp. 9 and 44, 45, §§ 4 and 111 in fine).

109. The Government refer to the language of the indication and submit that it is a recommendation which is not binding. They rely on a statement by the Court in the Soering judgment (paragraph 111 in fine) which reads as follows:

> "This finding (that the implementation of the extradition order would give rise to a breach of Article 3) in no way puts in question the good faith of the United Kingdom Government, who have from the outset of the present proceedings demonstrated their desire to abide by their Convention obligations, firstly by staying the applicant's surrender to the United States authorities in accord with the interim measures indicated by the Convention institutions and secondly by themselves referring the case to the Court for a judicial ruling".

110. In the Government's view, this statement by the Court implied that it was an act of good faith to follow the indications given by the Convention

institutions, but not an obligation under the convention to abide by the indications.

111. The Commission finds that the quoted statement by the Court can equally be read as supporting the opposite view, since the Court refers to the Government abiding by their Convention obligations in connection with staying the applicant's surrender in accord with the interim measures.

112. The Commission considers that the indication given must be seen in the light of the nature of the proceedings before the Convention organs and of the Commission's role in these proceedings.

113. As provided for in Article 19 of the Convention the Commission is one of the two organs set up by the Convention "to ensure the observance of the engagements undertaken by the High Contracting Parties in the ... Convention ...".

114. The machinery set up by the Convention must be seen as a whole. The proceedings before the Convention organs will terminate either with a decision declaring the application inadmissible or with a friendly settlement, or with a binding decision by the Court or the Committee of Ministers. The purpose of an indication under Rule 36 is to preserve the rights of the parties, and to safeguard the general interests, until a final decision has been taken by the Strasbourg organs.

115. As the Government rightly submit the proceedings before the Convention organs are of declaratory nature. The Commission cannot issue a binding decision at a High Contracting Party that has violated the Convention, whereas the Court and the Committee of Ministers have that power. The Commission's task is of preliminary nature as regards the merits of the case, and its opinion as to whether there is a violation is not binding. The terms of the Commission's indication under Rule 36 must be read against its background.

116. The Commission has noted that the question whether interim measures indicated by international tribunals are binding or not is the subject of controversy in international law and that no uniform legal view exists. The Commission is however not required in the present case to decide whether in general an indication under Rule 36 is binding on the respondent State. Its examination can be limited to the question whether in the circumstances of the present case, the fact that Sweden did not act in accordance with the Commission's indication under Rule 36 of its Rules of Procedure constituted a failure by Sweden to comply with its obligations under Article 25 of the Convention.

117. Under Article 25 § 1 in fine, the High Contracting Parties, who have recognised the right of individual petition, have undertaken not to hinder the effective exercise of this right. This undertaking does not imply a general duty on the State to suspend measures at the domestic level or to enforce domestic decisions when an individual has lodged an application with the Commission.

118. However, the Commission is of the opinion that there are special circumstances where the enforcement of a national decision would be in conflict with the effective exercise of the right to petition. That is the case, in particular, when enforcement of the decision would lead to serious and irreparable damage to the applicant and the Commission has given an indication under Rule 36 of its Rules of Procedure that it is desirable not to enforce that decision.

119. The Court has stated as follows in the Soering case (Soering judgment, loc. cit., pp. 34–35, §§ 87 and 90):

> "87. In interpreting the Convention regard must be had to its special character as a treaty for the collective enforcement of human rights and fundamental freedoms (see the Ireland v. the United Kingdom judgment of 18 January 1978, Series A no. 25, p. 90, § 239). Thus, the object and purpose of the Convention as an instrument for the protection of individual human beings require that its provisions be interpreted and applied so as to make its safeguards practical and effective (see, *inter alia*, the Artico judgment of 13 May 1980, Series A no. 37, p. 16, § 33). In addition, any interpretation of the rights and freedoms guaranteed has to be consistent with 'the general spirit of the Convention, an instrument designed to maintain and promote the ideals and values of a democratic society' (see the Kjeldsen, Busk Madsen and Petersen judgment of 7 December 1976, Series A no. 23, p. 27, § 53).
>
> ...
>
> 90. It is not normally for the Convention institutions to pronounce on the existence or otherwise of potential violations of the Convention. However, where an applicant claims that a decision to extradite him would, if implemented, be contrary to Article 3 by reason of its foreseeable consequences in the requesting country, a departure from this principle is necessary in view of the serious and irreparable nature of the alleged suffering risked, in order to ensure the effectiveness of the safeguard provided by that Article (see paragraph 87 above)".

120. In the Commission's view it follows from Article 25 § 1 and the above statement by the Court that, on the one hand, an applicant is entitled to the "effective exercise" of his right to petition the Commission, within the meaning of Article 25 § 1 in fine, i.e. a Contracting State shall not prevent the Commission from making an effective examination of the application and, on the other hand, an applicant who claims a violation of Article 3 of the Convention is entitled to an effective examination of whether an intended extradition or expulsion would be a violation of Article 3. An indication under Rule 36 of the kind at issue here serves the purpose of enabling the Commission, and subsequently the Court or Committee of Ministers, to examine effectively an application and to ensure the effectiveness of the safeguard provided by Article 3.

121. The Commission also notes that, before the present case, no Contracting State had ever failed to comply with an indication given by the Commission in expulsion cases. The Commission observes that, according to its own statistics, the Commission or its President had, at the time of Mr. Cruz Varas' expulsion, been seised with 182 cases in which the question arose of giving an indication under Rule 36 of its Rules of Procedure that an expulsion order should not be enforced, and that in 31 of these cases an indication was given by the Commission or its President.

122. Turning to the present case, the Commission therefore considers that to deport Mr Cruz Varas, although an indication under Rule 36 had been given, frustrated its examination and thereby rendered his right of petition ineffective. Such an action is, in the Commission's opinion, contrary to the spirit of the Convention and is incompatible with the effective exercise of the right to petition guaranteed by Article 25 § 1 of the Convention. These considerations apply notwithstanding the fact that the Commission has, after a full examination of the merits of the complaint under Article 3 of the Convention, concluded that there has been no violation of that provision.

123. Finally, the Government maintain that they were unable, as a matter of Swedish law, to comply with the Commission's indication under Rule 36.

124. The Commission recalls that Article 27 of the Vienna Convention on the Law of Treaties, to which Sweden is a Contracting Party, provides that a State may not invoke the provisions of its internal law as justification for its failure to perform a treaty. This rule also applies in the examination of cases under the European Convention on Human Rights.

125. Consequently, the Commission cannot accept the Government's defence that domestic law prevented them from complying with their obligations under the Convention.

126. The Government's arguments further prompt the Commission to clarify that the Convention does not leave the Contracting Parties with a choice between, on the one hand, complying with their obligations under the Convention and, on the other hand, failing to comply with their obligations under the Convention and instead trying to provide a remedy for the violation once it has been established. Their primary obligation must always be not to commit a breach of the Convention. This follows from the text of Article 1 of the Convention, which provides that the High Contracting Parties "shall secure" the rights and freedoms in the Convention, and from the Court's statements quoted above.

127. For these reasons, the Commission finds that Sweden failed to comply with its obligations under Article 25 § 1 of the Convention when it did not act in accordance with the Commission's indication under Rule 36 of the Rules of Procedure.

Conclusion

128. The Commission concludes, by twelve votes to one, that Sweden has failed to comply with its obligations under Article 25 § 1 of the Convention.

1. (b) Dissenting opinion of Mr. Sperduti

If only briefly, I must explain why, to my regret, I felt obliged to disagree with the other members of the Commission in the vote on Article 25 of the Convention.

I share the Commission's view that the Court's statements on the special character of the system for the collective enforcement of human rights and fundamental freedoms introduced by the European Convention must be taken into account. This is what the Court had to say recently in its judgment of 7 July in the Soering case, cited in paragraph 119 of the Commission's report:

> "87. In interpreting the Convention regard must be had to its special character as a treaty for the collective enforcement of human rights and fundamental freedoms (see the Ireland v. the United Kingdom judgment of 18 January 1978, Series A no. 25, p. 90, § 239). Thus, the object and purpose of the Convention as an instrument for the protection of individual human beings require that its provisions be interpreted and applied so as to make its safeguards practical and effective (see, *inter alia*, the Artico judgment of 13 May 1980, Series A no. 37, p. 16, § 33). In addition, any interpretation of the rights and freedoms guaranteed has to be consistent with 'the general spirit of the Convention, an instrument designed to maintain and promote the ideals and values of a democratic society' (see the Kjeldsen, Busk Madsen and Petersen judgment of 7 December 1976, Series A no. 23, p. 27, § 53)".

However I consider that any further development of the principles expressed above necessitates particular attention to the requirements of legal logic. It is my contention that it was only by going beyond the bounds of such requirements that the Commission in its report eventually envisaged a violation of the Convention by the Government in question, which violation consisted in the failure to comply with the measure indicated by the Commission, in application of Rule 36 of its Rules of Procedure, namely not to expel the applicant. The direct question of how this application of the Rules of Procedure affected the legal position was left unanswered; the Commission turned to Article 25 of the Convention and concluded that the conduct of the Swedish government amounted to a violation of that Article.

Admittedly, the undertaking given by Contracting Parties, in connection with the declaration on the right of individual petition provided for in Article 25, "not to hinder in any way the effective exercise of his right" is an important factor contributing to the effectiveness of the guarantee system set up by the Convention. But the meaning of the words "effective exercise" in Article 25 is to be interpreted in the light of that Article's purpose, i.e. firstly, the declaration recognising the right to petition the Commission, secondly, an undertaking to allow free exercise of that right in its different forms.

In the final analysis, my remarks can be reduced to a single criticism: correct interpretation of Article 25 does not justify agreement with the audacious solution adopted by the majority of the Commission, namely to raise Rule 36 of the Rules of Procedure to the status of a legal rule empowering the Commission – or, if the Commission is not sitting, its President – to impose on defendant States obligations additional to those deriving directly from the Convention.

My last observation is that Rule 36 does indeed have particular legal relevance, but this relevance may be expressed as follows: the responsibility of a State deporting a person to another State where there is a serious risk that the person will be subjected to treatment contrary to Article 3 of the Convention must be regarded as greater when the expulsion decision has been carried out in spite of a warning to the first State from the Commission in application of Rule 36 of its Rules of Procedure.

2. (a) Judgment of the Court of 20 March 1991

1. General considerations

94. As has been noted on previous occasions the Convention must be interpreted in the light of its special character as a treaty for the protection of individual human beings and its safeguards must be construed in a manner which makes them practical and effective (see, *inter alia*, the above-mentioned Soering judgment, Series A no.161, p. 34, § 87). While this approach argues in favour of a power of the Commission and Court to order interim measures to preserve the rights of parties in pending proceedings, the Court cannot but note that unlike other international treaties or instruments the Convention does not contain a specific provision with regard to such measures (see, *inter alia*, Article 41 of the Statute of the International Court of Justice; Article 63 of the 1969 American Convention on Human Rights; Articles 185 and 186 of the 1957 Treaty establishing the European Economic Community).

95. The European Movement, which first proposed the drafting of a European Convention on Human Rights, originally included in a draft

Statute of the European Court of Human Rights an interim measures provision (Article 35) based in substance on Article 41 of the Statute of the International Court of Justice (see Collected Edition of the *travaux préparatoires*, Vol. I, p. 314). The *travaux préparatoires* of the Convention are, however, silent as to any discussion which may have taken place on this question.

96. The absence of a specific interim measures provision in the Convention gave rise to a Recommendation by the Consultative Assembly of the Council of Europe calling on the Committee of Ministers to draft an additional Protocol to the Convention which would empower the Convention organs to order interim measures in appropriate cases (see Recommendation 623, Yearbook of the Convention, Vol. 14, pp. 68–71). The Committee of Ministers subsequently decided that the conclusion of such a protocol was not expedient on the ground, *inter alia*, that the existing practice of the Commission in requesting governments to postpone the measure complained of worked satisfactorily (see Doc. 3325, pp. 4–6, Working Papers of Consultative Assembly, 25th Ordinary Session, 25 September – 2 October 1973). The Assembly later recommended that the Committee of Ministers call on member States to "suspend extradition or expulsion to a non-Contracting State" where the Commission or the Court was called on to take a decision on, *inter alia*, allegations under Article 3 (see Recommendation 817 (1977) on Certain Aspects of the Right to Asylum, Yearbook of the Convention, Vol. 20, pp. 82–85). Finally the Committee of Ministers on 27 June 1980 adopted a similar recommendation to governments of member States in cases concerning extradition to a non-Contracting State (see Recommendation no. R (80) 9, Yearbook of the Convention, Vol. 23, pp. 78–79).

2. Can a power to order interim measures be derived from Article 25 § 1 or other sources?

97. The question arises for consideration in this case whether, notwithstanding the absence of a specific provision in the Convention, a power for the Commission to order interim measures can nevertheless be derived from Article 25 § 1 considered separately or in conjunction with Rule 36 of the Commission's Rules of Procedure or from other sources.

98. Firstly it must be observed that Rule 36 has only the status of a rule of procedure drawn up by the Commission under Article 36 of the Convention. In absence of a provision in the Convention for interim measures an indication given under Rule 36 cannot be considered to give rise to a binding obligation on Contracting Parties. Indeed this is reflected in the wording both of Rule 36 itself ("may indicate any interim measure the adoption of which seems desirable") and of the indications made under it in the present case ("to indicate to the Government of Sweden that it was desirable ... not to deport the applicants to Chile") (see paragraph 56 and similar wording in paragraph 61 above).

99. As to the Contracting Parties' obligation not to hinder the effective exercise of the right of petition it must first be noted that Article 25 § 1 is limited to proceedings before the Commission and to individual applications. It does not apply to inter-State cases where the interest in respecting an indication made under Rule 36 is essentially the same.

In its ordinary meaning Article 25 § 1 imposes an obligation not to interfere with the right of the individual effectively to present and pursue his complaint with the Commission. Such an obligation confers upon an applicant a right of a procedural nature distinguishable from the substantive rights set out under Section I of the Convention or its Protocols. However it flows from the very essence of this procedural right that it must be open to individuals to complain of alleged infringements of it in Convention proceedings. In this respect also the Convention must be interpreted as guaranteeing rights which are practical and effective as opposed to theoretical and illusory (see the above-mentioned Soering judgment, Series A no. 161, p. 34, § 87), and the authorities cited therein).

Nevertheless, as seen above, no specific provision in the Convention empowers the Commission to order interim measures. It would strain the language of Article 25 to infer from the words "undertake not to hinder in any way the effective exercise of this right" an obligation to comply with a Commission indication under Rule 36. This conclusion is not altered by considering Article 25 § 1 in conjunction with Rule 36 or – as submitted by the Delegate of the Commission – in conjunction with Articles 1 and 19 of the Convention.

100. The practice of Contracting Parties in this area shows that there has been almost total compliance with Rule 36 indications. Subsequent practice could be taken as establishing the agreement of Contracting States regarding the interpretation of a Convention provision (see, *mutatis mutandis*, the above-mentioned Soering judgment, Series A no. 161, pp. 40–41, § 103, and Article 31 § 3 (b) of the Vienna Convention of 23 May 1969 on the Law of Treaties) but not to create new rights and obligations which were not included in the Convention at the outset (see, *mutatis mutandis*, the Johnston and Others judgment of 18 December 1986, Series A no. 112, p. 25, § 53). In any event, as reflected in the various recommendations of the Council of Europe bodies referred to above, the practice of complying with Rule 36 indications cannot have been based on a belief that these indications gave rise to a binding obligation (see paragraph 96 above). It was rather a matter of good faith co-operation with the Commission in cases where this was considered reasonable and practicable.

101. Finally, no assistance can be derived from general principles of international law since, as observed by the Commission , the question whether interim measures indicated by international tribunals are binding is a controversial one and no uniform legal rule exists.

102. Accordingly, the Court considers that the power to order binding interim measures cannot be inferred from either Article 25 § 1 in fine, or from other sources. It lies within the appreciation of the Contracting Parties to decide whether it is expedient to remedy this situation by adopting a new provision notwithstanding the wide practice of good faith compliance.

103. In this connection, it must be borne in mind that Rule 36 indications are given by the Commission or its President only in exceptional circumstances. They serve the purpose in expulsion (or extradition) cases of putting the Contracting States on notice that, in the Commission's view, irreversible harm may be done to the applicant if he is expelled and, further, that there is good reason to believe that his expulsion may give rise to a breach of Article 3 of the Convention. Where the State decides not to comply with the indication it knowingly assumes the risk of being found in breach of Article 3 following adjudication of the dispute by the Convention organs. In the opinion of the Court where the State has had its attention drawn in this way to the dangers of prejudicing the outcome of the issue then pending before the Commission any subsequent breach of Article 3 found by the Convention organs would have to be seen as aggravated by the failure to comply with the indication.

3. Did the expulsion actually hinder the effective exercise of the right of petition?

104. The applicants claimed that the expulsion of the first applicant actually hindered the effective presentation of the application to the Commission.

Compliance with the Rule 36 indication would no doubt have facilitated the presentation of the applicants' case before the Commission. However, there is no evidence that they were hindered in the exercise of the right of petition to any significant degree. The first applicant remained at liberty following his return to Chile and was free to leave the country (see paragraphs 36–38 above). Their counsel was in fact able to represent them fully before the Commission notwithstanding the first applicant's absence during the Commission's hearing.

Nor is it established that his inability to confer with his lawyer hampered the gathering of evidence additional to that already adduced during the lengthy immigration proceedings in Sweden or the countering of the Government's submissions on questions of fact.

4. Recapitulation

105. In sum, there has been no breach of Article 25 § 1 in fine.

2. (b) Joint dissenting opinion of Judges Cremona, Thór Vilhjálmsson, Walsh, Macdonald, Bernhardt, De Meyer, Martens, Foighel and Morenilla

In our view there has been a violation of Article 25 insofar as the first applicant was expelled to Chile on 6 October 1989, that is, one day after the application was lodged with the European Commission of Human Rights and a few hours after the Commission had asked the Government "not to deport the applicants to Chile ...".

1. The present judgment confirms the view expressed in the Soering judgment that extradition and expulsion may contravene the Convention. It cannot be otherwise since the Convention provides for a real and effective protection of human rights for all persons present in the member States; their governments cannot be permitted to expose such persons to serious violations of human rights in other countries. This should be beyond doubt in cases where torture or violations of other basic human rights are to be feared.

The protection under the Convention would be meaningless if a State had the right to extradite or expel a person without any prior possibility of clarification – as far and as soon as possible – of the consequences of the expulsion. The Court has repeatedly underlined that "the object and purpose of the Convention as an instrument for the protection of individual human beings require that its provisions be interpreted and applied so as to make its safeguards practical and effective" (see the Soering judgment of 7 July 1989, Series A no. 161, p. 34, § 87). This basic principle must be kept in mind when we consider the procedural guarantees contained in the Convention.

2. It is true that Article 25 § 1, second sentence, of the Convention seems, according to its wording, to protect only the effective exercise of the right to lodge a complaint. However, this does not imply that States are permitted to make the possible result of an application devoid of any practical relevance. Otherwise States would be obliged to allow a person to lodge a petition with the Commission but would be able to expel him immediately thereafter irrespective of the consequences however serious they might be. We cannot accept such an interpretation. In our view, the procedural guarantee contained in Article 25 presupposes and includes the right of the individual to be afforded, at the least, an opportunity to have the application considered more closely by the Convention organs and to have his basic rights finally protected if need be.

3. These principles do not lead to the result that every application under Article 25 automatically inhibits extradition or expulsion to another country. The mere fact that a complaint under Article 25 has been lodged concerning a decision to extradite or expel should not restrict the power of governments to consider and to weigh the available evidence and to decide whether the decision should, nevertheless, be enforced. In reaching this decision they can

take into account that applications are often obviously unfounded. Considerations of State security and public policy and other facts (including the length of the procedure before the Convention organs) may also be relevant. But at this stage – and only at this stage – the indication of provisional measures under Rule 36 of the Commission's Rules of Procedure comes into play. Such an indication gives the respondent State the assurance that the Commission considers the application to be of great importance under the Convention and that it will investigate the matter speedily (see paragraphs 52–55 above). Seen in this perspective, measures indicated under Rule 36 bind the State concerned since this is the only means to protect the applicant against a possible violation of his or her rights causing irreparable harm. Furthermore, it is, in our view, implicit in the Convention that in cases such as the present the Convention organs have the power to require the parties to abstain from a measure which might not only give rise to serious harm but which might also nullify the result of the entire procedure under the Convention.

In the final analysis, it is incompatible with Article 25 of the Convention that the first applicant in this case was expelled immediately after he had lodged his complaint contrary to the indication made under Rule 36 of the Commission's Rules of Procedure.

4. It cannot be of any relevance in the present case that in the event the applicant was not tortured on his return to Chile and that he was able to take the necessary steps in the procedure before the Convention organs. The critical date is 6 October 1989. At that date a grave violation of human rights following deportation could not have been excluded and the Commission had clearly indicated that closer investigation appeared necessary and would be conducted speedily.

5. It is true that, unlike some other international instruments, the Convention does not contain any express provision as to the indication of provisional measures. But this does not exclude an autonomous interpretation of the European Convention with special emphasis placed on its object and purpose and the effectiveness of its control machinery. In this context, too, present-day conditions are of importance. Today the right of individual petition and the compulsory jurisdiction of the Court have been accepted nearly by all the member States of the Council of Europe. It is of the essence that the Convention organs should be able to secure the effectiveness of the protection they are called on to ensure.

Part Two: Colloquium

Opening Address

JOCHEN ABR. FROWEIN

Dear Professor Mosler, Ladies and Gentlemen, the purpose of our colloquium is to honour Professor Hermann Mosler on the occasion of his 80th birthday with a discussion of interim measures in international jurisdictions. We are quite happy that so many have accepted our invitation although regrettably the timetable of the International Court of Justice has made it impossible for its President and judges to attend our meeting.

We thought that the choice of the topic "interim measures in international jurisdictions" is on the one hand a very timely one, and on the other hand concerns a subject near the interests of our guest of honour as far as his scholarly work and also his experience as a judge at the International Court of Justice is concerned. We are particularly happy that Professor Francis Jacobs, Advocate-General of the European Court of Justice in Luxembourg, and Dr. Thirlway of the International Court of Justice have accepted to give, together with Professor Bernhardt, introductory reports for our discussion.

To his and our regret Professor Tom Buergenthal, longtime judge and president of the American Court of human rights, had to cancel his trip to Heidelberg because of a UN mission which he had to undertake unexpectedly. For the publication he will prepare his report.

Hermann Mosler's role for the doctrine as well as for the practice of public international law has been described earlier and I shall not repeat that. The Max Planck Institute for Comparative Public Law and International Law gained its profile from Hermann Mosler, the Institute's first post-war director from 1954 to 1976, and his successors try to guard this heritage.

Hermann Mosler has always seen the dangers existing for the legal order among nations, dangers which every German lawyer of his generation has experienced during his own lifetime. It is certainly due to this experience that Mosler has always clearly underlined the need for public international law to be based on a value system. According to him this system may either be derived from philosophical or religious views which may see the legal order based on natural law. However, it is also possible, according to Hermann Mosler, that the fundamental rules be seen as principles of a practical necessity without which co-existence and cooperation among the States in the international society could not be upheld.

During his mandate as judge of the International Court of Justice from 1976 to 1985 Hermann Mosler acted on the basis of these principles. Only rarely did he make use of the possibility of dissenting or concurring opinions. One should not draw the conclusion from this fact that his influence on the majority position must have been unimportant. The contrary may be nearer to the truth since the practice of institutions may show that those who are rare dissenters may have greater influence during deliberations. I shall try to show you some of the basic ideas of Hermann Mosler as a judge through his separate opinions.

In 1980 the Court gave its Advisory Opinion to the Interpretation of the Agreement of 25 March 1951 between the WHO and Egypt. Mosler wrote his second separate opinion in that context; I shall come back to the first one later.

In a careful interpretation of the agreement between a State and an international organization Mosler reaches the conclusion that a permanent obligation could not be reconciled with the character of the treaty.

> "I consequently conclude that by virtue of a right deriving from the provisions of the agreement as a whole ... either party may put an end to its operation ...".

It is of considerable interest in that context how Mosler develops the procedural conditions for the termination and arrives at the clarification that a two years period which was contained in a provision for the revision of the treaty could be applied by analogy for the termination.

In 1982 Mosler had the opportunity to come back to his earlier work on the law of international organizations in a separate opinion for the Advisory Opinion of the Court concerning the Application for Review of Judgment No. 273 of the United Nations Administrative Tribunal. The rule, well-known in municipal law, according to which the subject may assume that a legal norm is valid after it has been promulgated by the competent organ, is used to justify a similar rule for the law of United Nations. He also applies the principle of a hierarchy of norms within the system of the United Nations.

The Case concerning Military and Paramilitary Activities in and against Nicaragua was undoubtedly a particular challenge for all judges at the ICJ. However, nobody could foresee that concerning the jurisdiction of the Court complicated issues reminiscent of the coming into effect of individual declarations in private law would arise. Nicaragua had declared on 24 September

1929 that it would recognize the jurisdiction of the Permanent Court of International Justice without, however, ever ratifying the Protocol concerning the Permanent Court. When the Statute of the International Court of Justice came into force the declaration of 1929 existed and the question was whether it was a declaration "still in force", "pas encore expirée". The majority of the Court was of the opinion that the declaration of 1929 was "certainly valid, but not binding". Mosler detects a wrong construction of the legal act in that description. According to him the act was made dependent on a suspensive condition. He clarifies that with the choice of words by the majority the decision was already indicated that later a ratification might make the declaration valid. According to him "A potentially effective act however only acquires its validity if and when the condition is met." Since, according to him, the declaration is in no way legally valid it could not be seen as transformed according to Art. 36 para. 5 of the Statute of the International Court of Justice into a declaration valid for that Court.

Of considerable interest is Mosler's consideration concerning Nicaragua's behaviour by which an invalid declaration could have become effective. According to him this could be based on the following legal argument:

> "The legal reason for this view may be the clear and undoubted appearance of a valid submission which has been maintained over many years. The legal concept justifying such a consideration would be analogous to that of acquisitive prescription, a general principle of law within the meaning of Art. 38, para. 1 c, of the Statute, by which lapse of time may remedy deficiencies of formal legal acts. If one follows this theory the facts and the conduct must be absolutely unequivocal and must not leave room for any doubt".

However, Mosler came to the conclusion that such facts did not exist.

Mosler wrote a rather detailed dissenting opinion to the judgment concerning the continental shelf between Libya and Malta. At the beginning he refers to the role of the judge who should make the law "more determinable by objective criteria, and thus more predictable to potential parties". It seems clear that he has doubts whether the Court has followed that method in the complicated case.

Mosler makes a basic methodological remark in his separate vote:

> "... a relationship certainly exists between the principles and rules applicable in a given dispute and the method or choice of methods resulting from the determination of the principles and rules applicable in a concrete case. The determination of the method is therefore indicated by the applicable principles and rules, even when the choice of one method does not logically or necessarily follow from the definition of the principles and rules ...".

The first separate opinion written by Mosler in 1976 concerns interim measures by the Court under Art. 41. Without encroaching on Dr. Thirlway's report I would like to refer to one consideration in the rather short separate opinion by Mosler. The problem of jurisdiction for interim measures which leads into a logical dilemma as long as the jurisdiction for the merits is uncertain is solved by Mosler in a surprisingly clear way:

> "Art. 41 is, however, in so far an autonomous grant of jurisdiction that it permits that the grounds conferring jurisdiction in conformity with the basic article are to be examined only to the extent that this can be done without endangering the urgency with which a request for interim measures must be considered".

This must mean that every State which has accepted the jurisdiction of the Court must respect an interim order as soon as the Court could provisionally establish its jurisdiction. It may be that Mosler will come back to this problem today.

After these introductory remarks delivered as the opening address of the colloquium, the reports published in Part One were delivered.

Discussion

Steinberger, Chairman: Ladies and gentlemen, the discussion is now open. Without wishing to impose any constraints on the discussion I would like to suggest that it may be appropriate for the purpose of our debate to be guided by the structure and divisions of the three reports which have been presented.

The reports have concentrated on the following main themes. First, the normative foundations for possible interim measures of protection, i.e. the normative basis in the relevant convention, statute, and rules of procedure; also the question whether the indication of interim measures of protection can be regarded as inherent in international adjudication as a general principle of law. The German Federal Constitutional Court has held that the constitutional princple of effective recourse to a legal remedy, which is contained in Art. 19 (4) of the Basic Law, includes the principle of allowing the indication of interim measures of protection at least for all types of public law proceedings and in the case in question for proceedings before the *Sozialgerichten*; the law on these courts had excluded such measures in certain areas.

The second main theme is concerned with the conditions for the permissible indication of interim measures in a broad sense, e.g. the question of the established or probable or prima facie established jurisdiction on the merits. Is it an autonomous and independent jurisdiction for interim measures? What is the relationship of this jurisdiction to the jurisdiction in the subject matter of the main case on the merits, in particular with regard to the requirement of a link between the indication of interim measures and the law involved in the main proceedings. The procedural questions that arise in this connection include the court's indication of interim measures *proprio motu* or *ex officio*. There are also questions of urgency, of necessity, of impending irreversible damage and similar matters.

The third aspect is the permissible content of interim measures of protection, e.g. the question of the provisional establishment of facts. What is the significance in this connection of the *status quo* that should not be altered? Moreover, there is the question of different types of interim measures, depending also on the different forms of legal action that may be available, e.g. before the Luxembourg Court.

The fourth theme concerns the binding force and enforceability of provisional measures, including their normative foundations as well as special features which arise under Rule 36 of the rules of procedure of the European Commission and the European Court of Human Rights, and the relationship to Art. 25 of the European Convention on Human Rights. There is also the question of the effect of decisions, which is a most important matter for the Member States of the European Community, including the legal effects on national courts and national proceedings of decisions taken in indicating interim measures of protection by the Court of Justice of the Community.

The final theme concerns the legal consequences of interim measures of protection which are later found to be unjustified, for example when in the main proceedings an action is held to be unfounded. Are damages applicable in such a case?

Before requesting the names of speakers in the debate, I give the floor to Mr. *Tomuschat* who would like to explain some aspects of interim measures of protection within the framework of UN commissions.

Tomuschat: I would like briefly to comment on the procedure of the Human Rights Committee under the International Covenant on Civil and Political Rights. As you know, the [First] Optional Protocol to the Covenant provides for an individual "communication". This remedy enables individuals to submit complaints to the Human Rights Committee, which eventually makes a pronouncement in the form of "views". These "views" are not binding, and hence injunctions would appear to be logically excluded. Nonetheless, there is a substitute remedy. Art. 86 of the Rules of Procedure of the Committee may inform the government concerned about its view that interim measures "may be desirable to avoid irreparable damage" to the alleged victim. In this regard, an interesting practice has evolved, in particular in connection with Jamaica. In a series of cases petitioners contended that capital sentences had been rendered on the basis of national proceedings vitiated by serious defects. Responding to these allegations, the Committee has on many occasions turned to the government of Jamaica, requesting it to desist from carrying out the death sentences until the completion of the proceedings on the merits. Generally, the Government of Jamaica has indeed heeded the appeals made by the Committee. Undoubtedly, the indication of such interim measures constitutes a useful complement to the procedure under the Optional Protocol. The Human Rights Committee has thus shaped an important institution which is well suited effectively to protect the rights under the Covenant.

Steinberger: Thank you very much, Mr. *Tomuschat*. Even though the number of such cases of interim measures may be limited, when they do arise they are mostly of a very controversial and far-reaching nature.

Rodríguez Iglesias: Very briefly, with regard to precisely the question you have raised about the existence of a general principle of law as a basis for interim injunctions, I should like to point out that the case-law of the European Court of Justice in the matter of interim measures or provisional legal protection before national courts is based precisely on such a principle of effective legal protection. Unlike the situation before the Court of Justice there is no express basis. The Court of Justice speaks of a general principle of effective legal protection. This could also be regarded as a fundamental right to effective legal protection and that is quite clear in the two judgments which Advocate-General *Jacobs* cited at the end of his address, *Factortame* and *Zuckerfabrik*. And I would also like to stress in this respect that in *Zuckerfabrik* the Court pointed out that the requirements of legal protection are the same before the national courts as they are before the Court of Justice. Indeed they must be the same since they arise from the same principle. And Mr. *Jacobs* has said, quite rightly, that *Zuckerfabrik* is criticized in Germany because that would represent a diminution of legal protection. In other countries that is called a raising of the standard of protection. But we must realise that in the context of Community law *Zuckerfabrik* in itself constitutes an exception, since after the judgment in *Foto-Frost* the consequence would be that a national court could never in such circumstances suspend a national administrative measure which implements a Community regulation. And that is an exception that has been established as a consequence of the principle of effective legal protection. Thank you very much.

Pescatore: My observations relate also to the legal basis, and I think that we must start by taking a systematic view of our problem which means in this case a comparative law view. That is what we are here to do today: to compare the different international courts with each other. But I think that we should also include in this comparison the uses and methods of national courts, of national jurisdictions, in the field of interim measures. Prof. *Steinberger* gave a very striking example of the practice of the German Constitutional Court in this respect. Years ago I prepared a comparative study on this matter. I looked up the uses and methods of national courts of the different legal civilizations, and what struck me particularly is the injunctive power of the common law courts of the United Kingdom. I think that the convergences which we can find in the national organization of tribunals and in the powers given to these tribunals can constitute general principles of international law as they are envisaged by Art. 38 of the Statute of the Court. Let us not forget that all international tribunals have been created with a view to the model of national courts and not vice-versa.

And in this light I have two observations to make on the question of the legal basis. Interim measures in my opinion take place within the framework of proceedings on the substance of each case. Interim measures are generally the first incident in substantive proceedings. They are the first step towards the final solution of a given case. Interim measures are – could I say – a provisional anticipation of the final decisions. Interim measures – this has been explained very well this morning – are aimed at preserving not only the integrity of the parties' rights, but also at preserving the integrity of the powers of each court and tribunal. And therefore I would be strongly opposed, and I apologize for this to Mr. *Thirlway*, to the doctrine of distinct jurisdiction. One jurisdiction on substance and one jurisdiction on interim measures? No! The jurisdiction on interim measures is an enclosure and a part of substantive jurisdiction and it must be viewed as such. That is my first observation.

My second observation is a consequence of what I have tried to say. Interim measures in that perception are inherent in any judicial power. Not only implicit, but they are necessarily inherent in any judicial power. A meaningful judicial power must include the possibility of taking interim measures. Therefore, express provisions as we find them in some treaties or statutes of international courts are basically declarative of the powers of these tribunals and not constitutive of these powers. They are regulative, they show how this particular power is to be exercised, but even if – as is the case in the European Court of Human Rights – the Statute is silent on it, there is an inherent right and I would say an inherent obligation of legal protection to take these measures. I therefore deeply regret the majority decision in the *Cruz Varas* Case and most so the outrageous behaviour of the Swedish government in this matter which flouted the request addressed to it by the Human Rights Commission in a most dramatic way. To me it is, I must say, a deep scandal that a majority of the Human Rights Court has failed to single out and to condemn that inadmissible behaviour of a government which had accepted the Human Rights Convention. For the idea of inherent powers of the judiciary it could be worthwhile to look also into the case-law of the ICJ. I am referring to the two opinions of the International Court on the effect of the judgments of the ILO or rather the United Nations and the ILO Administrative Tribunals. There the question was raised whether these were genuine judicial decisions and the International Court has said in these opinions, especially in the first one relating to the United Nations Tribunal, that by its very essence judicial decisions are binding, that the concept itself implies that when there is a court it must be independent and its decisions must be binding on everybody. By necessity judicial decisions are binding, and if I consider the interim measures to be only a provisional anticipation of what might be the final outcome of a court's decision, I think that whatever is said or left unsaid in the different statutes the interim measures must be binding on everybody.

von Mangoldt: Mr. Chairman, like the previous speaker I am in a somewhat awkward position when commenting on the question whether it is possible to generally derive jurisdiction to issue temporary orders as an inherent power from general principles of law or something comparable. In my opinion, this problem is closely connected with others, also on the agenda, especially with the question whether there are specific procedural rules rendering temporary orders compulsory; the only alternative construction for coming to such binding force, its foundation on substantive law, the law to be applied in the matter *sub iudice*, is obviously inconceivable.

Let me first take up the general principles approach, the idea of determining international law rules by means of comparative law. In my opinion, the presentation of Mr. Advocate-General *Jacobs*, at least with regard to the question of suspensive effect of interim measures of protection, clearly indicated fundamental differences between German and French conception: The more judicial control aims at a preservation of objective legality, the less temporary orders (with suspensive effect) are available; the more the protection of individual rights, however, is aimed at, the more interim measures with suspensive effect may be obtained in favour of the person concerned.

If the protection of human rights above all has to be conceived with a view to guaranteeing the rights of the individual directly concerned, as Prof. *Bernhardt* suggested, and if the question of a suspensive effect of interim measures is considered in terms of effectivity of the individual's petition (taking effectivity as a principal guideline for judicial control, as has been reported from the jurisprudence of the German Federal Constitutional Court with its concept of effective judicial protection), this may indeed open ways and means of protection, even of wishes which may have been expressed by the European Commission of Human Rights in the course of its own proceedings. On the other hand, it has to be recognized with regard to international litigation, especially in the case of protection of human rights, that applications may be brought in by States and that such applications may not so much aim at the protection of any given individual, but may ask for judicial control of objective situations, as in the Greek case after the military *coup d'état*.

The persuasiveness of the idea of effectivity, underlying the concept of interim measures with mandatory suspensive effect, is reduced even more if it is taken into consideration that there are many means of frustrating international adjudication, and thus the idea of effectivity in international litigation, with no effective remedy at hand; let me just point to the contention that an award was null and void as the ultimate technique of escaping from international obligations. As long as in international adjudication, in contrast to national adjudication, effectivity of judicial protection has not been recognized and realized as a principal guideline for the organization of judicial proceedings, it does not necessarily seem to be convincing that, because of effectivity of judicial proceedings, the possibility of indicating interim measures should be considered an implied power of every international court or tribunal. And it seems to me even less convincing if the implied powers approach is taken in order to defend the proposition that in international litigation interim measures should be considered to be mandatory, as long as treaty-practice of States continues to provide for examples in which the use of the term "to indicate" in connection with interim measures obviously is meant to make it clear that temporary orders should not be vested with any specific procedural binding force. If so cautious an approach is taken, an interrelationship with the problem of disputed jurisdiction becomes obvious: Even though a decision without jurisdiction to the merits would constitute intervention into the exclusive jurisdiction of the parties concerned, courts and tribunals may be allowed to show much more reluctance in positively ruling upon their own jurisdiction before making temporary orders if such orders are only recommendatory, not having any specific procedural binding force.

Golsong: At this point of the discussion I would like to refer only to the issue of the existence of a general principle of law which empowers any international court of law to order with binding effect provisional measures of protection. Mr. *Pescatore* has submitted that such a principle is presently covered by Art. 38 of the ICJ Statute as a general principle of law; he has further stressed that one could infer such a principle from comparison of existing domestic legal systems.

It is with regret that I must say I cannot share the opinion of Mr. *Pescatore*.

First of all, international tribunals are not operating within a fully structured legal system comparable to a domestic legal order. They exercise what is clearly a specifically assigned jurisdictional power, mostly if not always assigned to them by virtue of an international treaty. If the treaty does not provide for a power to order provisional measures of protection with binding effect, then there is no such power given.

Even the ICJ Statute does not recognize that such power would exist as a general principle of law. If it were so, there would not have been any need to insert Art. 41 in that instrument. There are a number of other international tribunals which do not have the assigned power of ordering provisional measures and for which no one would recognize the existence of a similar implied power. This observation is also valid for international arbitration panels.

In matters of jurisdictional power, we have to respect the clear meaning of the underlying statute. This is also true for the ECHR and its decision-making bodies. There is no inherent power to order provisional measures, even not inherent in Art. 25 of the Convention. If the Contracting States had envisaged such power, they would have said so explicitly in the Convention. It should be noted in this connection that the Statute of the ICJ has served as the guideline for the institutional part of the Convention. The fact that even a provision like Art. 41 of the ICJ Statute was not inserted in the Convention seems to me sufficient proof of the will of the Contracting Parties *not* to grant the Commission and the Court such a power on provisional matters. I therefore subscribe fully to the opinion of the majority in the *Cruz Varas* judgment of the European Court.

Hailbronner: I would like to add some brief thoughts on the efficiency of legal redress. As far as the efficient protection of individual rights by judicial remedy from violations by the State is concerned, it appears problematical to me to draw conclusions from national law for public international law. It is a basic principle in national law that public interest in enforcement must give way to an examination of the decision, if rights of the individual are in danger of permanent injury. This is – with differences as to details – the uniform state of law in Western European States. But even before the courts this does no longer hold uniformly true, and has, therefore, to be taken into account when transferring rules which were developed in national law to an examination of procedures in public international law. In applying the principle of due process one therefore has to bear in mind that a changeover from quantity to quality is taking place. As a rule there has already been a national examination; the balancing of interests, which lies at the core of the due process principle, has already taken place. By giving the injured the right of effective redress at the hands of national authorities, Art. 13 ECHR is based on this notion, too. The basic conditions are therefore different, when the Commission and the Court are called upon to adjudicate over possible violations of the ECHR by the State.

Furthermore, I would like to pursue another related idea concerning the question of a binding effect of the Commission's Orders which in itself is closely linked to the problem of effective legal redress. One could argue that an effective protection of individual rights is only possible if any execution is stayed before the Commission's decision. Bearing in mind the *Cruz Varas* Case one has to take into account that the individual case must not be the only relevant factor in the weighing of interests. If I may exaggerate a little, the whole system of the ECHR could only function so far because barely ten per cent of all lawyers in Western Europe know the difference between the Luxembourg Court and the Strasbourg Court. If a larger number of lawyers had better knowledge of the decisions rendered by the European Commission of Human Rights and the European Court a serious problem would be posed concerning the limited amount of international protection of human rights available. Furthermore, the numbers given by Mr. *Bernhardt* are sufficient proof that even now the call on Strasbourg is comparatively common.

Taking a look at the group of cases concerned by *Cruz Varas*, namely foreigners who are concerned by immigration law measures, one has to bear in mind the consequences if the criteria mentioned by Mr. *Bernhardt* were used in every day immigration procedures. He introduced the notion that one should refrain from any action which would void a subsequent coming into effect of Court decisions. The most important pattern of cases falling under this rule would be cases of *refoulement* on the one hand and repatriation measures, like deportation, expulsion and extradition on the other. However, the Court has not yet ruled whether this applies to the refusal of entrance, though every day procedure treats it that way. The assumption of an application of the *refoulement* interdiction in Art. 3 ECHR to cases of a turnback at the border is currently predominant, too. In practice this means that persons who claim to have been the victims of torture in their respective countries of origin could demand a preliminary entrance permit as well as a residence permit until the end of the ECHR procedure; permanent injury could not be excluded in case of their dismissal in any event. Therefore, the Commission might as a rule not only be entitled but may be even obligated to suspend planned state measures of execution to protect the effective enjoyment of ECHR rights (bearing in mind the idea of effective legal redress). This would lead to a large number of potential cases with subsequent suspensory effect which often comes next after national measures with suspensory effect. A last remark in this direction: there are good reasons to disagree with the points made by the majority in *Cruz Varas*; if one does align with the minority opinion it would at least be necessary to introduce a modifying element and include national interests of enforcement in the weighing of interests on the international level or in the decision-making process of the Commission or the Court. At the same time, the possibility of generalization of those cases, i.e. the effects of the individual decision on a larger number of similar cases, has to be taken account of. It should not only be the individual case which comes into focus. A binding effect of provisional orders could, therefore, only be advocated if an overbearing possibility indicates a violation of ECHR rights in the execution of a national measure.

Herdegen: Mr. Chairman, I should like to touch again upon the question whether interim measures of protection flow from a kind of "inherent power". In my opinion, there is no general principle of law that could establish such a power. The actual practice in international litigation, even having regard to new trends in international arbitration, does not support a sufficiently close connection between the jurisdiction on the merits of a case and interim measures. In this respect I would follow the restrictive view formulated by Mr. *Golsong*. I would go even further and deny, as a matter of principle, the possibility to define jurisdictional competences in disputes between States on the basis of general principles of law. In this context, only international agreements or customary law can be relied upon for the establishment or delimitation of judicial (or quasi-judicial) competences. General principles of law do not offer a proper basis for definig the subjection of States under the jurisdiction of international institutions. Moreover, the general rules on the interpretation of international agreements bar the presumption that States, by submitting themselves to an international forum, automatically consent to juridical intervention into their rights which rests only upon a summary assessment of the facts and the law.

In this context, Mr. *Thirlway* has advocated an interesting substantive rule: i.e. that, once the dispute is pending before the agreed forum, the States concerned should have to refrain from any actions that might aggravate the controversy. It may well be that such a demand finds some support in the present doctrine of international law. However, I do not find such a limitation of the States' freedom of action very persuasive. Why should a State be precluded from exercising territorial rights of use under dispute or from availing itself of other controversial benefits only because these rights or benefits are the object of pending proceedings before an international forum? On the other hand, it seems to be all the more important to enhance the effectivity of explicit norms on interim measures on the level of interpretation. Thus, Art. 41 of the Statute of the ICJ should be construed as vesting the Court with a power to render binding decisions.

Mosler: What I am going to discuss is still related to the question of the so-called "general principle" that the jurisdiction on the merits implies the competence to decide on interim measures. I look at it, however, from the opposite point of view, that is: To what extent a court must ascertain its jurisdiction on the merits in order to assume jurisdiction on indicating or imposing provisional measures.

But before taking up the issue, and without abusing this opportunity to have the floor, Mr. Chairman, I request your permission to express my deep gratitude and great pleasure that my crossing of the 80 years line should have provided the occasion, without any merit of my own, for this impressive and fruitful symposium of colleagues who are experts on the various aspects of international judicial settlement of disputes, and for such profoundly elaborated presentations as we have heard from the three speakers. Recourse to judicial settlement aims at avoiding self-help and excluding force in international relations. The International Law Commission has dealt with the subject under discussion today from the perspective of countermeasures taken in a legal dispute not necessarily pending before a court or tribunal. The problem of interim measures may also find its place in the mosaic of proposals or adopted solutions which will be the achievement, as we hope, of the United Nations Decade of International Law. For the first time in such a context, the resolution of the United Nations General Assembly initiating the Decade urgently recommended States to have resort to the international judiciary and, in particular, the ICJ, as means for the peaceful settlement of disputes.

I would like to raise two points: The first relates to the role of the examination of the jurisdiction on the merits in the proceedings on interim measures, the second to the binding effect of the order imposing such measures. To avoid misunderstanding, let me clarify one matter. The *Aegean* Case has been repeatedly referred to this morning. There was a tendency within the Court to a more thorough examination of the jurisdictional question in the proceedings on the indication of provisional measures against Turkey. The Court did not define this point explicitly but denied the application made by Greece because the circumstances of the case did not require measures of interim protection. In other orders indicating or denying such measures one finds a stereotype sentence which reads approximately as follows: "It is required that the provisions invoked by the applicant appear prima facie to afford a basis on which the jurisdiction of the Court might be founded." On the basis of this formulation the Court coped well with the cases in which it indicated interim measures. In some cases of denying an application it left the question of its prima facie jurisdiction aside because in its view the circumstance of the case did not require provisional measures, whether or not the Court could assume jurisdiction on the merits. As regards the circumstances requiring interim measures, the question must be answered: "Does there exist a danger of irreparable damage?". This is the typical criterion applied to weigh up the situation. Logic requires, in my view, that there first has to be considered prima facie whether or not jurisdiction might exist.

The second point on which I would like to comment is the "general principle" that judicial bodies have an inherent competence to indicate or order provisional measures, and that this competence may include their binding effect on the parties. As an example, I recall the elaboration in 1959 of the Rules of Procedure of the European Court of Human Rights. The ECHR was silent on interim measures. One then took the view that an inherent power to "indicate" such measures did exist. The Statute of the ICJ and the term "indicate" in Art. 41 was taken as a model. I remember that the approach of the Strasbourg Court to the questions of structure and procedure was at that time to make use, as far as possible, of the Statute and Rules of the Hague Court. Accordingly, the European Court of Human Rights considered itself – despite its character of protecting human and individual rights, and despite its close interconnection with the national law of the Member States – as an international court set up by an international treaty. There existed already some precedents in international treaties to the effect that interim measures were binding, for instance in the Geneva General Act for the Pacific Settlement of International Disputes of 1928. The Rules of Procedure of the European Court of Human Rights followed the language of the Statute of the ICJ which did not explicitly include the binding force, and thus left it to development through interpretation. There are examples of provisions which show that meanwhile the view that orders are binding has made progress, for instance, if I remember correctly, in the Rules of the Iran-United States Claims Tribunal and the Uncitral Rules.

The answer to the question if and with what force a court or tribunal has an interim jurisdiction depends, as the case may be, on the legal character of the judicial institution, or on the subject-matter, or on the recognition of jurisdiction, or on its compulsory character. This morning, Advocate-General *Jacobs* explained various situations, particularly interesting because the European Court of Justice is organized as two instances, because of its jurisdiction on individual rights, and because of its direct interference with national legal systems.

The arguments in favour of the binding effect of orders of courts and tribunals competent to "indicate" interim measures have considerably increased. One of the main reasons for the obligations of the parties to comply with such orders remains – as already has been put forward in the discussion – the fact that these measures form part of judicial proceedings, and that this phase should be treated in the same way as the phase relating to the merits and the judgment. The obligations in the preliminary phase cannot be less than those in the other phases. All this is not cogently convincing, but it strengthens the argumentation in favour of the binding effect.

Delbrück: Following your line of argument, Mr. *Mosler*, would it not then be necessary to distinguish between international judicial institutions proper and those bodies which are more of a conciliatory type like the Human Rights Commission or the UNESCO Committee on Recommendations? The enforcement procedures before these conciliatory committees are designed to win the cooperation of the "indicted" states. Now, if one would go about ordering binding interim measures when a new complaint has been lodged with the competent commission or committee, this could actually frustrate the substantive goal of the proceedings just beginning, that is to induce the respondent State to cooperate with the committee or commission in order to end the human rights violation at issue. Thus, I am in full agreement with your argument with regard to the international judicial bodies proper. But I should then want to draw a clear line between those judicial bodies and the quasi judicial or conciliatory institutions.

Mosler: I share your opinion to distinguish judicial proceedings in the proper sense from quasi judicial or other forms of interference or settlement.

Zemanek: I am now tempted to comment on the point presently under discussion, although I wish to address myself primarily to another point.

To deduce that a tribunal must necessarily possess certain powers because it is called a "tribunal", seems a circular argument. This is because before calling a "tribunal" one would have to show that it possesses the very powers which are now deduced from the term. In other words: it is faulty logic to deduce from a term the necessity of certain conditions which would have to exist before the term could be properly applied.

Be that as it may, I wanted to address myself to Mr. *Thirlway's* interesting proposition that the jurisdiction of the ICJ for provisional measures is independent of its jurisdiction on merits. If I understood him correctly, he submitted that whereas the jurisdiction on the merits depends on the consent of the parties, expressed in one or other of the forms enumerated in Art. 36

of the Statute, jurisdiction for provisional measures originates from ratifying the Statute. This brought a hypothetical case to my mind, which has puzzled me for some time.

On 23 October 1992 Hungary, wishing to institute proceedings against the Czech and Slovak Federal Republic in respect of the Gabcikovo-Nagymaros Barrage System, submitted an application to the ICJ. In the absence of a declaration under Art. 36 (2) of the Statute by the CSFR, no prima facie jurisdiction of the Court was claimed by Hungary, but the hope was expressed that the CSFR might consent to the proceedings in this particular case (*forum prorogatum*).

If I follow Mr. *Thirlway's* proposition, the Court would, in spite of the obvious lack of jurisdiction on the merits at this instant, have had jurisdiction to prescribe provisional measures, had Hungary requested them. That seems somewhat absurd. What would happen if the CSFR did not agree to the proceedings on the merits? Would the "provisional measures" then stand forever?

Klein: The first question is whether the anticipated outcome of the main proceeding should influence the result of provisional measures proceedings. The accepted wisdom is that a court should not allow the anticipated outcome of the main action to affect the provisional proceedings unless the outcome of the main action is evident. In practice, it is difficult for a court to divorce the decision on provisional measures from the main action.

In some cases provisional rulings even necessarily anticipate the outcome of the main action. Here the courts have no choice but to consider the issues presented by the main action in the provisional proceedings. This approach is particularly appropriate when the provisional measure will have a legitimizing effect that continues after the measure's lapse. Although to my knowledge, no international court has rendered a decision on this point, a recent decision by the German Federal Constitutional Court is illustrative. The case involved the Federal Election Act's application to the first all-German elections. In granting provisional relief, the Court held that the provisional order's effect would continue regardless of the main action's outcome. As it turned out, since the election was held before the main action was resolved, the provisional order controlled the election and had far greater impact than usual provisional orders do normally. A dissenting judge argued that the Court should have explicitly considered the outcome of the main issue in granting provisional relief. I believe that the majority did in fact anticipate the outcome of the main action, but I think that they should have done so explicitly.

The second point that I wish to discuss involves the interaction between procedural law and substantive law. Prof. *Bernhardt* has illustrated this interaction in his discussion of the *Soering* Case. Substantive guarantees provided by the ECHR may be violated when a contracting State permits a State not bound by the Convention to interfere with an individual's rights. Any provisional measure made to prevent harm occuring will thus at the same time require to be extended accordingly. I think that this result is absolutely correct and logical. The scope of the provisional measures should follow the scope of the protection, especially when the provisional measures have a binding character.

The third and last point involves a question that to my recollection has not been discussed before. How much discretion should courts have regarding the imposition of provisional measures? The relevant legal norms state that courts "may" or "can" or "shall have the power" to impose provisional measures. These norms may provide courts with the jurisdictional basis for imposing provisional measures, but they may also grant a discretionary power to the courts to impose such measures. Probably both interpretations could be correct. Unfortunately, there is little authority on the point. My sense is that such norms at any rate do not grant an unlimited discretion, since each legal instance will cover but one legally-determined discretion. Yet such a question may be a merely theoretical one, since the courts we are speaking about are not under the authority of a higher court. There is, however, one particular control concerning the ICJ. The Court may indicate provisional measures when it fears that the Security Council will otherwise assume jurisdiction and impose a political solution on a dispute. There is overlapping jurisdiction between the Security Council and the Court that has its impact even on the field of provisional measures.

Stein: I would like to address a problem which crossed my mind when Prof. *Bernhardt* in his report mentioned the *Soering* Case and the question whether there was an obligation to extradite under the existing treaty or not. A problem, which may not be a very frequent one in practice, could arise if an international court is asked to order interim measures in a given legal context, and that order might find itself in contradiction to an obligation which stems from a different legal context, the latter not falling as such entirely under the jurisdiction of that international court.

For example, an older extradition treaty might require extradition under certain circumstances without enabling the requested State to make extradition in the case of imminent capital punishment dependent upon assurances by the requesting State that the death penalty will not be carried out. Could, for example, the Court in Strasbourg by interim measure prevent a State party to the ECHR from extraditing the requested person and thus require that State to violate the extradition treaty, at least for some time? Could the Court of Justice of the European Communities in Luxembourg order interim measures which would prevent a Member State from fulfilling its obligations under a treaty with a third State, a treaty which remains valid under Art. 234 of the EEC Treaty and which might recently have been confirmed by the EEC Commission?

In both cases the Courts have jurisdiction over the obligations of Member States under the Human Rights Convention and the EEC Treaty, but they do not have, at least not exclusive, jurisdiction over the validity, applicability or interpretation of a treaty which links Member States to third States.

The situation is different if a national court gives precedence to the Human Rights Convention over a bilateral extradition treaty *within its own national legal order*, as the Swiss Federal Court did some years ago.

And the situation is different if the ICJ rules that an interim measure may not be ordered after the Security Council has taken a decision under Chapter VII of the UN Charter which runs counter to the requested interim measure, as in the *Lockerbie* Case; the hierarchy of contradicting legal obligations is here clearly fixed by Art. 103 of the UN Charter. But neither the Court in Strasbourg nor the Court in Luxembourg have the power to give "their" conventions precedence over other international treaties.

The problem is, of course, very similar for the main action, if obligations under the Convention and other international treaties are in conflict. But the final judgments in the main action of both the Strasbourg and Luxembourg Courts are *declaratory* judgments, leaving it to the Member States to solve the problem of conflicting international obligations, in the same way as they leave it to the Member States to amend national legislation which has been found to be in violation of the Convention or the EEC Treaty. Interim orders, however, require immediate and absolute obedience, and they are the result of only summary proceedings.

One could perhaps argue that an interim order prevents a State only for a certain period of time from living up to its treaty obligations *vis à vis* a third State, but there may be circumstances under which even an only belated fulfilment of treaty obligations could be unacceptable for the third State.

I am inclined to say that an international court may *not* order interim measures which would bring the State concerned into conflict with another of its international obligations, if those other obligations do not fall under the jurisdiction of that international court, but I am not entirely sure in this respect and would be grateful to hear the opinion of the panelists on that question.

Partsch: I would like to address a question to Mr. *Bernhardt* concerning the practice of the American Human Rights Court to admit an application for preliminary measures before a substantial claim has been submitted. This has the advantage of inducing the claimant eventually to abstain from submitting the substantial claim if he has no success with his request for a preliminary order.

My question is whether the claimant or petitioner is obliged to present his arguments concerning his substantial claim in order to have his request for a preliminary measure admitted or whether it is sufficient to affirm the urgency of his request.

The Court may be in a difficult situation in view of the possibility that the reasons for urgency may under certain circumstances change even in the period between the pronouncement of the decision and its delivery in written form.

Sir Ian Sinclair: I shall endeavour to be brief. I am very tempted to take up and comment on the points made by Mr. *Stein*, but that was in fact not the reason why I asked for the floor. It was really simple to express the view that, despite all that has been said this afternoon and what has been said this morning by various speakers, I am personally not convinced that there is a general principle of law which sustains the idea that any international tribunal has an inherent power to order interim measures of protection or provisional measures whatever you may designate them. It seems to me from studying the various provisions that are made in the constituent instruments governing the jurisdiction and functioning of these tribunals, that the power to indicate interim measures is an attributed power, a power given in the constituent instrument, and it cannot be and is not a derived power from some extra-statutory general principle of law. At least I do not believe that that case is proven. And the other general thought that occurred me having heard our various speakers this morning is that in fact, if you look at the three institutions which we have been discussing in the course of today, the power of the International Court to indicate interim measures, the power of the European Court of Justice so to do and the power of the European Court of Human Rights to indicate interim measures, you will see that the functions of these courts are quite different, and that in fact different considerations arise in considering the conditions under which interim measures may be actually ordered or indicated in any particular instance. In the case of the International Court, the one with which I am perhaps most familiar, there clearly is in many cases a basic question of jurisdiction to hear the merits which may arise and therefore the question of the link between the actual power to indicate interim measures and the question of jurisdiction on the merits is a very close one. And we know from what Prof. *Mosler* has so rightly said this morning that the Court has on a number of occasions considered this and has worked out some kind of a threshold formular which has worked relatively satisfactorily, at least since the mid-1970s. The threshold point at which the Court will be prepared to indicate interim measures, other considerations being equal, is where the Court is satisfied that there is a prima facie case for it to be able to exercise jurisdiction etc. etc. etc. This does not arise, as far as I can judge, in the context of the other Courts that we have been discussing this morning. In the case of the European Court of Justice, of course, there is, because of the very nature of the body, and the interaction between national systems of law and the Community legal order, a quite different and quite distinct perspective. In the case of the European Court of Human Rights, as Prof. *Bernhardt* rightly said, its main function is the protection of the individual. I recognize and acknowledge that in the cases of the functioning of the European Court of Human Rights, there are certain types of cases particularly involving asylum, deportation etc. where there may be a felt necessity to try to persuade a State to withhold action pending the outcome of the proceedings on the merits. But I do not see that Art. 25 of the ECHR in and by itself provides a sufficient basis for the actual ordering of interim measures as such. It may be that it could provide a basis for an appeal to the State concerned to withhold action. In the particular case which has been referred to, I do not know whether I would be on the side of the majority or the minority. I suspect I would be on the side of the majority, but I very much regret the fact that Sweden did not comply with a request from the Court in that particular case. But this, again, is a question of particular circumstances. I am certainly not in a position to make any judgment, not having read the case in detail.

Macdonald: A question for Mr. *Thirlway*, if I may, Mr. Chairman. I am not sure whether it fits in exactly under the two headings that we are considering at the moment, but since this subject has been alluded to by one of the earlier speakers, I thought that it would be right to put it on the floor and perhaps ask Mr. *Thirlway* if he could respond at the appropriate time. And the question really goes to the second set of considerations in the *Lockerbie* or the *Libyan* Case and that is of course the question of the relationship between the Court and the Security Council. It seems to me, Mr. Chairman, that this is going to be an extremely important question in the year just ahead especially with so many suggestions as to improvements or reforms of the United Nations in the near future. And I am wondering whether the reasoning that we find in the majority judgment particularly gives us very much to go on insofar as relating the interim measures or the interim measures provision with this question of delineating the respective spheres of these two parties. So I just put this matter before you and ask if we could have some discussion on that at the appropriate point.

Seidl-Hohenveldern: I would like to contribute my experience as arbitrator in international commercial arbitration to the debate on the ICJ's implied powers to indicate interim measures. The common denominator appears to be that neither the ICJ nor commercial arbitral tribunals command any effective power to enforce such measures. Both, however, have an implied power to indicate such measures, as this term is understood by *Sir Ian Sinclair*, i.e. to draw the attention of the parties to the possibilitiy of adopting an attitude capable of preventing a worsening of the situation during the proceedings. Such a recommendation appears so obviously desirable that the power to "indicate" such measures appears to be implied in the task of any adjudicatory organ, be it the ICJ or a modest commercial arbitral tribunal.

Bos: Mr. Chairman, one very short question to Mr. *Thirlway*. I have listened with great interest to his lecture this morning. In view of the time, I merely ask a question and I do not try to answer it myself. Is there any possibility of internal appeal before the ICJ on provisional measures that have been indicated? Can a party come back to the subject in the course of the proceedings, even on the merits, and express the wish for it to be discussed again? If that is a possibility, I would have another view of the binding force of provisional measures.

Thirlway: Thank you, Mr. Chairman. Rather than trying to make a general statement in answer or to sum up, if I might just give my reactions to one or two observations that have been made in the course of the debate, in the hope of stimulating further discussion. May I also make one disclaimer beforehand: many of the speeches have been made in German, and I have been following the interpretation, which, however competent, always puts a glass wall between oneself and the speaker. It is possible that I may not have fully grasped a speaker's point. If that appears to be the case, I hope that perhaps somebody who is more bilingual than I will put the point again in English. Now it would perhaps be simplest if I could work backwards, and take up some of the more recent observations.

First of all, the extremely interesting point just made by Mr. *Zemanek* about the recent proceedings brought by Application by Hungary against Czechoslovakia. That Application has not been published because the Rules (Art. 38, para.5) do not allow it at this stage. The Application does in fact contain a sentence hinting at the possibility of a request for provisional measures, and so this matter has been considered, not by the Court but at Registry level. For my own part, I see no difficulty in the Court having at this moment power to receive and examine a request for provisional measures from Hungary, the only point being that it is necessarily doomed to disappointment because there is admittedly no jurisdiction on the merits. I would still maintain the distinction between the two sorts of jurisdiction on the basis that the Court in this case does have jurisdiction to deal with a request for provisional measures, and theoretically to indicate such measures. When there is admittedly no jurisdiction to deal with the merits, then whether you call this fact a "circumstance" or simply a "preliminary issue" as suggested by Judge *Mosler*, it is so fatal an objection that the matter is foredoomed.

Turning now to the point raised by Prof. *Macdonald* on the *Lockerbie* Case and the relationship between the Court and the Security Council: Prof. *Macdonald* was kind enough to warn me during the lunch hour that he was proposing to put this point, so I had time to do a little homework! I would like if I may to read one sentence from the separate opinion of Judge *Shahabuddeen* in that case which I think puts the decision of the Court in the clearest and shortest terms:

"In this case, it happens that the decision which the Court is asked to give is one which would directly conflict with a decision of the Security Council. That is not an aspect which can be overlooked. Yet it is not the juridical ground of today's Order. This results not from any collision between the competence of the Security Council and that of the Court, but from a collision between the obligations of Libya under the decision of the Security Council and any obligations which it may have under the Montreal Convention".

That I think sums up the essence of the Court's decision; and the result is that the answer to Judge *Macdonald's* question is that the Court's Order gives no help at all on the basic question of the conflict or possible conflict between the competences of the Court and of the Security Council, conflict which can arise, of course, not only at the provisional measures stage but at the merits stage of any case; in fact the matter has already been discussed in a number of previous cases, the *Aegean Sea* Case for example.

Now if I might return to the intervention of President *Pescatore*, clearly we differ to a considerable extent on this question of whether the Court has one jurisdiction or two, and on the question of whether there is a general principle of law. There is one difficulty that I see, on which I would be interested to hear further comment: if you hold the theory that there is only a single jurisdiction, basically a merits jurisdiction which embraces a jurisdiction to deliver provisional measures, then what is the theoretical position in a case like *Anglo-Iranian Oil Co.* Case, where measures were indicated, and the court subsequently decided that it had no merits jurisdiction? The conclusion would apparently have to be that there had been no jurisdiction to indicate measures. It seems to me the only way out of the dilemma is to postulate a separate ground of jurisdiction, jurisdiction to indicate provisional measures, which is not dependent on the existence of merits jurisdiction. There may be other ways out; I would be very interested to hear suggestions.

On the question of a general principle of law, authorizing an international tribunal to indicate provisional measures, I think I said this morning that at The Hague the question hardly arises, because the Court has a specific text in the Statute. So the only relevance of the question of a general principle is either the possibility that a general principle overrides the specific text, and I do not think anybody argues that, or that the general principle supplements the specific text. This is a point I tried to bring out this morning in discussing the question of indication of measures designed to prevent aggravation or extension of the dispute, and the question whether the general principle might add to the specific text in the sense of making measures binding when the text itself does not contemplate measures which were binding.

If it is accepted – as I would suggest it should be – that the Statute of the Court was intended to give the Court simply a power of the kind referred to by Prof. *Seidl-Hohenveldern* just now, not a power to compel but simply a power to point out what was desirable, is it possible for a general principle of law to not merely go beyond what was the treaty-law intention of the Statute, but actually to contradict it by giving the Court power to indicate binding measures? I would suggest that that is doubtful.

There was also a suggestion that the dicta of the Court in the Administrative Tribunal cases were of interest. I agree they are, in the sense that they suggest that there are certain aspects of a court which are inherent in the nature of a court, so that if you create a court, you attach to it those powers automatically. That is a view that I myself would find more attractive in this context than the argument based on a general principle of law; it is more a principle of inherency, and possibly even a principle of treaty interpretation. But I would hesitate to follow President *Pescatore* so far as to say that the fact that a judicial decision is necessarily binding, meaning by that a decision on the merits, after hearing both sides, as to what the legal rights of the parties are, necessarily implies the equally binding effect of a decision as to what practical arrangements are desirable on the basis of what the parties' rights are believed to be. I think that possibly is where we part company, and that is all one can say on that.

Mr. Chairman, if I may address an area which is not mine, I was most interested in the discussion of the case before the European Court of Human Rights of the Chilean who was being extradited from Sweden (*Cruz Varas* v. *Sweden*, Series A, Vol.201). Like *Sir Ian Sinclair* I do not know the terms of decision, so I am dependent on what I have heard today but I would like to raise a question on that, on which the experts in the field can perhaps enlighten me. As I understand it, the view of the minority in the Court was that interim measures directing a non-extradition could be based on the Article of the Convention, I think it is Art. 25, which imposes on contradicting States a duty "not to hinder in any way the effective exercise" of the right of individual petition. The difficulty which I see, perhaps naïvely, is this: that duty is a duty which exists independently of any Order of the Court, so that whether or not the Court had made any Order, Sweden would have been bound not to hinder the effective exercise of the right of individual petition, and therefore (arguably) no to extradite the person concerned. But if that is so, is the Court entitled to declare a breach of the Convention at an interim stage without a full hearing and argument? It may be so; but surely the basis for doing so cannot be found in Art. 25. It must lie somewhere behind that provision, so that Art. 25 does not help on the procedural point of whether an interim decision can be taken.

Jacobs: I really have very little to say. I shall again profess my remarks with a disclaimer. Mr. *Thirlway* said that because he was listening through the interpreters he might have missed some of the nuances. I think that because I was not listening through interpreters I may be in the same position. I hope you will forgive me that. But I really think that most of the discussion was not directed to the Court of Justice. I could perhaps just comment on the question of Mr. *Bos* which was directed specifically to the ICJ and which concerns the possibility of varying interim measures. There is a specific procedure in the Luxembourg Court, Art. 87 of the rules, which says on application by a party the order may at any time be varied or cancelled on account of a change in circumstances. And I suspect that even if that provision were not there, the Court might have assumed some power to act in that way. In fact, it is perhaps interesting that in the English system the courts commonly give the parties expressly what is called liberty to apply, where there may be a need for an order to be varied. And I suppose that it is possible that such a right to come back to the Court could be included in the terms of the initial interim order itself. On the more substantive point, I think this was the main point that was raised in the discussion so far as it concerns the Court of Justice, the question whether there is some general principle involved; Judge *Rodríguez Iglesias* pointed out that the case-law of the Court in the *Zuckerfabrik* case does seem to suggest that there is a general principle providing for interim relief, and of course since the provisions are contained in the treaty in very clear and expressed terms, the problem raised in the discussion does not really apply to our Court, although it might perhaps be interesting purely from a speculative point of view to ask the question whether in the absence of those treaty provisions the Court would nevertheless have held that it did have some inherent power to order interim measures. And I think if one looks at the more recent case-law on judicial protection which is a very highly developed body of case-law there is no doubt, at least in the light of that recent case-law, that the Court would have been likely to take that view, but we do not really need to consider that question. But perhaps I could mention a case which has some relevance, though only indirect, and that is a case concerned not with the powers of the Court itself, but with the powers of the Commission, that is the powers of the Commission in competition proceedings, because some years ago a question arose whether the Commission had any inherent powers to order interim measures in competition proceedings. The case arose on a Complaint by a company that another company was abusing a dominant position. The complaint company asked the Commission to protect it, while the Commission proceedings were going on, to prevent it from being driven out of the business which it feared would be the result if the alleged infringement continued. The Commission replied that it had no power to take such measures because under the legislation under which it operated which was a regulation of the Council, Regulation No.17, which lays down the powers of the Commission on the procedures to be followed in competition proceedings, there was no provision for the Commission to take interim measures. So we had really exactly the question whether there was any implied power. The Commission said it had no power, the company appealed to the Court, and in that appeal, the Case *Camera Care* in 1980 I think, the Court held that the Commission must be regarded as having an implied power to take interim measures to protect the position of private parties, because such a power was necessary if the provisions of the Treaty were to have their effect. So the Court has recognized in those circumstances a power of the Commission to adopt interim measures in circumstances which the Court gave some indication of its judgment from which the Commission subsequently spelled out in a practice statement. I do not think we can make any analogy with the position under for example ECHR to argue that the Court of Human Rights might thus have accepted the notion that the European Commission of Human Rights must be regarded as having an implied power to adopt interim measures in the course of proceedings before the Commission. I think the scope here for making analogies is rather limited for the reasons indicated by *Sir Ian Sinclair*. The systems are each governed by their own particular functions and the position in particular I think is very different with a system like the Community system which is a system based on compulsory and automatic jurisdiction. Might one nevertheless at least express the hope that in the course of time as the European Convention becomes a normal feature of our legal systems and as the jurisdiction of the Court and Commission of Human Rights, too, comes to be recognized as tantamount to a form of automatic jurisdiction, that one day the position in the Strasbourg system may follow the Community system.

Thirlway: I would first like to apologize to Prof. *Bos*: I quite forgot to answer the question which he was good enough to address to me personally. In fact, Prof. *Jacobs* has virtually dealt with it by citing the Rules of the European Court, because the Rules of the ICJ contain a very similar provision, Art. 76, para. 1:

> "At the request of a party the Court may, at any time before the final judgment in the case, revoke or modify any decision concerning provisional matters if, in its opinion, some change in the situation justifies such revocation or modification".

In fact the Court has in some cases itself taken the initiative. In the *Fisheries Jurisdiction* Cases, the Orders indicating measures provided that they were to run for a year and then to be re-examined. And they were re-examined.

The only case I can remember where a party did come back and ask for exercise of this power was the *Nicaragua* v. *United States* Case. Nicaragua came back to the Court complaining specifically that the United States had not complied with the measures indicated; but it did not argue that this non-compliance was a breach of an international obligation. It argued that fresh measures should be indicated. The President of the Court replied that at the jurisdictional stage of the proceedings, then in progress, it was not appropriate to go into the matter, and Nicaragua then thought better of it, and the matter was allowed to drop. For myself I find that little incident significant as suggesting that the measures were not regarded as binding, as themselves creative of international obligations.

Bernhardt: The discussion has in my opinion shown, and this is underlined in the contribution by Prof. *Seidl-Hohenveldern,* that there is at least a general principle of law which accords to an international tribunal the competence, implicitly and without any express provision in a treaty, to ask the parties to do or not to do something. Neither the relevant provision in the Rules of the Committee under the International Covenant on Civil and Political Rights nor the provision in the Rules of the European Commission on Human Rights has ever been drawn into doubt. These institutions, and international courts even more so, can ask the parties not to prejudice the result of their future findings.

But I am still not convinced that one cannot go further and find a general principle of law permitting, at least in extreme situations, courts and tribunals to order interim measures with binding effect for the parties. It is clear that at first the relevant conventional text must be consulted and interpreted. Insofar the Statute of the International Court of Justice may raise some doubts. But is it not possible to deduce a general principle of law from national legal systems which give courts the power to intervene when the danger exists that one party takes measures which may be incompatible with the final judgment to be delivered?

But I would not only rely on a general principle of law, but also on the rules of treaty interpretation. This was underlined in the dissenting opinion of the minority in the *Cruz Varas* Case. In this respect, my conclusion is different from that drawn by Mr. *Golsong* and Mr. *Herdegen.* The *travaux préparatoires* are often neither convincing nor decisive. I would instead lay stress on the teleological interpretation, the *effet utile* aspect. If an international convention gives a tribunal or other institution the competence to take binding decisions *vis-à-vis* States, is it not in conformity with the object and purpose of the convention that the tribunal can, by interim measures, prevent the final decision from becoming meaningless or ineffective?

Doehring: Let me add some remarks to those of Mr. *Bernhardt.* I wonder why we should be so reluctant in regard to the existence of a general principle of law under which provisional measures not expressly provided for by the written law should be applicable. We generally accept and presuppose so many principles of procedural law the existence of which no one would deny even if they were not written down in a code. For example, we find the principle of equality of the parties in litigation, and it will also be applied when not expressly provided for. We never would neglect the principle *audiatur et altera pars.* We stress the principle that the parties must be enabled to duly prepare the case. We do not expect a judgment which does not deal with the main arguments of the litigants. We stress the principle of the independence of the judges and their impartiality. We find so many principles of procedural law which everybody will respect as non-written rules too. These rules do not stem from natural law, but from general principles of positive law generally applied in all civilized legal systems. For me the decisive test will always be the question of whether such a principle emanates from the well established national legal systems and developed independently in each system because it is based on the so-called nature of things. To this extent, I would like to deviate somewhat from the opinion of Mr. *Bernhardt*. It is not the *effet utile* but the fact that without the application of such a principle the process would be meaningless, i.e. it is not the question of whether a principle commanding the admissibility of a provisional measure will further the work of the Court, but of whether without this legal possibility the further work of the Court will become meaningless.

Whether this situation will occur depends mainly on the type of the subject matter to be dealt with by the Court. Let me give an example. In former times, we did not have the so-called *Anfechtungsklage* in German law. People had to accept the decision of the public authority and only then the question arose whether a claim for compensation due to a wrongful act would be well founded. But when the action of the administration might produce an irreparable damage, no later compensation can repair that damage. In that case, a legal process against the public authority would become meaningless. For just that reason we introduced the *Anfechtungsklage* long ago. If, for example, a political party would be prevented from participating in an electoral campaign which will end in few days due to the completion of the election, only a provisional measure could be helpful, not a judgment rendered in half a year or even later. That is the reason why I consider that the subject matter to be dealt with by the Court is decisive when one asks whether or not the Court must have the opportunity to order a provisional measure even when not foreseen in the procedural law code.

Frowein: With your permission, Mr. Chairman, I would like to make two brief remarks on the basis of the discussion which we have heard. When we speak of a general principle it is of great importance to realize that we must differentiate between general principles in different jurisdictions and in different contexts. It is difficult to deny, as *Francis Jacobs* implied, that for the European Court of Justice even without a rule one would have accepted an implied power for interim measures. By the way in Germany we had a lengthy discussion on these issues in the Weimar period, when the then Constitutional Court, the *Staatsgerichtshof für das Deutsche Reich*, had no formal power for interim measures. However, there was a prevailing doctrine that you could imply it. This is quite different on the international level. If one realizes that within the European Convention on Human Rights the States have clearly refrained from giving any power to the Convention organs to quash national decisions this is one argument, I do not say it is the final one, but one argument to be reluctant to imply a full power for binding interim measures. I am fully in line with Mr. *Seidl* that indications in the sense of non-binding measures must be possible. It was unfortunate that the European Court of Human Rights was faced with the *Cruz Varas* Case. As is frequently stated, hard cases make bad law. In *Cruz Varas* already the Commission had been of the opinion, after a comparatively short investigation of the facts, that there could be no violation. At the same time, the Commission had been confronted with another case from Sweden, where Sweden also disregarded the Art. 36 indication. This was the case of *Mansi* where somebody was deported to Jordan. In all likelihood, in fact there was very good evidence for it, Mr. Mansi was tortured in Jordan. This case was immediately settled by Sweden by paying compensation to Mr. Mansi. This would have been a much better case where at least the aggravating circumstance that a State should have acted against a clear indication by the Commission was present. Even if one should come to the conclusion that the indication as such is not binding, the aggravation of a violation by such an attitude or procedure could hardly be denied.

Schiedermair: I would like to follow up on the stimulating remarks made by Mr. *Doehring* and turn the test into a practical one. Do interim measures of protection really form a necessary part of the judicial process, in the same way as the independence and impartiality of judges? That is just the question! Let us consider the case discussed today of the deportation from Sweden, the abuse of human rights as the man was deported to Chile. Can the pronouncement of the European Court of Human Rights prevent that? No: It remains for the Court to determine at liberty, and this is its role, that Sweden is in breach of the Convention on Human Rights as a consequence of the deportation. But the matter appears in a quite different light when Mr. *Bernhardt* states that the protection of human rights and individual recourse to the courts, along the lines of Art. 19 (4), is an inherent part of the Strasbourg judicial process.

I cannot assume that is the case, because that is just the problem: has the judicial process been sufficiently developed under the Convention on Human Rights so that individual recourse necessarily forms a part of the process of adjudication? A clear indication that this is not the case is provided by the very lack of a developed system of interim measures of protection. The procedural law of individual recourse under the Convention on Human Rights provides only limited guarantees. As Mr. *Herdegen* and others said this morning, and this is a further clear indication of the situation, the Strasbourg Court was created, in the form of an ordinary international court, as a legal instrument in the full implementation of the treaty. Therefore in this regard we cannot rely on an argument which refers to an inherent quality of the process of adjudication: that is precisely the problem. Indeed, as Mr. *Zemanek* indicated, when we operate with arguments based on the essence of the matter and the inherent characteristics of the process of adjudication, we are, I fear, moving rather within the framework of a *petitio principiae*. Thank you very much.

Tomuschat: I would agree with Mr. *Frowein* and Mr. *Schiedermair*. I think there are different standards of fairness: fairness in proceedings between States, and standards of fairness as far as proceedings before national courts are concerned. Those standards are laid down in Art. 6 of the European Convention and in Art. 14 of the International Covenant on Civil and Political Rights. Additionally, as a third group there exist proceedings before international institutions concerning individual rights. Consequently, it should not be assumed that the same solution must apply in all fields. There is a basic difference in particular between proceedings between States and proceedings before national courts, because States can arrange their judicial relationships in the manner they see fit, whereas the individual in national proceedings is subject to the jurisdictional power of the State. Therefore, distinctions must be drawn. What is fair and equitable in national proceedings may not be fair and equitable in proceedings between States.

Let me just move on to a second point. Prof. *Mosler* has already raised it. He said that there is a relationship between the binding character of provisional measures and the right to take reprisals. To the extent that the binding character of such provisional measures is affirmed, the right of States to take reprisals in defense of their rights or alleged rights may be curtailed or should be restricted. But if they constitute no more than recommendations or indications, then probably States cannot be denied the right to take reprisals or countermeasures, as the modern terminology runs, in defense of their rights. This is presently being discussed in the International Law Commission. According to the rapporteur Arangio-Ruiz, any procedure of peaceful settlement of disputes would exclude the possibility to take reprisals. This limitation goes much too far. In particular, since it would also exclude the right of countermeasures in cases where only diplomatic negotiations are available, the wrongdoer would clearly be favoured and the affected State would be put in a very bad position indeed. The only situation where one can and must reflect on whether the right to take countermeasures should be excluded is when parties have access to an international institution for the settlement of disputes, to the extent that the institution does indeed have the power to take countermeasures unilaterally; the parties should rely on the authority of the international body to make appropriate orders.

But if that power does not exist, States should remain free to protect their rights as they see fit, of course without resorting to measures which are prohibited under Art. 2 para. 4 of the United Nations Charter. Thank you.

Rodríguez Iglesias: I want to take up the question put by the Advocate-General *Jacobs* as to whether the Court could have founded its own jurisdiction to grant interim measures on a general principle if there were no basis in the Treaty. I very much agree with Prof. *Tomuschat* and all the previous speakers that there are very important differences between proceedings between States, which are more in the nature of international proceedings, and proceedings in which you have to protect the rights of individuals. It seems to me quite certain that the Court of Justice would have affirmed its jurisdiction to grant interim measures in proceedings where the rights of individuals were in question. And, at the end of the day, that is what it did for the national courts in *Factortame* and in *Zuckerfabrik*. But it appears doubtful whether it would have affirmed its jurisdiction to grant interim measures in infringement proceedings. I think that, in the absence of any basis in the Treaty, this would be a sort of enlargement of its own power to order interim measures against the States which it would have been very difficult to base on a general principle.

The other point I would like to make concerns the invitation of Mr. *Thirlway* to take a position on the distinction or the relation between jurisdiction on the merits and jurisdiction to grant interim measures. I disagree with him. I agree with Prof. *Pescatore* that both jurisdictions are one and the same thing. I would put it very simply: If a case comes before a court, and that court has jurisdiction on the merits, then it has jurisdiction to grant interim relief. If it clearly does not have jurisdiction on the merits, then neither does it have jurisdiction to grant interim relief. The problem arises only where the jurisdiction on the merits is doubtful. But then, just as it must have a sort of provisional jurisdiction to determine whether it has jurisdiction on the merits as a preliminary issue, it also has a provisional jurisdiction to grant interim measures. That is the way I would put it. Thank you.

Puente Egido: My intention was not to take part in the debate but simply to listen. However, I have decided to say something because it is my impression that we are labouring under a certain amount of conceptual confusion. The very notion of precautionary measures may have many applications, so that if we map out the necessary distinctions we will be able to talk about different categories of precautionary measures.

First of all, I would like to say that the idea of closely linking the competence over the adoption of precautionary measures by a court to the competence over the central issue exercised by the same court seems inexact to me. If we look at the techniques of private international law, we can see that it is a generally accepted practice in different conflicting systems for a court to have the competence to adopt precautionary measures in a matter on whose central issue the said court clearly lacks the competence to rule from the outset. Among precautionary measures, these can be considered protective or security measures. An example taken from Spanish law of Conflict can serve as an illustration. It is Art. 33 of the former Royal Decree on Aliens, promulgated in the last century. According to this article, Spanish courts are competent both in civil and criminal law to adopt precautionary measures "should it be necessary to prevent fraud or adopt urgent provisional measures in order to detain a debtor who may try to abscond with the intention of evading his debts, or to act as temporary guardian for a person of unsound mind or similar cases."

The *Soering* Case has already been mentioned by previous speakers. In fact, an important part of the judicial acts involved in extradition proceedings by the different States can be seen as precautionary measures since, if no State surrenders any of its own offenders, there is clearly a lack of jurisdiction on the part of the courts of the surrendering State to give a ruling on the central issue, regarding the imputed crimes which constitute the basis of the request for extradition by the requesting State. This, therefore, means that courts which in principle lack jurisdiction over the central issue are nevertheless competent to adopt decisions which to a large extent can be called precautionary measures.

Mention has previously been made of the general rules of international law and of the possibility of implicitly deducing from them powers for the adoption of precautionary measures. Having consulted and analysed the decisions of the two international courts of The Hague, I believe that it is impossible to conclude that in these decisions precautionary powers are necessarily linked to the powers of the court over the central issue. The question has been raised in separate votes and dissenting opinions, but not in the decisions themselves. That is, the Court of The Hague may or may not have adopted precautionary measures, but it has not linked these obligatorily to powers over the central issue. This is not to deny the problem that competence over precautionary matters may be exercised, outside a strictly conventional framework, and therefore be deduced from general rules of international law.

It is in this sense that the *Soering* Case, tested before the European Court of Human Rights, seems to me to be of interest. The risk that, if Soering had been surrendered by Great Britain to the United States, he would have suffered the death penalty was not a determinig factor. The decisive factor was the degrading and inhuman treatment, contrary to Art. 3 of the European Convention, that Soering was likely to have undergone if he had been surrendered. The infringement of the Convention's obligations was to be found in the long period of appeals before American courts (eight to ten years) that Soering would have faced in order to avoid execution if he had been sentenced to death, as was probable. In so doing, the Court in my opinion made a decision laden with consequences. In ruling that the surrender of Soering by the British authorities to those of the United States in fulfillment of the bilateral extradition treaty between the two States was incompatible with the obligations undertaken by Great Britain as a signatory to the ECHR, it is thus really asserting a rule of *ius cogens*, although only in a regional context. Furthermore, in my opinion, the doctrine of the *Soering* Case leads to the assertion that the criminal jurisdiction of the signatory

States to the European Convention is limited, since this rule of *ius cogens* has modified their original criminal jurisdiction. Thus there also arises the complex question of the effect of the rules derived from this Convention on the obligations and rights springing from a treaty with a third State (in this case the United States) and a signatory State to the European Convention. The precautionary measures adopted by the European Court forbidding the British authorities to surrender until a ruling has been made on the central issue cannot be satisfactorily explained from a strictly conventional point of view. They have to be explained through reference to this norm of *ius cogens* which lies at the basis of the European Court's decision.

Oellers-Frahm: I would like to make a remark concerning the binding force of interim measures which demonstrates the manner in which the different components forming the system of interim protection are intertwined. I have always pleaded for the binding character of interim measures. The main reasons, to give at least some brief explanation, lie in the fact that a State which voluntarily has accepted binding jurisdiction of an international court or tribunal has to accept as equally binding all those steps which the court or tribunal considers necessary in order to reach its judgment. This line of argument almost inevitably leads to the conclusion that international courts and tribunals have an implied power to indicate interim measures even in a case where their statutes do not explicitly provide for such a power.

With regard to the binding force of interim measures I want to come back to a remark made by Mr. *Thirlway* in his report stating that the question of the binding force of interim measures has to be resolved by applying the law of treaties in interpreting the statute of the court or tribunal in question. This procedure, however, in my opinion, necessarily leads to the result that such measures are binding. If we look, for example, at Art. 41 of the Statute of the ICJ we find the term "to indicate" which as we all agree is not unambiguous. The term "indicate" must consequently, according to the opinion of Mr. *Thirlway*, be construed by applying the rules of the law of treaties and by doing this we come, as Prof. *Bernhardt* has already said, to the principle of *effet utile* and that means that in the case of a court with binding jurisdiction we can only reach the conclusion that the interim measures must be binding too.

I think that however we may approach the problem we will reach the conclusion that interim measures are binding and even the argument that this opinion is not backed by a state practice is not convincing. States have likewise not always implemented a binding judgment and as far as I know nobody ever has drawn the conclusion that state practice therefore no longer supports the binding character of judgments. That is why I think that the consequence of the submission to the binding jurisdiction of an international court or tribunal logically implies under all aspects the binding character of provisional measures.

I want to add that to my feeling it seems – to use a term that is perhaps slightly exaggerated – somehow cynical to hear Prof. *Schiedermair's* statement that the European Court of Human Rights was not prevented from giving its judgment in the *Cruz Varas* Case by the fact that the complainant, Mr. Cruz Varas himself, had been extradited. And the Court itself has made a remark going in the same direction by stating that the fact of not respecting the interim measures could be regarded as an aggravating factor in the final judgment. This, however, does not correspond to the primary aim of the ECHR, namely the protection of the individual, and even less to Art. 25 of the Convention. That is why I would like to stress that in my view more reasons plead in favour of the binding force, also of interim measures indicated by the Commission which must be regarded as a part of the global process of binding decision-making of the Court.

Pescatore: Mr. *Thirlway* has a legitimate expectation to have a reply from me on a question he returned to me. He said the following: Interim measures having been taken, what is the way out if the court in the end finds that there was no case? And my reply is that in such a situation it is the court which has the first word and the last word. The first word is the institution of interim measures and the last word is a final decision, and this fits perfectly into my framework, the single framework theory. If in the end the court finds that it even had no jurisdiction at all, it will declare the interim measures terminated and it may add that the provisional measures have been taken nonetheless for a very worthy purpose, which was to keep the way open for the free exercise of its own function without prejudging itself; and that is precisely why the measures are not final but are provisional. I would add that even internationally, we live in a legally structured society and not in a legal jungle, and when I say this I would like to remind you of the case on the *French Nuclear Experiments in the Pacific Area*. If there is a sort of prima facie case to bring to a court, if there is a free access to a court, it is quite natural that interim measures may be taken from the court. So the only conclusion I deduce from all this is that a judge must be extremely cautious when he institutes interim measures. I am among those who have been in the situation of having to decide on interim measures. If you wish to see an example of how to handle these matters I direct you to the *Moratori* Case which was about the construction of a dam in Ethiopia not unlike the Case of the *Bridge over the Belt*, and you will see, that you compare the order on interim measures and the final decision in that case, and you can see how cautious the interim judge was. So I refer you to the collection of the Court's judgments. You can find it under the name Moratori.

Hailbronner: I would like to refer shortly again to *Cruz Varas*. Mr.*Bernhardt*, I am still not convinced. You said there should not be any automatic suspensory effect. On the other hand: everything which was said here leads to exactly this result, at least for the area which we are talking about. Mr.

Frowein has pointed to the *Cruz Varas* decision and to the differences in comparison to another case. In *Cruz Varas* there were no indications for a violation of the Convention in the end. Everything would hinge on the "irreparable damage", i.e. the frustration of theoretically possible individual rights in case of a different outcome of the procedure. If this is the decisive issue for the binding effect of a provisional order, it is difficult to see how the Commission could say "we demand the suspension of a state measure" in one case and yet accept execution before a decision on possible ECHR violations in another. Consequently the suspension of state measures should take place in every case in which the enforcement of possible rights would in fact be irrevocably frustrated in case of execution; in the end, this means suspension as a rule. In my opinion, everything which was said here therefore does not take into account the necessary distinction between mass procedures and a suspension of enforcement in accordance with all aspects of the individual case to the degree which is necessary. Naturally a suspension of this kind can be required and based on a factual need within the ECHR procedure, too. On this point much of what was said relating to the effectiveness of ECHR legal redress convinces me; still I think it is necessary to recognize that a general suspensory procedure can only function if it is used by relatively few. As soon as it is claimed by too many it may not work anymore. In this case there is a substantial danger that we shall have a second procedure of legal redress on the European level in addition to a substantial national procedure, therefore creating serious difficulties in executing national measures.

von Mangoldt: I should like to make a brief comment concerning the effect of temporary orders under Art. 41 of the ICJ Statute. In my opinion, interpretation of this provision should not leave aside the developments which had occured in respect of the same article of the original Statute of the Permanent Court of International Justice, but which did not cause the drafters of the present Statute to provide for changes in the wording of the provision. An important part of this development is the Geneva General Act, formerly in its original, now in its revised version. Art. 33 (1) of the Act, after having referred to the authority of the Court to indicate interim measures under Art. 41 of the Statute, finally states: "The parties to the dispute shall be bound to accept such measures." This gives an answer to the disputed question whether temporary orders of the court were to be binding by explicitly providing for pertinent obligations of the parties concerned. The revised version of the Act follows the same pattern.

There is still another example of dispute with regard to the correct interpretation of a provision of the original Statute, namely Art. 36. In this case however, the drafters of the 1945 Statute showed their willingness for change by departing from the wording of the original Statute of the Permanent Court. Since this has not been done in the case of Art. 41 of the Statute, even though the question of a binding force of temporary orders had been taken up by the Geneva General Act and had been decided in the affirmative, the conclusion can only be that the term "to indicate" (measures) was meant not to include specific procedural binding force of temporary orders which had been added by the pertinent provision of the Geneva General Act.

My second point is closely related to the question which was raised by Prof. *Hailbronner*. The construction of a duty of the State concerned to follow the wishes of the Human Rights Commission in proceedings under Art. 25 of the ECHR not to frustrate the individual's petition, which Prof. *Bernhardt* has suggested in view of the *Cruz Varas* Case, leads me to the question whether the binding nature of such recommendations of the Commission could vary depending on whether the proceedings before the Commission had been initiated by an individual's petition or by State complaint. If not, a construction similar to the one suggested for proceedings upon petition would be indispensable.

My second question in respect of temporary orders under the ECHR goes to Prof. *Bernhardt's* reliance on *effet utile*. Under the Convention there is an alternative to reaching a final decision in a given case, either by applying to the European Court of Human rights or by referring the matter to the Committee of Ministers of the European Council. If the *effet utile*-approach which has been suggested actually starts from the idea of effective protection of substantive rights, this would not only apply in cases of temporary orders to be issued by the Court but also in respect of those which might be considered by the Committee of Ministers. Would you come to this conclusion, Prof. *Bernhardt*?

Bernhardt: I would first like to make a few remarks on the last two contributions to the discussion.

In the *Cruz Varas* Case, the Commission and Court were convinced that at the date when Cruz Varas was expelled the possibility of irreparable damage, namely the danger of torture in Chile, could not be excluded. In respect of interim measures, the situation and the information available at the time of expulsion are decisive. If it later turns out that the danger did in fact not exist, this does not change the legal evaluation.

The question has also been raised whether the Committee of Ministers may have comparable competences under the European Convention. This is in my view not relevant. The question is whether the indication of interim measures by the Commission at the time when a violation of the Convention cannot be excluded is obligatory or not. In order to answer this question, the competences of the Committee of Ministers play no role.

I now come to a more general remark. In my view, it can no longer be disputed that the procedure in Strasbourg mainly serves the protection of individual rights and not primarily any general public interest. This is shown *inter alia*, as Professor *Mosler* has already pointed out, by the position of the applicant in the Strasbourg proceedings; he/she is now considered to be a party even if he/she cannot bring his/her case to the Court. This last remaining defect will be eliminated with Protocol No. 9. Also Art. 50 of the Convention shows that the protection of individual rights is the essential element. States must seek, as far as possible, to remedy the violation of the Convention in favour to the individual concerned; if this is not possible, pecuniary damages must be paid.

Several participants in the discussion have considered the following point: An individual petition to the human rights institutions cannot have the automatic effect that a State cannot take further steps against the individual concerned. The international institution must have the possibility to see provisionally whether it is competent in the case and whether the application is not obviously unfounded. Neither the jurisdiction of the institution and the admissibility of an application nor the possible outcome of the procedure on the merits can entirely be excluded from the consideration whether interim measures should be indicated or not. In this respect, the situation in international human rights cases may be different from the situation in disputes between States or, for example, before the German Federal Constitutional Court.

Another difficult question, which has been raised by Professor *Delbrück*, concerns the fact that the European Commission on Human Rights cannot take binding decisions on the merits. Does this hinder binding interim orders? I am not convinced that the answer is in the affirmative. The procedure before the Commission is part of legal proceedings which can later lead to a binding decision of the European Court, and these proceedings must be seen as a unity. If the Court decision is preceded by proceedings before the Commission, either the Commission itself or the Court (as under the American system) should be able to indicate interim measures with binding force, right from the beginning of the whole procedure. But it should also be clear that the competence can and should be used only in exceptional cases.

Thirlway: Very briefly, because I have had a look at the clock, I would like to comment, if I may, particularly on the remarks made by Dr. *Oellers*, because I know that she is very much an expert in this field, and I therefore listened to her with some trepidation. We differ over the question of the binding element of provisional measures, and I was struck by her suggestion that States which freely agree to recognize the binding force of a future judgment must accept the "steps leading up to the decision" as equally binding. I think possibly the question on which we differ is: What are the steps leading up to the decision? I am myself not satisfied that this category covers provisional measures; but it does cover, for example, the point which I think was referred to by Prof. *Rodríguez Iglesias*, the determination of the court's own jurisdiction. There must be a possibility of a binding decision on jurisdiction even if Art. 36, para. 6, of the Statute were not there; but I would distinguish that requirement from Art. 41 of the Statute.

I was challenged, I think, on my argument that if provisional measures are binding, they must be so only on a basis of treaty law. I would stand by that, and I would rather doubt the force of the *effet utile* argument as applied to the International Court, whatever its value may be in the Human Rights Court. Has the International Court not shown that even without a power clearly to indicate binding measures of protection its operations are satisfactory? If so, may we not conclude that the *effet* is not *utile*? Furthermore, the Vienna Convention recognizes the relevance of State practice in interpretation, just as much as that of the *effet utile*. Dr. *Oellers* pointed out that the fact that States do not comply with judgments does not mean that they are not binding. I entirely agree on that, but I think of the fact that States, whether or not they comply with provisional measures, have not in their practice acted as though they believed such measures were binding. Even more significant, and this is a point I did not have time to go into this morning, is the fact that the Court itself has not acted as though it believed provisional measures to be binding. I know a number of examples, with which I am sure Dr. *Oellers* is acquainted, but we have not time to go into them now.

I would entirely agree with President *Pescatore* that this is a field in which the judge must be cautious, and I am not suggesting that a State is free to ignore provisional measures. As I think I said earlier, a decision indicating measures is a decision which has to be complied with to the extent that the State must take very careful account of those measures, and , on the lines indicated bei Prof. *Seidl-Hohenveldern*, consider whether they should not be complied with; but the State remains free to depart from them without being in breach of a judicial decision. That is the position which I have been trying to defend. Mr. Chairman, I think that is all I wish to say, thank you very much.

Jacobs: I just have two remarks to make, first of all I would like to return to the question of the distinction in the context of the Community Court between cases involving individuals and cases involving member States. I am not convinced that such a distinction is very fruitful. As regards the powers of the Court to order interim measures against member States, I think it is interesting to know that this is precisely the area in which the Court can be said to have innovated, because it has held that in the final judgment it can only make a declaration against the State. So there is the analogy, I think, between the Community system and the European Convention.

The other point that I would make on measures that in the context of the Community system infringements by member States are simply infringements of individual rights on a larger scale. And it would be somewhat paradoxical therefore to say that member States should not be subject to interim measures simply because it is not just one individual that is liable to be affected but a larger number. I think the second comment that I would like to make is simply because I seem to have the last word. I should like to thank, perhaps on behalf of the participants also, the organizers of the Colloquium for giving us the opportunity of taking part in today's proceedings which I found immensely interesting, for their hospitality and for the arrangements that we have so much enjoyed. Thank you very much.

Steinberger: We have reached the end of the discussion, ladies and gentlemen. But kindly allow me a few concluding remarks. This morning we listened to three excellent reports. I would like to repeat now the thanks which were expressed earlier this morning to the reporters. I also thank, in particular, all those who contributed to the discussion. It was a most fruitful discussion which concentrated on essential matters and did not get lost in the pursuit of details.

Many thanks to you all for your participation. We are honoured that you could come. For those who must depart today, I wish you a safe journey home; for those who can remain, I wish you a very pleasant evening and a happy stay in Heidelberg. Thank you very much.

List of Participants

Dr. Hans Ballreich, München
Professor Dr. Rudolf Bernhardt, Vice-President of the European Court of Human Rights, Heidelberg
Privatdozent Dr. Ulrich Beyerlin, Heidelberg
Professor Dr. Denise Bindschedler-Robert, former Judge at the European Court of Human Rights, Bern
Professor Marten Bos, Epe (The Netherlands)
Professor Dr. Michael Bothe, Frankfurt
Professor Thomas Buergenthal[1], Lobingier Professor of International and Comparative Law at the National Law Center, The George Washington University, Washington D. C., Former Judge and President of the Inter-American Court on Human Rights
Professor Dr. Juan Manuel Castro-Rial, Madrid
Professor Dr. Jost Delbrück, Kiel
Professor Dr. Karl Doehring, Heidelberg
Professor Christian Dominicé, Geneva
Professor Dr. Tono Eitel, Legal Adviser and Head of the Legal Department of the Foreign Office, Bonn
Professor Dr. Ulrich Everling, former Judge of the Court of Justice of the European Communities, Wachtberg-Pech
Professor Dr. Jochen Abr. Frowein, First Vice-President of the European Commission on Human Rights, Heidelberg
Professor Dr. Heribert Golsong, Washington
Professor Dr. Walter J. Habscheid, Lindau
Professor Dr. Kay Hailbronner, Konstanz
Dr. Gerda Heidel, Charlottesville/Virginia
Professor Dr. Matthias Herdegen, Konstanz
Professor Dr. Roman Herzog, President of the Federal Constitutional Court, Karlsruhe
Professor Dr. Meinhard Hilf, Hamburg

---

[1] Prof. Buergenthal could not personally attend the Symposium, but submitted his paper.

Professor Francis G. Jacobs, Advocate-General of the Court of Justice of the European Communities, Luxembourg
Professor Dr. Othmar Jauernig, Heidelberg
Professor Dr. Erik Jayme, Heidelberg
Professor Dr. Paul Kirchhof, Judge at the Federal Constitutional Court, Heidelberg
Professor Dr. Eckart Klein, Mainz
Privatdozentin Dr. Dr. Juliane Kokott, Heidelberg
Professor Richard B. Lillich, Charlottesville/Virginia
Professor Ronald St. J. Macdonald, Judge at the European Court of Human Rights, Toronto
Professor Dr. Hans von Mangoldt, Nehren
Professor Dr. Hermann Mosler, former Director of the Max Plack Institute for Comparative Public Law and International Law, former Judge of the International Court of Justice
Professor Dr. Fritz Münch, Heidelberg
Dr. Karin Oellers-Frahm, Heidelberg
Professor Dr. Thomas Oppermann, Tübingen
Professor Dr. Georgios Papadimitriou, Athens
Professor Dr. Karl Josef Partsch, Ingelheim
Professor Dr. Pierre Pescatore, former Judge at the Court of Justice of the European Communities, Luxembourg
Professor Dr. Ernst-Ulrich Petersmann, St. Gallen
Professor Dr. Herbert Petzold, Deputy Registrar of the European Court of Human Rights, Strasbourg
Professor Dr. José Puente Egido, Madrid
Professor Gil Carlos Rodríguez Iglesias, Judge at the Court of Justice of the European Communities, Luxembourg
Professor Dr. Walter Rudolf, Mainz
Professor Dr. Hartmut Schiedermair, Köln
Professor Dr. Hans Schneider, Heidelberg
Professor Dr. Theodor Schweisfurth, Heidelberg
Professor Dr. Ignaz Seidl-Hohenveldern, Vienna
Sir Ian Sinclair, London
Professor Dr. Torsten Stein, Heidelberg
Professor Dr. Helmut Steinberger, former Judge at the Federal Constitutional Court, Heidelberg
Dr. H. W. A. Thirlway, Principal Legal Secretary, International Court of Justice, The Hague
Professor Dr. Christian Tomuschat, Bonn
Brian Walsh, Judge at the European Court of Human Rights, Dublin
Professor Dr. Rüdiger Wolfrum, Kiel
Dr. Norbert Wühler, Geneva
Professor Dr. Karl Zemanek, Vienna

Max-Planck-Institut für ausländisches öffentliches Recht und Völkerrecht

Beiträge zum ausländischen öffentlichen Recht und Völkerrecht

Hrsg.: J. A. Frowein, H. Steinberger, R. Wolfrum

Bde. 27–59 erschienen im Carl Heymanns Verlag KG Köln, Berlin (Bestellung an: Max-Planck-Institut für Völkerrecht, Berliner Str. 48, 69120 Heidelberg); ab Band 60 im Springer-Verlag Berlin, Heidelberg, New York, London, Paris, Tokyo, Hong Kong, Barcelona, Budapest

---

116 Thilo *Marauhn:* **Der deutsche Chemiewaffen-Verzicht.** 1994. XXII, 400 Seiten (7 Seiten English Summary). Geb. 128,– DM

115 Andreas *Zimmermann:* **Das neue Grundrecht auf Asyl.** 1994. XXVI, 437 Seiten (8 Seiten English Summary). Geb. 128,– DM

114 Axel *Wilke:* **Der völker- und gemeinschaftsrechtliche Schutz der Tätigkeit des Auslandskorrespondenten.** 1994. XVI, 317 Seiten (5 Seiten English Summary). Geb. 148,– DM

113 Peter-Tobias *Stoll:* **Technologietransfer. Internationalisierungs- und Nationalisierungstendenzen.** 1994. XXXII, 452 Seiten (11 Seiten English Summary). Geb. 128,– DM

112 Jörg *Polakiewicz:* **Die Verpflichtungen der Staaten aus den Urteilen des Europäischen Gerichtshofs für Menschenrechte.** 1993. XXI, 392 Seiten (8 Seiten English Summary). Geb. 138,– DM

111 Matthias *Hartwig:* **Die Haftung der Mitgliedstaaten für Internationale Organisationen.** 1993. XXI, 371 Seiten (9 Seiten English Summary). Geb. 148,– DM

110 Juliane *Kokott:* **Beweislastverteilung und Prognoseentscheidungen bei der Inanspruchnahme von Grund- und Menschenrechten.** 1993. XXIV, 482 Seiten (11 Seiten English Summary). Geb. 198,– DM

109 **Das Minderheitenrecht europäischer Staaten. Teil 2** (In Vorbereitung)

108 Jochen Abr. *Frowein*/Rainer *Hofmann*/Stefan *Oeter* (Hrsg.): **Das Minderheitenrecht europäischer Staaten. Teil 1.** 1993. XIII, 536 Seiten. Geb. 90,– DM

107 Stefan *Richter:* **Die Assoziierung osteuropäischer Staaten durch die Europäischen Gemeinschaften.** 1993. XIX, 285 Seiten (11 Seiten English Summary). Geb. 128,– DM

106 Jochen Abr. *Frowein* (Hrsg.): **Die Kontrolldichte bei der gerichtlichen Überprüfung von Handlungen der Verwaltung.** 1993. XIV, 370 Seiten. Geb. 165,– DM

105 Georg *Nolte:* **Beleidigungsschutz in der freiheitlichen Demokratie.** 1992. XX, 294 Seiten. (7 Seiten English Summary). Geb. 128,– DM

104 Thomas *Giegerich:* **Privatwirkung der Grundrechte in den USA.** Die State Action Doctrine des U.S. Supreme Court und die Bürgerrechtsgesetzgebung des Bundes. 1992. XXIII, 518 Seiten (18 Seiten English Summary). Geb. 198,– DM

103 Stefan *Oeter:* **Neutralität und Waffenhandel.** 1992. XVI, 290 Seiten (6 Seiten English Summary). Geb. 128,– DM

102 Rüdiger *Wolfrum:* **The Convention on the Regulation of Antarctic Mineral Resource Activities.** An Attempt to Break New Ground. 1991. VII, 205 Seiten. Geb. 85,– DM

101 Jochen Abr. *Frowein*/Torsten *Stein:* **Rechtliche Aspekte einer Beteiligung der Bundesrepublik Deutschland an Friedenstruppen der Vereinten Nationen.** 1990. IX, 129 Seiten. Geb. 78,– DM

100 Wolfgang *Benedek:* **Die Rechtsordnung des GATT aus völkerrechtlicher Sicht.** 1990. XXIII, 557 Seiten. Geb. 248,– DM

99 Matthias *Herdegen:* **Gewissensfreiheit und Normativität des positiven Rechts.** 1989. XV, 330 Seiten. Geb. 148,– DM

98 **Staat und Völkerrechtsordnung, Festschrift für Karl Doehring.** 1989. XIV, 1067 Seiten. Geb. 380,– DM

97 Rainer *Hofmann:* **Die Ausreisefreiheit nach Völkerrecht und staatlichem Recht.** 1988. XIV, 337 Seiten (7 Seiten English Summary). Geb. 148,– DM

96 Ulrich *Beyerlin:* **Rechtsprobleme der lokalen grenzüberschreitenden Zusammenarbeit.** 1988. XXII, 571 Seiten (6 Seiten English Summary, 6 Seiten Résumé français). Geb. 178,– DM

95 Ulrich *Wölker:* **Zu Freiheit und Grenzen der politischen Betätigung von Ausländern.** Der politische Gebrauch der Meinungs-, Versammlungs- und Vereinigungsfreiheit der Ausländer nach innerstaatlichem Recht, Völkerrecht und Europarecht. 1987. XXI, 264 Seiten (7 Seiten English Summary, 7 Seiten Résumé français). Geb. 98,– DM

94 Jochen Abr. *Frowein*/Torsten *Stein* (Hrsg.): **Die Rechtsstellung von Ausländern nach staatlichem Recht und Völkerrecht/The Legal Position of Aliens in National and International Law/Le régime juridique des étrangers en droit national et international.** 1987. XLVI, 2.135 Seiten. (In zwei Bänden, die nur zusammen abgegeben werden.) Geb. 480,– DM

93 Rudolf *Bernhardt*/John Anthony *Jolowicz* (Eds.): **International Enforcement of Human Rights.** Reports submitted to the Colloquium of the International Association of Legal Science, Heidelberg 28–30 August 1985. 1987. VIII, 265 Seiten. Geb. 84,– DM

92 Juliane *Kokott:* **Das interamerikanische System zum Schutz der Menschenrechte.** 1986. XII, 166 Seiten (6 Seiten English Summary). Geb. 78,– DM

91 Rolf *Kühner:* **Vorbehalte zu multilateralen völkerrechtlichen Verträgen.** 1986. XI, 307 Seiten (6 Seiten English Summary). Geb. 98,– DM

90 Daniel *Thürer:* **Bund und Gemeinden.** Eine rechtsvergleichende Untersuchung zu den unmittelbaren Beziehungen zwischen Bund und Gemeinden in der Bundesrepublik Deutschland, den Vereinigten Staaten von Amerika und der Schweiz. 1986. XVII, 352 Seiten (7 Seiten English Summary). Geb. 118,– DM

89 Helmut *Damian:* **Staatenimmunität und Gerichtszwang.** Grundlagen und Grenzen der völkerrechtlichen Freiheit fremder Staaten von inländischer Gerichtsbarkeit in Verfahren der Zwangsvollstreckung oder Anspruchssicherung. 1985. XV, 261 Seiten (11 Seiten English Summary). Geb. 78,– DM

88 Rudolf *Dolzer:* **Eigentum, Enteignung und Entschädigung im geltenden Völkerrecht.** 1985. XIII, 331 Seiten (3 Seiten English Summary). Geb. 118,– DM

87 Norbert *Wühler:* **Die internationale Schiedsgerichtsbarkeit in der völkerrechtlichen Praxis der Bundesrepublik Deutschland.** 1985. XIII, 239 Seiten (5 Seiten English Summary). Geb. 88,– DM

86 Peter *Malanczuk:* **Region und unitarische Struktur in Großbritannien.** Die verfassungsrechtliche und verwaltungsorganisatorische Bedeutung der Region in England, Wales und Schottland. 1984. XIII, 296 Seiten (5 Seiten English Summary). Geb. 98,– DM

85 Rüdiger *Wolfrum:* **Die Internationalisierung staatsfreier Räume.** Die Entwicklung einer internationalen Verwaltung für Antarktis, Weltraum, Hohe See und Meeresboden. 1984. XX, 757 Seiten (11 Seiten English Summary). Geb. 198,– DM

84 Wolfram *Karl:* **Vertrag und spätere Praxis im Völkerrecht.** Zum Einfluß der Praxis auf Inhalt und Bestand völkerrechtlicher Verträge. 1983. XX, 438 Seiten (17 Seiten English Summary). Geb. 98,– DM

MIX
Papier aus verantwortungsvollen Quellen
Paper from responsible sources
FSC® C105338

If you have any concerns about our products,
you can contact us on
ProductSafety@springernature.com

In case Publisher is established outside the EU,
the EU authorized representative is:
Springer Nature Customer Service Center GmbH
Europaplatz 3, 69115 Heidelberg, Germany

Printed by Libri Plureos GmbH
in Hamburg, Germany